ARIUS DIDYMUS
Epitome of Stoic Ethics

SBL
Society of Biblical Literature

TEXTS AND TRANSLATIONS
GRAECO-ROMAN SERIES

edited by
Elizabeth Asmis and
John T. Fitzgerald

Texts and Translations 44
Graeco-Roman 14

ARIUS DIDYMUS
EPITOME OF STOIC ETHICS

ARIUS DIDYMUS

Epitome of Stoic Ethics

edited by

Arthur J. Pomeroy

Society of Biblical Literature
Atlanta, Georgia

ARIUS DIDYMUS

Epitome of Stoic Ethics

edited by
Arthur J. Pomeroy

Copyright © 1999 by the Society of Biblical Literature

All rights reserved. No part of this work may be reproduced or transmitted in any form or by any means, electronic or mechanical, including photocopying and recording, or by means of any information storage or retrieval system, except as may be expressly permitted by the 1976 Copyright Act or in writing from the publisher. Requests for permission should be addressed in writing to the Rights and Permissions Office, Scholars Press, P.O. Box 15399, Atlanta, GA 30333-0399, USA.

> **Library of Congress Cataloging-in-Publication Data**
> Didymos, ho Areios.
>   [Epitome of Stoic ethics. English & Greek]
>   Epitome of Stoic ethics / Arius Didymus ; edited by Arthur J. Pomeroy.
>   p.   cm. — (Texts and translations ; 44. Graeco-Roman series ; 14)
>   English and Greek.
>   Includes bibliographical references (p.   ).
>   ISBN 0-88414-001-6 (alk. paper)
>   1. Stoics. 2. Ethics, Ancient.   I. Pomeroy, Arthur John, 1953– .
> II. Title. III. Series: Texts and translations ; no. 44.
> IV. Series: Texts and translations. Graeco-Roman religion series ; 14.
> B528.D53513   1999
> 188—dc21   99-41529
>   CIP
>
>   08 07 06 05 04 03 02 01 00 99   5 4 3 2 1

Printed in the United States of America
on acid-free paper

CONTENTS

Preface	vii
Abbreviations	ix
Introduction	1
Text and Translation	9
Notes to the Text	105
Select Bibliography	129
Greek-English Glossary	131

PREFACE

Above all I am indebted to Elizabeth Asmis. When I was a graduate student at Cornell University, she asked me to prepare a translation of the section of Stobaeus which provides an outline of Stoic ethics. Two decades later, as editor of this series, she suggested a revision of my juvenile efforts. I readily agreed, only to discover the task growing more complicated as my awareness of the difficulties involved increased. As editor, Liz has offered excellent advice and corrected numerous egregious errors. Those which remain should be taken as indicative of my own linguistic and philosophical deficiencies and should in no way be attributed to her.

Next, I should acknowledge the constant encouragement of my other editor, John Fitzgerald, who has offered advice on the inclusion and deletion of material and has turned his skilled eye to the final version, picking up inconsistencies and misprints and expertly querying my translation in numerous places.

I also wish to thank my colleagues in the Classics Department at Victoria University of Wellington, especially Tim Parkin and David Rosenbloom, for encouragement and advice. Janet Watson was an invaluable assistant in indexing the glossary to the text — a task which would have taken much longer without a grant from the Research Committee of the Faculty of Humanities and Social Sciences at Victoria University. The Leave Committee of Victoria University provided funds for travel and the Department of Classics, University of California, Berkeley, assisted in providing access to their university's library resources which were invaluable in completing this project. I would also like to acknowledge the invaluable assistance of the resources of the *Thesaurus Linguae Graecae* on CD-ROM in setting the text, composing the glossary, and in seeking parallels for Arius' Greek usage.

Finally, I wish to dedicate this to Poppy, who ensures that I arise each morning.

Arthur Pomeroy
Victoria University of Wellington,
Wellington, New Zealand
Arthur.Pomeroy@vuw.ac.nz

ABBREVIATIONS

LS A. Long and D. Sedley (eds.), *The Hellenistic Philosophers*, 2 vols (Cambridge 1987): referred to by section numbers and letter (e.g. 68 G) for a specific ancient text, or by volume and page number (e.g. 1.156) for philosophical commentary or commentary on the text.

LSJ H.G. Liddell, R. Scott, H.S. Jones, *A Greek-English Lexicon*, 9th Edition and Supplement (Oxford 1996).

SVF H. von Arnim, *Stoicorum Veterum Fragmenta*, 3 vols (Leipzig 1903-5; Vol. 4, Index, compiled by M. Adler, 1924): citations by volume and fragment number (e.g. 3.223) — references to volume 3, unless identified as fragments of other Stoics, are to fragments of Chrysippus.

INTRODUCTION

In order to educate his son, Septimius, and to assist him to remember what he had read,[1] Ioannes from Stobi (Skopje in the modern Republic of Macedonia) produced a collection of excerpts culled from pagan philosophers, poets, orators, and politicians, arranged topically.[2] The anthology is probably to be dated to the early fifth century AD, since Stobaeus makes use of various Neoplatonist writers, the latest of whom, Themistius, died in 388. Despite the author's clear pagan sympathies — he never quotes Christian authors and seeks to instill a traditional classical education — the work was read and favourably reviewed by the Byzantine patriarch, Photius, in the mid-ninth century. After a series of adventures, during which the introduction and numerous topics were lost and some surviving sections of the second book were wrongly attributed to Book Three, the collection survived, divided into two works, the *Eclogues* (Books 1-2) and the *Florilegium* (Books 3-4).[3]

Stobaeus was able to draw on earlier compilations when seeking material which would lead to his son's moral improvement.[4] Collections of *Chreiai*, witty sayings attributed to famous persons, were popular in the ancient world, as was doxography, the summary of various philosophical doctrines. In his second book, amongst a range of topics dealing with moral philosophy, Stobaeus preserves a summary (ἐπιτομή) of the ethical teachings of the ancient philosophical schools (2.7). Included is a section entitled, "The beliefs [*dogmata*] of Zeno and the other Stoics about the ethical part of philosophy". In the mid-nineteenth century,

---

[1] Photius, *Bibl.*, cod. 167 [p.112a Bekker]: ἐπὶ τῷ ῥυθμίσαι καὶ βελτιῶσαι τῷ παιδὶ τὴν φύσιν ἀμαυρότερον ἔχουσαν πρὸς τὴν τῶν ἀναγνωσμάτων μνήμην.
[2] Name: Ἰωάννης Στοβεύς - *Suda*, sv. Ἰωάννης; Photius, *Bibl.*, cod. 167: ΙΩΑΝΝΟΥ ΣΤΟΒΑΙΟΥ ἐκλογῶν ἀποφθεγμάτων ὑποθηκῶν βιβλία τέσσαρα (" John of Stobi : four books of choice extracts, pointed sayings, and didactic advice.")
[3] For a history of the vicissitudes of the text, see C. Wachsmuth, *Ioannis Stobaei Anthologii Libri Duo Priores* (Berlin 1884), Prolegomena.
[4] For the techniques of Stobaeus and his predecessors in anthologising, see David E. Hahm, "The Ethical Doxography of Arius Didymus", *Aufstieg und Niedergang der römischen Welt* 2.36.4 (1990) 2938-43: generally texts were simply copied word-for-word, but abridgement was frequent and occasionally texts were paraphrased or altered to suit the new context.

August Meineke noted that this summary bore notable similarities in style and content to the following section, "The teachings of Aristotle and the other Peripatetics on ethics". A passage from this discussion of Peripatetic ethics is later quoted as deriving from "The Epitome of Didymus" (Stobaeus 4.39) . By identifying this work as part of the doxography referred to by Eusebius as "The Epitomes of Arius Didymus",[5] Meineke was able to deduce that the author of both the Peripatetic and Stoic sections was Arius Didymus.[6]

The philosophical writer Arius Didymus may be assumed to be the same as Arius, a prominent Alexandrian philosopher, who accompanied Augustus when he entered Alexandria in 30 BC.[7] A close associate of the emperor throughout his life, Arius is known to have composed a work of consolation to comfort the emperor's wife, Livia, after the death of her son Drusus in 9 BC.[8] There is insufficient evidence to give more precise details of Arius' life,[9] but what is known is consonant with the career of the writer on ethical philosophy. The latter quotes from Hecaton (late 2nd or early 1st century BC), probably from Posidonius (ca. 135-ca. 51BC), and also Eudorus (1st century BC), so a dating in the latter half of the first century BC for his composition fits well. Furthermore, a thirteenth century manuscript (Parisinius gr. 1759) contains a list of Stoic philosophers which may have originally have come from the end of Diogenes Laertius' *Lives of the Philosophers*, Book Seven. Here Arius follows Posidonius, but precedes Cornutus, the first century AD Stoic. In sum, the philosopher-companion of Augustus, well-known at Alexandria, and the writer with a particular interest in ethics are likely to be the same person.

[5] *Praep. Ev.* 15.15.1; 15.20.1.
[6] A. Meineke, "Zu Stobaeus", *Sokrates: Zeitschrift für das Gymnasialwesen* 13 (1859) 563-5; id., *Ioannis Stobaei Eclogarum physicarum et ethicarum libri duo*, vol. 2 (Leipzig 1860) cliv-clv. The argument was expanded by H. Diels, *Doxographi Graeci* (Berlin 1879) 69-88. More recently, the identification of the writer in Stobaeus with the Alexandrian philosopher has been questioned by Tryggve Göransson, *Albinus, Alcinous, Arius Didymus* (Göteborg 1995). For a well-reasoned defence of the traditional linkage of the two, see Brad Inwood's review of Göransson in *BMCR* 95.12.8 (1995)[electronic] = 7 (1996) 25-30.
[7] Plutarch, *Ant.* 80, *Praecept. ger. rei publ.* 814d, *Apophth.* 207a-b; Dio 51.16.3-4.
[8] Seneca, *Cons. ad Marc.* 4-5.
[9] Hahm, *loc. cit.* 3035-3047, offers a judicious treatment of this topic.

INTRODUCTION

From what is known of Arius Didymus, it is likely that he was regarded by his contemporaries as a Stoic. However, his ability to detail the ethical systems of other philosophical schools in his general introduction (2.7.37-57) and account of Peripatetic ethics (2.7.116-152), his friendship with the Peripatetic Xenarchus (Strabo 14.5.4), and his praise for the Academic Eudorus (2.7.42) all suggest considerable philosophical tolerance. His very aim of offering a clear outline of Stoic principles probably means that he harmonized conflicting theories in earlier Stoic thought in order to create logical consistency. It is also likely that he incorporated syncretising elements from other systems where this assisted his aim. The result is not a history of the development of Stoic doctrine, but a quite individualistic example of Stoic thought as it existed in the late first century BC.

* * * * *

The text of Arius Didymus' Epitome of Stoic Ethics used for this translation and commentary is generally that of Wachsmuth, who produced the last major edition of Stobaeus' *Eclogues* in 1884. The following comments are largely a summary of Wachsmuth's investigations, supplemented by David Hahm's remarks in his *Aufstieg und Niedergang* article on Arius.

In general, Stobaeus appears to have copied selections of ancient writers, indicating the name of the author and the title of the work being quoted in a marginal note (*lemma*). These notes were later incorporated in the text as headers before the quotations, but occasionally the copyist failed to note correctly to which passage a marginal heading referred and so misattributed selections. Thus, in our text, there is the possibility that the introductory heading is misplaced before some introductory remarks of the compiler. This need not be due to Stobaeus himself, but could be an intermediate compilation. Elsewhere the text itself is generally copied verbatim, but could be adjusted to fit the context — for instance, if a passage in the original text was deleted, minor changes in grammar might be needed to create a "seamless" fit across the gap. Minor copying errors and (hopefully, rarely) major mistakes, such as the insertion of two loose pages from Book 2 in Book 4, occurred as part of the normal transmission of the text. In the medieval period, further abridgement occurred by the deletion of sections which were not

of interest to the copyist — particularly in Book 1, which is now half the size of Book 4. This is obvious from a comparison of the section headings recorded by Photius. It is uncertain whether abridgements were also made inside sections, such as in the treatment of Stoic ethics. Clearly the archetype from which the earliest surviving manuscripts are derived had suffered considerable damage. Not only had this version lost its introduction, but also the last thirty-seven topics of Book 2, which is now only a quarter of the size of Book 4. Sometimes too the archetype was illegible: the copyist of the Farnese manuscript of Stobaeus (F) often leaves gaps in these places, while the report of the Paris manuscript (P) indicates that these illegible passages had increased over the next century. The latter two manuscripts, both belonging to the late medieval period, are the only direct copies of the archetype and as such form the basis of the most "modern" text of Stobaeus, Wachsmuth's 1884 edition.

Book 2, Chapter 7 ("On the ethical type of philosophy"), which includes the description of Stoic ethics, is now almost half of the surviving text of the second book. This suggests that little of Stobaeus' text for this section has been lost. The general lemma for the Stoic section also suggests that Stobaeus has copied this passage as one single quotation from an earlier source.[10] It is possible that medieval copyists made some abridgements, but whether these changes are as extensive as suggested by David Hahm[11] is a moot point. Hahm's arguments for the Lucianic scholia often preserving a better version of Stobaeus' text require careful examination of each individual case. The text of the Stoic section, in accord with the history of the text, displays a large number of errors in the manuscripts. Some are trivial, but many display considerable corruption in the transmission, including loss of text and a probable misinsertion of section 5b after 5g. The most important of these textual problems will be individually noted in the commentary.

---

[10] There is a second heading at 5h ("On what is to be chosen and what is to be avoided") which Wachsmuth deletes but may indicate a lost system of sub-headings.
[11] *Loc. cit.* 2943-2975

TEXT

As already indicated, the text of Stobaeus is derived from the Farnese (F) and Paris (P) manuscripts, from which all other manuscripts derive. Printed editions have been produced by W. Canter (Antwerp, 1575 — the first publication), A. Heeren (Göttingen, 1792-1801), T. Gaisford (Oxford, 1850), A. Meineke (Leipzig: Teubner, 1860-3), and finally C. Wachsmuth and O. Hense (Berlin: Weidemann, 1894-1912). Wachsmuth in the section on Stoic ethics makes considerable use of suggestions from German scholars of the nineteenth century, particularly Usener, Hirzel, Diels, and Hense. In the twentieth century there has been a reaction against Wachsmuth's readiness to change the text, as can be seen in the not infrequent reversion to the manuscript readings in the selections printed in H. von Arnim, *Stoicorum Veterum Fragmenta* and, more recently, in A. Long and D. Sedley, *The Hellenistic Philosophers*.

The following is a list of the places where the text varies from Wachsmuth's edition. Reversion to the manuscript readings is noted; for other changes, see the *apparatus criticus*.

	Wachsmuth's Text	**This Edition**
5a	ἡδονὴν πόνον ... ὑγίειαν νόσον	πόνον ἡδονὴν ... νόσον ὑγίειαν (FP)
5b	Ἀφροσύνην μὲν οὖν... καὶ ἀδυναμίαν	Ἀφροσύνην μὲν οὖν ⟨καὶ ἀκολασίαν⟩ ...καὶ ἀδυναμίαν ⟨καὶ ἀσθένειαν⟩
5b1	πολιτικοῦ ⟨λογικοῦ⟩ ζῴου	πολιτικοῦ ζῴου (FP)
5b7	ἡ αὐτὴ διανοίᾳ	ἡ αὐτὴ ⟨τῇ⟩ διανοίᾳ
5b9	ἔρωτα ...	ἔρωτα ⟨τὸν σπουδαῖον φιλίας⟩
5b10	καὶ ὅσα ποιεῖ ναὶ [οὔ] μὰ Δία καὶ ἃ μὴ ποιεῖ.	καθ' ὅσα ποιεῖ καὶ οὔ μὰ Δία, καθ' ἃ μὴ ποιεῖ.

5b13	ἐναντίαν κακίαν τῇ φρονήσει	ἐναντίαν κακίαν τῇ σωφροσύνῃ (FP)
5f	τὴν τῆς σωφροσύνης κτῆσιν	τὴν τῆς σωφροσύνης χρῆσιν
5i	ἀρεστόν· ⟨καθ' ὃ δὲ ... δοκιμαστόν⟩· καθ' ὃ δὲ πάλιν ... εἶναι, ⟨ἐπαινετόν⟩.	ἀρεστόν· καθ' ὃ δὲ πάλιν ... εἶναι, ⟨ἐπαινετόν⟩.
5k	Τῶν δὲ ἐν σχέσει τὰς μὲν καὶ ἐν ἕξει εἶναι, οἷον τὰς ἀρετάς· τὰς δ' ἐν σχέσει ...	Τῶν δὲ ἐν σχέσει τὰ μὲν καὶ ἐν ἕξει εἶναι, οἷον τὰς ἀρετάς· τὰ δ' ἐν σχέσει ...
5l	ἑτέρως δὲ ἐπιστήμην σύστημα ἐκ καταλήψεων τοιούτων... ἄλλως δὲ σύστημα ἐξ ἐπιστημῶν τεχνικῶν	ἑτέραν δὲ ἐπιστήμην σύστημα ἐκ ἐπιστημῶν τοιούτων... ἄλλην δὲ σύστημα ἐξ ἐπιστημῶν τεχνικῶν (FP)
5m	Ἔστι δ' ἡ μὲν εὐτεκνία κτῆσις τέκνων κατὰ φύσιν ἔχουσα σπουδαία, ἡ δὲ εὐγηρία χρῆσις σπουδαία γήρως κατὰ φύσιν ἔχουσα	Ἔστι δ' ἡ μὲν εὐτεκνία χρῆσις τέκνοις κατὰ φύσιν ἔχουσι σπουδαία, ἡ δὲ εὐγηρία χρῆσις σπουδαία γήρᾳ κατὰ φύσιν ἔχοντι (FP)
6a	ἔλαττον εἶναι κατηγόρημα	ἔλαττον εἶναι ⟨ἢ⟩ κατηγόρημα
7a	ψυχῆς κατάστασιν καὶ σώματος, καθ' ἣ ...	ψυχῆς κατάστασιν καὶ σώματος, καθ' ἃς ... (FP)

INTRODUCTION

7e	ὅσα ἐστὶν ὁρμῆς κινητικὰ προστρεπτικῶς ἐφ᾽ ἑαυτά...ὅσα ἐστὶν ὁρμῆς κινητικὰ ἀνετικῶς ἐφ᾽ ἕτερα καὶ μὴ προστρεπτικῶς ⟨ἐφ᾽ ἑαυτά⟩	ὅσα ἐστὶν ὁρμῆς κινητικὰ καταστρεπτικῶς ἐφ᾽ ἑαυτά...ὅσα ἐστὶν ὁρμῆς κινητικὰ ἀν⟨εν⟩εκτικῶς ἐφ᾽ ἕτερα καὶ μὴ κατατρεπτικῶς ⟨ἐφ᾽ ἑαυτά⟩
8a	τοιαύτην δ᾽ εὐφυίαν προσφερομένοις	τοιαύτην δ᾽ εὔροιαν προσφερομένοις
9	φοράν τινα ⟨διανοίας ἀπό τινος τῶν ἐν τῷ μὴ πράττειν⟩	φοράν τινα ⟨διανοίας ἀπό τινος τῶν ἐν τῷ πράττειν⟩
9b	Ἤδη δὲ ἄλλῳ μὲν εἶναι συγκαταθέσεις, ἐπ᾽ ἄλλο δὲ ὁρμάς· ... τὰ περιεχόμενά πως ἐν τοῖς ἀξιώμασιν, οἷς συγκατατίθεσθαι.	Ἤδη δὲ ἄλλων μὲν εἶναι συγκαταθέσεις, ἐπ᾽ ἄλλο δὲ ὁρμάς· ... τὰ περιεχόμενά πως ἐν τοῖς ἀξιώμασιν, οἷς συγκαταθέσεις. (FP, Madvig)
11a	καθῆκον πάντας ἀπέχον τοὺς ἀριθμούς	καθῆκον πάντας ἐπέχον τοὺς ἀριθμούς (FP)
11m	κατὰ τοῦτο δικαιοπραγεῖν	κατὰ τοῦτο ἀδικοπραγεῖν
11m	ἐν τῷ διαψευστῶς τὸ ψεῦδος λέγειν	ἐν τῷ διαψευστικῶς τὸ ψεῦδος λέγειν
11n	οὔτε ὀρεγόμενόν τινος οὔτε νομίζειν βουλόμενον ἔν τινι τῶν ἐν τῷ βούλεσθαι εἰδικῶν	οὔτε ὀρεγόμενόν τινος οὔθ᾽ ὅλως γινόμενον ἔν τινι τῶν ἐν τῷ βούλεσθαι εἰδικῶν
11q	οὔ τι μὴν πάντα ἀστεῖα τέκνα ἔχοντα, δεῖν γὰρ τὸν εὐτεκνοῦντα χρήσασθαι αὐτοῖς ὡς τοιούτοις.	οὔ τι μὴν πάντα· δεῖν γὰρ τὸν εὐτεκνοῦντα ἀστεῖα τέκνα ἔχοντα χρήσασθαι αὐτοῖς ὡς τοιούτοις.

In the translation of the text I have sought wherever possible to be consistent in my rendering of the Greek into English, since the Stoics aimed at developing a distinct technical vocabulary to assist their philosophical efforts. There is, of course, some resulting loss of fluency in the English version, but I hope that the gain of greater accuracy in the presentation of the philosophical arguments will be some compensation. The endnotes are consequently aimed at offering continuous assistance to the reader by clarifying the translation, by explaining technical terms, and by highlighting important ethical statements as they occur. But for more detailed consideration of their philosophical importance, the reader should consult Long and Sedley or other specialised investigations of Hellenistic philosophy, of which a selection is listed in the bibliography. In my notes I have felt it particularly important to offer cross-references to other parts of Arius' summary, since his account of Stoic ethics often relies on premises whose full exposition will only occur later or which have been set out already, but in somewhat different contexts. Because of the strong interconnections between aspects of Stoic ethical thought, some overlapping in the endnote material is unavoidable. I can only hope that the convenience to the reader will be felt to excuse any repetition which may occur.

ARIUS DIDYMUS
EPITOME OF STOIC ETHICS

TEXT AND TRANSLATION

ΙΩΑΝΝΟΥ ΣΤΟΒΑΙΟΥ ΕΚΛΟΓΑΙ ΑΠΟΦΘΕΓΜΑΤΑ ΥΠΟΘΗΚΑΙ,
LIB. II CAP. VII. 5-12

Ζήνωνος καὶ τῶν λοιπῶν Στωικῶν δόγματα περὶ τοῦ ἠθικοῦ μέρους τῆς φιλοσοφίας.

Περὶ δὲ τῶν ἠθικῶν ἑξῆς ποιήσομαι τὸν ὑπομνηματισμὸν τὰ κεφάλαια τῶν ἀναγκαίων δογμάτων ἀναλαβών. Ἄρξομαι
5a δ' ἐντεῦθεν·
Ταῦτ' εἶναί φησιν ὁ Ζήνων, ὅσα οὐσίας μετέχει· τῶν δ' ὄντων τὰ μὲν ἀγαθά, τὰ δὲ κακά, τὰ δὲ ἀδιάφορα. Ἀγαθὰ μὲν τὰ τοιαῦτα· φρόνησιν, σωφροσύνην, δικαιοσύνην, ἀνδρείαν καὶ πᾶν ὅ ἐστιν ἀρετὴ ἢ μετέχον ἀρετῆς· κακὰ δὲ τὰ τοιαῦτα· ἀφροσύνην, ἀκολασίαν, ἀδικίαν, δειλίαν καὶ πᾶν ὅ ἐστι κακία ἢ μετέχον κακίας· ἀδιάφορα δὲ τὰ τοιαῦτα· ζωὴν θάνατον, δόξαν ἀδοξίαν, πόνον ἡδονήν, πλοῦτον πενίαν, νόσον ὑγίειαν, καὶ τὰ τούτοις ὅμοια.
5b Τῶν δὲ ἀγαθῶν τὰ μὲν εἶναι ἀρετάς, τὰ δ' οὔ. Φρόνησιν μὲν οὖν καὶ σωφροσύνην ⟨καὶ δικαιοσύνην⟩ καὶ ἀνδρείαν ⟨καὶ μεγαλοψυχίαν καὶ ῥώμην καὶ ἰσχὺν ψυχῆς⟩ ἀρετάς· χαρὰν δὲ καὶ εὐφροσύνην καὶ θάρρος καὶ βούλησιν καὶ τὰ παραπλήσια οὐκ εἶναι ἀρετάς. Τῶν δὲ ἀρετῶν τὰς μὲν ἐπιστήμας τινῶν καὶ τέχνας, τὰς δ' οὔ. Φρόνησιν μὲν οὖν καὶ σωφροσύνην καὶ δικαιοσύνην καὶ ἀνδρείαν ἐπιστήμας εἶναι τινῶν καὶ τέχνας· μεγαλοψυχίαν δὲ καὶ ῥώμην

W 2.57

2.58

SVF 3.95
LS 60K

Ζήνωνος ... φιλοσοφίας: Heeren transposed after Περί ... ἐντεῦθεν   8 δικαιοσύνην, σωφροσύνην: transposed by Wachsmuth   11 ἀδικίαν, δειλίαν: P; δειλίαν, ἀδικίαν: F   13 πόνον ἡδονὴν ... νόσον ὑγίειαν: FP; ἡδονὴν πόνον ... ὑγίειαν νόσον: Wachsmuth.   17 ⟨καὶ δικαιοσύνην⟩ καὶ ἀνδρείαν ⟨καὶ μεγαλοψυχίαν καὶ ῥώμην καὶ ἰσχὺν ψυχῆς⟩: supplemented by Meineke and Wachsmuth   24 δικαιοσύνην καὶ ἀνδρείαν: Meineke; ἀνδρείαν καὶ δικαιοσύνη: FP   25 μεγαλοψυχία: FP; μεγαλοψυφία: doubtfully, Wachsmuth

John of Stobi: Extracts, Sayings, and Advice
Book Two, Chapter 7. 5-12

The beliefs of Zeno and the other Stoics[1] about the ethical part[2] of philosophy.

Next I will offer a summary of their ethics, repeating the essentials of their principal beliefs. I will begin here.

5a Those things exist, according to Zeno, which participate in substance.[3] Of the things which exist, some are good, some are bad, and some are indifferent.[4]

These are examples of good things: intelligence, self-restraint, justice, bravery, and everything which is a virtue or participates in virtue.[5]

These are examples of bad things: stupidity, lack of self-restraint, injustice, cowardice and everything which is a vice or participates in vice.

These are examples of indifferent things: life, death; reputation, lack of reputation; toil, pleasure; riches, poverty; sickness, health;[6] and things of this sort.[7]

5b Of good things, some are virtues, others are not.

So intelligence, self-restraint, <justice>, bravery, <great-heartedness, strength of mind, and power of the soul> are virtues;[8] joy, cheerfulness, confidence, wish,[9] and the like are not virtues.[10]

Of the virtues, some are types of knowledge and expertises in certain matters,[11] others are not.

Intelligence, self-restraint, justice, and bravery are types of knowledge and expertises in certain matters; great-heartedness,

καὶ ἰσχὺν ψυχῆς οὔτ' ἐπιστήμας τινῶν εἶναι
οὔτε τέχνας. Ἀνάλογον δὲ καὶ τῶν κακῶν τὰ
μὲν εἶναι κακίας, τὰ δ' οὔ. Ἀφροσύνην μὲν οὖν
⟨καὶ ἀκολασίαν⟩ καὶ ἀδικίαν καὶ δειλίαν καὶ
μικροψυχίαν καὶ ἀδυναμίαν ⟨καὶ ἀσθένειαν⟩ 5
κακίας εἶναι· λύπην δὲ καὶ φόβον καὶ τὰ
παραπλήσια οὐκ εἶναι κακίας. Τῶν δὲ κακιῶν
τὰς μὲν εἶναι ἀγνοίας τινῶν καὶ ἀτεχνίας, τὰς
δ' οὔ. Ἀφροσύνην μὲν οὖν καὶ ἀκολασίαν καὶ
ἀδικίαν καὶ δειλίαν | ἀγνοίας εἶναι τινῶν καὶ 10
ἀτεχνίας· μικροψυχίαν δὲ καὶ ἀδυναμίαν ⟨καὶ
ἀσθένειαν⟩ οὔτε ἀγνοίας τινῶν οὔτε ἀτεχνίας.
5b1   Φρόνησιν δ' εἶναι ἐπιστήμην ὧν ποιητέον
καὶ οὐ ποιητέον καὶ οὐδετέρων, ἢ ἐπιστήμην
ἀγαθῶν καὶ κακῶν καὶ οὐδετέρων φύσει 15
πολιτικοῦ ζῴου (καὶ ἐπὶ τῶν λοιπῶν δὲ
ἀρετῶν οὕτως ἀκούειν παραγγέλλουσι)·
σωφροσύνην δ' εἶναι ἐπιστήμην αἱρετῶν καὶ
φευκτῶν καὶ οὐδετέρων· δικαιοσύνην δὲ
ἐπιστήμην ἀπονεμητικὴν τῆς ἀξίας ἑκάστῳ· 20
ἀνδρείαν δὲ ἐπιστήμην δεινῶν καὶ οὐ δεινῶν
καὶ οὐδετέρων· ἀφροσύνην δὲ ⟨ἄγνοιαν⟩
ἀγαθῶν | καὶ κακῶν καὶ οὐδετέρων, ἢ
ἄγνοιαν ὧν ποιητέον καὶ οὐ ποιητέον καὶ
οὐδετέρων· ἀκολασίαν δὲ ἄγνοιαν αἱρετῶν καὶ 25
φευκτῶν καὶ οὐδετέρων· ⟨ἀδικίαν δὲ ἄγνοιαν
μὴ ἀπονεμητικὴν τῆς ἀξίας ἑκάστῳ⟩· δειλίαν
δὲ ἄγνοιαν δεινῶν καὶ οὐ δεινῶν καὶ
οὐδετέρων. Παραπλησίως δὲ καὶ τὰς ἄλλας
ἀρετὰς καὶ κακίας ὁρίζονται, τῶν εἰρημένων 30
ἐχόμενοι. Κοινότερον δὲ τὴν ἀρετὴν διάθεσιν
εἶναί φασι ψυχῆς σύμφωνον αὑτῇ περὶ ὅλον
τὸν βίον.

W
2.59

SVF
3.262
LS
61H

2.60

---

4 ⟨καὶ ἀκολασίαν⟩ καὶ ἀδικίαν καὶ δειλίαν καὶ μικροψυχίαν καὶ ἀδυναμίαν ⟨καὶ ἀσθένειαν⟩:
I have supplemented from the conclusion of 5b below; P omits καὶ δειλίαν
7 κακιῶν: κακῶν FP, corr. Heeren.   11 καὶ ἀσθένειαν: suppl. Meineke   13 5b1-5b13 are transposed by Wachsmuth from after 5g   16 Wachsmuth supplements with ⟨λογικοῦ⟩, comparing Chrysippus *Peri nomou* in Plut. *Stoic. rep.* 11, Cic. *Fin.* 5.66
18 δ' εἶναι: δὲ καὶ FP, corr. Heeren   22 ἄγνοιαν: suppl. Heeren   26 ἀδικίαν δὲ ἄγνοιαν μὴ ἀπονεμητικὴν τῆς ἀξίας ἑκάστῳ: suppl. Heeren, μὴ suppl. Mullach

strength of mind,[12] and power of the soul are neither types of knowledge of particular matters nor expertises.[13]

Analogously, of bad things some are vices, others are not.

So stupidity, <lack of restraint>, injustice, cowardice, small-mindedness, and mental incapacity <and feebleness> are vices;

pain and fear and the like are not vices.

Of the vices, some are failures to understand certain matters and failures in expertise, but others are not.

So stupidity, lack of restraint, injustice, and cowardice are failures to understand certain matters and failures in expertise;

small-mindedness, incapacity, <and feebleness> are neither failures to understand particular things nor failures in expertise.

5b1[14] Intelligence is a knowledge of what things must be done and what must not be done and of what are neither, or a knowledge of what are good things and what are bad and what are neither for a naturally political creature[15] (and they prescribe that it is to be so understood with regard to the other virtues);

self-restraint is a knowledge of what things are worth choosing and what are worth avoiding and what are neither;

justice is a knowledge of apportioning to each its due;

bravery is a knowledge of what things are terrible and what are not and what are neither;

stupidity is <ignorance of> what things are good and what are bad and what are neither, or ignorance of what things are to be done and what not to be done and what are neither;

lack of restraint is ignorance of what things are worth choosing and what are worth avoiding and what are neither;

<injustice is ignorance not apportioning to each its due;>

cowardice is ignorance of what things are terrible and what are not and what are neither.

They define the other virtues and vices as well in a similar fashion, keeping to what has been stated. More generally, they say that virtue is a disposition of the soul in harmony with itself concerning one's whole life.[16]

5b2 Τῶν δ' ἀρετῶν τὰς μὲν εἶναι πρώτας, τὰς δὲ ταῖς πρώταις ὑποτεταγμένας· πρώτας δὲ τέτταρας εἶναι, φρόνησιν, σωφροσύνην, ἀνδρείαν, δικαιοσύνην. Καὶ τὴν μὲν φρόνησιν περὶ τὰ καθήκοντα γίνεσθαι· τὴν δὲ σωφροσύνην περὶ τὰς ὁρμὰς τοῦ ἀνθρώπου· τὴν δὲ ἀνδρείαν περὶ τὰς ὑπομονάς· τὴν δὲ δικαιοσύνην περὶ τὰς ἀπονεμήσεις. Τῶν δὲ ὑποτεταγμένων ταῖς ἀρεταῖς ταύταις τὰς μὲν τῇ φρονήσει ὑποτετάχθαι, τὰς δὲ τῇ σωφροσύνῃ, τὰς δὲ τῇ ἀνδρείᾳ, τὰς δὲ τῇ δικαιοσύνῃ. Τῇ μὲν οὖν φρονήσει ὑποτάττεσθαι εὐβουλίαν, εὐλογιστίαν, ἀγχίνοιαν, νουνέχειαν, ⟨εὐστοχίαν⟩, εὐμηχανίαν· τῇ δὲ σωφροσύνῃ εὐταξίαν, κοσμιότητα, αἰδημοσύνην, ἐγκράτειαν· τῇ δὲ ἀνδρείᾳ καρτερίαν, θαρραλεότητα, μεγαλοψυχίαν, εὐψυχίαν, φιλοπονίαν· τῇ δὲ δικαιοσύνῃ εὐσέβειαν, χρηστότητα, εὐκοινωνησίαν, εὐσυναλλαξίαν. Εὐβουλίαν μὲν οὖν εἶναι λέγουσιν ἐπιστήμην τοῦ ποῖα καὶ πῶς πράττοντες πράξομεν συμφερόντως· εὐλογιστίαν δὲ ἐπιστήμην ἀντanaιρετικὴν καὶ συγκεφαλαιωτικὴν τῶν γινομένων καὶ ἀποτελουμένων· ἀγχίνοιαν δὲ ἐπιστήμην εὑρετικὴν τοῦ καθήκοντος ἐκ τοῦ παραχρῆμα· νουνέχειαν δὲ ἐπιστήμην ⟨τῶν χειρόνων καὶ βελτιόνων· εὐστοχίαν δὲ ἐπιστήμην⟩ ἐπιτευκτικὴν τοῦ ἐν ἑκάστῳ σκοποῦ· εὐμηχανίαν δὲ ἐπιστήμην εὑρετικὴν διεξόδου πραγμάτων· εὐταξίαν δὲ ἐπιστήμην τοῦ πότε πρακτέον, καὶ τί μετὰ τί, καὶ καθόλου τῆς τάξεως τῶν πράξεων· κοσμιότητα δὲ ⟨ἐπιστήμην⟩ πρεπουσῶν καὶ ἀπρεπῶν κινήσεων· αἰδημοσύνην δὲ ἐπιστήμην

SVF 3.264

W 2.61

---

14 εὐστοχίαν: suppl. Wachsmuth, comparing Chrysippus in Andronicus Rhodius *De Passionibus* p. 752   24 συγκεφαλαιωτικήν: Heine; μὴ κεφαλαιωτικήν: FP   27 τῶν χειρόνων καὶ βελτιόνων· εὐστοχίαν δὲ ἐπιστήμην: suppl. Wachsmuth, comparing Chrysippus in Andronicus Rhodius *De Passionibus* p. 753   34 ἐπιστήμην: suppl. Heeren

5b2 Of the virtues, some are primary, while others are subordinate to the primary virtues.

There are four which are primary: intelligence, self-restraint, bravery, and justice.
  Intelligence deals with appropriate acts;[17]
  self-restraint deals with man's impulses;[18]
  bravery deals with acts of endurance;
  justice deals with the apportioning of what is due.

Of the virtues which are subordinate to these, some are subordinate to intelligence, others subordinate to self-restraint, others to bravery, others to justice.
  To intelligence are subordinated soundness of judgement, circumspection, shrewdness, sensibleness, <soundness of aim>, and ingenuity;
  to self-restraint are subordinated orderliness, propriety, modesty, and self-control;
  to bravery are subordinated perseverance, intrepidness, great-heartedness, stout-heartedness, and industriousness;
  to justice are subordinated piety, kindness, good fellowship, and fair dealing.

  They say, then, that soundness of judgement is a knowledge of what sort of things to do and how to do them so we will act expediently.
  Circumspection is a knowledge which marks off and summarises what is still in process and what is completed.[19]
  Shrewdness is a knowledge which is able to discover the appropriate act on the spot.
  Sensibleness is a knowledge <of what is worse and what is better.
  Soundness of aim is a knowledge> which is able to hit the target in each case.
  Ingenuity is a knowledge which is able to discover a way out of difficulties.

  Orderliness is a knowledge of when something must be done and in what sequence and, overall, of the order of actions.
  Propriety is <a knowledge> of suitable and unsuitable motions.[20]

εὐλαβητικὴν ὀρθοῦ ψόγου· ἐγκράτειαν δὲ
ἐπιστήμην ἀνυπέρβατον τῶν κατὰ τὸν ὀρθὸν
λόγον φανέντων· καρτερίαν δὲ ἐπιστήμην
ἐμμενητικὴν τοῖς ὀρθῶς κριθεῖσι·
θαρραλεότητα δὲ ἐπιστήμην καθ' ἥν οἴδαμεν
ὅτι οὐδενὶ δεινῷ μὴ περιπέσωμεν·
μεγαλοψυχίαν δὲ ἐπιστήμην ὑπεράνω
ποιοῦσαν τῶν πεφυκότων ἐν σπουδαίοις τε
γίνεσθαι καὶ φαύλοις· εὐψυχίαν δὲ ἐπιστήμην
ψυχῆς παρεχομένης ἑαυτὴν ἀήττητον·
φιλοπονίαν ι δὲ ἐπιστήμην ἐξεργαστικὴν τοῦ
προκειμένου, οὐ κωλυομένην διὰ πόνον·
εὐσέβειαν δὲ ἐπιστήμην θεῶν θεραπείας·
χρηστότητα δὲ ἐπιστήμην εὐποιητικήν·
εὐκοινωνησίαν δὲ ἐπιστήμην ἰσότητος ἐν
κοινωνίᾳ· εὐσυναλλαξίαν δὲ ἐπιστήμην τοῦ
συναλλάττειν ἀμέμπτως τοῖς πλησίον.

5b3 Πασῶν δὲ τούτων τῶν ἀρετῶν τὸ τέλος
εἶναι τὸ ἀκολούθως τῇ φύσει ζῆν· ἑκάστην δὲ
τούτου διὰ τῶν ἰδίων παρέχεσθαι
τυγχάνοντα τὸν ἄνθρωπον. Ἔχειν γὰρ
ἀφορμὰς παρὰ τῆς φύσεως καὶ πρὸς τὴν τοῦ
καθήκοντος εὕρεσιν καὶ πρὸς τὴν τῶν ὁρμῶν
εὐστάθειαν καὶ πρὸς τὰς ὑπομονὰς καὶ πρὸς
τὰς ἀπονεμήσεις. Καὶ ⟨κατὰ⟩ τὸ σύμφωνον καὶ
τὸ ἑαυτῆς ἑκάστη τῶν ἀρετῶν πράττουσα
παρέχεται τὸν ἄνθρωπον ἀκολούθως τῇ φύσει
ζῶντα.

5b4 Ταύτας μὲν οὖν τὰς ῥηθείσας ἀρετὰς
τελείας εἶναι λέγουσι περὶ τὸν βίον καὶ
συνεστηκέναι ἐκ θεωρημάτων· ἄλλας δὲ
ἐπιγίνεσθαι ταύταις, οὐκ ἔτι τέχνας οὔσας,
ἀλλὰ δυνάμεις τινάς, ἐκ τῆς ἀσκήσεως
περιγιγνομένας, οἷον τὴν ὑγίειαν τῆς ψυχῆς
καὶ τὴν ἀρτιότητα καὶ τὴν ἰσχὺν αὐτῆς καὶ τὸ

---

2 ἀνυπέρβατον: Wachsmuth, comparing Diog. Laert. 7.53; ἀνυπέρβλητον: FP
16 τοῦ: Wachsmuth; ἐν τῷ: FP   20 τούτου: Heeren; τούτων: FP
25 ἀπονεμήσεις: Canter; ὑπονεμήσεις: FP   25 κατὰ: suppl. Usener
26 ἑαυτῆς: Heine; ἑξῆς: FP   30 τελείας: τέχνας Hirzel   33 ἐκ: Meineke; ἐπὶ: FP

Modesty is a knowledge which is able to avoid correct reproach.

Self-control is a knowledge that does not overstep the bounds of what has come to light in accord with correct reasoning.[21]

Perseverance is a knowledge ready to persist in what has been correctly decided.

Intrepidness is a knowledge through which we know that we shall not encounter anything terrible.

Great-heartedness is a knowledge acting above what occurs naturally in both worthwhile and worthless matters.[22]

Stout-heartedness is a knowledge belonging to a soul as it shows itself invincible.

Industriousness[23] is a knowledge which is able to accomplish what is proposed, without being prevented by the toil.

Piety is a knowledge of the service of the gods.
Kindness is a knowledge which is disposed to do good.
Good fellowship is a knowledge of equality in partnership.
Fair dealing is a knowledge of how to deal with one's neighbours without incurring blame.

5b3 The goal of all these virtues is to live consistently with nature.[24] Each virtue through its individual properties enables man to achieve this. For from nature he has initial impulses for the discovery of what is appropriate, for the balancing of his impulses, for acts of endurance, and for acts of apportioning. Each of the virtues, by acting in concert and by its own particular properties, enables man to live consistently with nature.

5b4 So they say that the above-mentioned virtues are complete concerning life and are comprised from rules of behaviour.[25] There are other virtues in addition to these, no longer expertises but particular capacities, resulting from practice,[26] such as the health of the soul, its soundness and strength, and its beauty. For just as

κάλλος. "Ωσπερ γὰρ τὴν τοῦ σώματος ὑγίειαν εὐκρασίαν εἶναι τῶν ἐν τῷ σώματι θερμῶν καὶ ψυχρῶν καὶ ξηρῶν καὶ ὑγρῶν, οὕτω καὶ τὴν τῆς ψυχῆς ὑγίειαν εὐκρασίαν εἶναι τῶν ἐν τῇ ψυχῇ δογμάτων. Καὶ ὁμοίως ὥσπερ ἰσχὺς τοῦ 5 σώματος τόνος ἐστὶν ἱκανὸς ἐν νεύροις, οὕτω καὶ ἡ τῆς ψυχῆς ἰσχὺς τόνος | ἐστὶν ἱκανὸς ἐν τῷ κρίνειν καὶ πράττειν ἢ μή. "Ωσπερ τε τὸ κάλλος τοῦ σώματός ἐστι συμμετρία τῶν μελῶν καθεστώτων αὐτῷ πρὸς ἄλληλά τε καὶ 10 πρὸς τὸ ὅλον, οὕτω καὶ τὸ τῆς ψυχῆς κάλλος ἐστὶ συμμετρία τοῦ λόγου καὶ τῶν μερῶν αὐτοῦ πρὸς ⟨τὸ⟩ ὅλον τε αὐτῆς καὶ πρὸς ἄλληλα.

SVF 1.563

W 2.63

5b5 Πάσας δὲ τὰς ἀρετάς, ὅσαι ἐπιστῆμαί εἰσι 15 καὶ τέχναι, κοινά τε θεωρήματα ἔχειν καὶ τέλος, ὡς εἴρηται, τὸ αὐτό, διὸ καὶ ἀχωρίστους εἶναι· τὸν γὰρ μίαν ἔχοντα πάσας ἔχειν, καὶ τὸν κατὰ μίαν πράττοντα κατὰ πάσας πράττειν. Διαφέρειν δ' ἀλλήλων τοῖς 20 κεφαλαίοις. Φρονήσεως μὲν γὰρ εἶναι κεφάλαια τὸ μὲν θεωρεῖν καὶ πράττειν, ὃ ποιητέον, προηγουμένως, κατὰ δὲ τὸν δεύτερον λόγον τὸ θεωρεῖν καὶ ἃ δεῖ ἀπονέμειν ⟨καὶ ἃ δεῖ αἱρεῖσθαι καὶ ἃ δεῖ ὑπομένειν⟩, χάριν 25 τοῦ ἀδιαπτώτως πράττειν ὃ ποιητέον. τῆς δὲ σωφροσύνης ἴδιον κεφάλαιόν ἐστι τὸ παρέχεσθαι τὰς ὁρμὰς εὐσταθεῖς καὶ θεωρεῖν αὐτὰς προηγουμένως, κατὰ δὲ τὸν δεύτερον λόγον τὰ ὑπὸ τὰς ἄλλας ἀρετάς, ἕνεκα τοῦ 30 ἀδιαπτώτως ἐν ταῖς ὁρμαῖς ἀναστρέφεσθαι· καὶ ὁμοίως τὴν ἀνδρείαν προηγουμένως μὲν πᾶν ὃ δεῖ ὑπομένειν, κατὰ δὲ τὸν δεύτερον λόγον τὰ ὑπὸ τὰς ἄλλας· καὶ τὴν δικαιοσύνην προηγουμένως μὲν τὸ κατ' ἀξίαν ἑκάστῳ 35 σκοπεῖν, κατὰ δὲ τὸν δεύτερον λόγον καὶ τὰ

3.280

LS 61D

---

8 ἢ μή: Wachsmuth; καὶ μή: FP   8 τε: Davisius; γε: FP   12 μερῶν: Meineke; μελῶν: FP
13 τὸ: suppl. Mullach   13 αὐτῆς: Wachsmuth; αὐτοῦ: FP
25 καὶ ἃ δεῖ αἱρεῖσθαι καὶ ἃ δεῖ ὑπομένειν: suppl. Usener   30 τὰ: Heeren; τὰς: FP

the health of the body is a correct mixture of the hot, cold, dry, and wet elements in the body,[27] so too the health of the soul is a correct mixture of the beliefs in the soul. And likewise, just as bodily strength is an adequate tension in the sinews, so mental strength is adequate tension when deciding and acting or not.[28] And just as the beauty of the body is a due proportion of the limbs as they stand in relation to each other and in relation to the whole, so too the beauty of the soul is a due proportion in reasoning and in the parts of reasoning in relation to the whole of the soul and in relation to each other.

5b5 All the virtues which are types of knowledge and expertises have rules of behaviour in common and the same goal, as has been stated.[29] Because of this they are also inseparable. For he who has one has them all and he who acts in accordance with one acts in accordance with them all.[30] They differ from one another in their main functions. For the main functions of intelligence are primarily to view and do what must be done, but secondarily to view what one needs to apportion, <what one needs to choose, and what one needs to endure>, in order to do unerringly what must be done. Self-restraint's particular main function is primarily to provide balanced impulses and to view them, but secondarily to view those things which are under the control of the other virtues so that one conducts oneself unerringly in one's impulses. Likewise bravery is primarily to endure everything that one must, secondarily what is under the control of the other virtues. Justice is primarily to view what is in accord with the merit of each person, but secondarily —

λοιπά. Πάσας γὰρ τὰς ἀρετὰς τὰ πασῶν βλέπειν καὶ τὰ ὑποτεταγμένα ἀλλήλαις. Ὅμοιον γὰρ ἔλεγεν εἶναι ὁ Παναίτιος τὸ συμβαῖνον ἐπὶ | τῶν ἀρετῶν, ὡς εἰ πολλοῖς τοξόταις εἷς σκοπὸς εἴη κείμενος, ἔχοι δ᾽ οὗτος 5 ἐν αὑτῷ γραμμὰς διαφόρους τοῖς χρώμασιν· εἶθ᾽ ἕκαστος μὲν στοχάζοιτο τοῦ τυχεῖν τοῦ σκοποῦ, ἤδη δ᾽ ὁ μὲν διὰ τοῦ πατάξαι εἰς τὴν λευκὴν εἰ τύχοι γραμμήν, ὁ δὲ διὰ τοῦ εἰς τὴν μέλαιναν, ἄλλος ⟨δὲ⟩ διὰ τοῦ εἰς ἄλλο τι χρῶμα 10 γραμμῆς. Καθάπερ γὰρ τούτους ὡς μὲν ἀνωτάτω τέλος ποιεῖσθαι τὸ τυχεῖν τοῦ σκοποῦ, ἤδη δ᾽ ἄλλον κατ᾽ ἄλλον τρόπον προτίθεσθαι τὴν τεῦξιν, τὸν αὐτὸν τρόπον καὶ τὰς ἀρετὰς πάσας ποιεῖσθαι μὲν τέλος τὸ 15 εὐδαιμονεῖν, ὅ ἐστι κείμενον ἐν τῷ ζῆν ὁμολογουμένως τῇ φύσει, τούτου δ᾽ ἄλλην κατ᾽ ἄλλον τυγχάνειν.

5b6 Διττῶς δέ φησιν ὁ Διογένης λέγεσθαι τὰ δι᾽ αὑτὰ αἱρετά, ⟨τὰ⟩ καὶ τελικῶς αἱρετά, ὡς 20 ἔχει τὰ ἐν τῇ προειρημένῃ διαιρέσει κατατεταγμένα, τὰ δὲ ὅσα ἐν αὑτοῖς ἔχει τὴν αἰτίαν τοῦ αἱρετὰ εἶναι, ὅπερ παντὶ ἀγαθῷ ὑπάρχει.

5b7 Ἀρετὰς δ᾽ εἶναι πλείους φασὶ καὶ 25 ἀχωρίστους ἀπ᾽ ἀλλήλων, καὶ τὰς αὐτὰς τῷ ἡγεμονικῷ μέρει τῆς ψυχῆς καθ᾽ ὑπόστασιν, καθ᾽ ὃ δὴ καὶ σῶμα πᾶσαν ἀρετὴν εἶναί τε καὶ λέγεσθαι, τὴν γὰρ διάνοιαν καὶ τὴν ψυχὴν σῶμα εἶναι· τὸ γὰρ συμφυὲς πνεῦμα ἡμῖν 30 ἔνθερμον ὂν ψυχὴν ἡγοῦνται. |

Βούλονται δὲ καὶ τὴν ἐν ἡμῖν ψυχὴν ζῷον εἶναι, ζῆν τε γὰρ καὶ αἰσθάνεσθαι· καὶ μάλιστα τὸ ἡγεμονικὸν μέρος αὐτῆς, ὃ δὴ καλεῖται διάνοια. Διὸ καὶ πᾶσαν ἀρετὴν ζῷον εἶναι, 35

---

2 ἀλλήλαις: Usener; ἀλλήλοις: FP   4 ἐπὶ: FP; ἀπὸ: von Arnim   6 αὑτῷ: Meineke; αὐτῷ: FP   8 τοῦ: Usener; τὸ: FP   8 τοῦ πατάξαι: Usener; τὸ ὑποτάξαι: FP   10 δὲ: suppl. Heeren   17 ἄλλην: Heine; ἄλλον: FP   18 ἄλλον: Canter; ἄλλαν: P, ἄλλην: F   20 τὰ: suppl. Wachsmuth.

et cetera. For all the virtues consider what belongs to them all and those things subordinate to each of the other virtues. Thus Panaetius[31] said what happens in the case of the virtues is just as if there were one target set up for many archers and this had on it markings different in their colours. Then each archer would aim at hitting the target, one, however, by striking the white marking if he could make a hit, another by striking the black, and another by striking yet another colour marking. Just as these above all make it their goal to hit the target, but then each proposes its attainment in a different way, so in the same way all the virtues make it their goal to be happy, which depends on living in agreement with nature, but each attains this in its own way.[32]

5b6 Diogenes[33] says that the things which are worth choosing for themselves are spoken about in two senses: those which are completely worth choosing, as are those things classified in the above-mentioned division; and all those which have in themselves a cause for being chosen, which exists in every good thing.[34]

5b7 They say the virtues are both plural and inseparable from one another,[35] and are the same as the controlling part of the soul in substance; accordingly, then, every virtue is a body and is spoken of as such, since the mind and soul are body. For they think that the inborn breath in us, as it is warm, is our soul.[36]

They also want the soul in us to be a living creature, since it lives and has awareness. This is particularly true of the controlling part of it, which is called mind. Hence also every virtue is a living creature since it is the same as mind in essence. In accordance with

ἐπειδὴ ἡ αὐτὴ ⟨τῇ⟩ διανοίᾳ ἐστὶ κατὰ τὴν οὐσίαν. Κατὰ τοῦτο γάρ φασι καὶ τὴν φρόνησιν φρονεῖν, ἀκολουθεῖ γὰρ αὐτοῖς τὸ οὕτως λέγειν.

5b8 Ἀρετῆς δὲ καὶ κακίας οὐδὲν εἶναι μεταξύ. Πάντας γὰρ ἀνθρώπους ἀφορμὰς ἔχειν ἐκ φύσεως πρὸς ἀρετήν, καὶ οἱονεὶ τὸν τῶν ἡμιαμβείων λόγον ἔχειν κατὰ τὸν Κλεάνθην· ὅθεν ἀτελεῖς μὲν ὄντας εἶναι φαύλους, τελειωθέντας δὲ σπουδαίους.

Φασὶ δὲ καὶ πάντα ποιεῖν τὸν σοφὸν ⟨κατὰ⟩ πάσας τὰς ἀρετάς. Πᾶσαν γὰρ πρᾶξιν τελείαν αὐτοῦ εἶναι, διὸ καὶ μηδεμιᾶς ἀπολελεῖφθαι ἀρετῆς.

5b9 Ἀκολούθως γὰρ τούτοις δογματίζουσι καὶ ὅτι καὶ νουνεχόντως καὶ διαλεκτικῶς ποιεῖ καὶ συμποτικῶς καὶ ἐρωτικῶς. Τὸν δὲ ἐρωτικὸν καὶ διχῇ λέγεσθαι, τὸν μὲν κατὰ τὴν ἀρετὴν ποιὸν σπουδαῖον ὄντα, τὸν δὲ κατὰ τὴν κακίαν ἐν ψόγῳ, ὡς ἂν ἐρωτομανῆ τινα. εἶναι δ' ἔρωτα ⟨τὸν σπουδαῖον φιλίας⟩· τόν τ' ἀξιέραστον ὁμοίως | λέγεσθαι τῷ ἀξιοφιλήτῳ, καὶ οὐ τῷ ἀξιαπολαύστῳ· τὸν γὰρ ἄξιον σπουδαίου ἔρωτος, τοῦτον εἶναι ἀξιέραστον. Ὁμοίως δὲ τῇ ἐρωτικῇ τὴν συμποτικὴν παραλαμβάνουσιν εἰς τὰς ἀρετάς, τὴν μὲν περὶ τὸ ἐν συμποσίῳ καθῆκον ἀναστρεφομένην ἐπιστήμην οὖσαν τοῦ πῶς δεῖ ἐξάγεσθαι τὰ συμπόσια καὶ τοῦ πῶς δεῖ συμπίνειν· τὴν δ' ἐπιστήμην νέων θήρας εὐφυῶν, προτρεπτικὴν οὖσαν ἐπὶ τὰ κατ' ἀρετήν, καὶ καθόλου ἐπιστήμην τοῦ καλῶς ἐρᾶν· διὸ καί φασιν ἐρασθήσεσθαι τὸν νοῦν ἔχοντα. Τὸ δὲ ἐρᾶν αὐτὸ μόνον ἀδιάφορον

SVF
1.566
LS
61L

3.557

3.717

W
2.66

---

1 τῇ: suppl. von Arnim   8 ἡμιαμβείων: Wachsmuth; ἡμιαμβειαίων: FP; μιμιαμβείων: Meineke   12 κατὰ: suppl. Heeren   16 ὅτι καὶ νουνεχόντως: Usener; ὅτι κατὰ νουν ἔχων : FP; ὅτι ὁ νοῦν ἔχων: Mullach   19 ποιὸν: FP; ἐν ἐπαίνῳ: Hirzel   21 εἶναι δ' ἔρωτα ⟨τὸν σπουδαῖον φιλίας⟩: Wachsmuth, who supplements the lacuna after ἔρωτα, *exempli gratia*; εἰ δ' : FP; ἔτι δ': Heine; εἶναι δ' ἔρωτα τὴν ἐπιστήμην νέων θήρας: Asmis, transposing τόν τ' ἀξιέραστον ... συμπίνειν after ἔμφασιν   28 τοῦ πῶς: Heeren; τὸ πῶς: FP — repeated below   31 προτρεπτικὴν: Wachsmuth; πρὸς τρέψιν: P; πρὸς τέρψιν: F; πρὸς τέρψιν, ⟨ἄγ⟩ουσαν ἐπὶ τ⟨ὰ⟩ κατ' ἀρετήν: Schofield, Pomeroy   31 τὰ: Wachsmuth in his notes; τὴν: FP; ἐπὶ τ⟨ὸ ζ⟩ῆν: Meineke   34 ἀδιάφορον: Heeren; διάφορον: FP

this, they also say that intelligence is intelligent; for it is consistent with these things to speak in this way.

5b8 There is nothing in-between virtue and vice. All men have from nature initial impulses for virtue and they have, as it were, the logic of iambic half-lines according to Cleanthes:[37] while they are incomplete they are worthless, but once complete they are worthwhile.[38]

They also say that the wise man does everything in accord with all the virtues. For every action of his is complete; hence he also lacks none of the virtues.[39]

5b9 So, consistent with this, they hold the belief that he also acts sensibly and dialectically, and convivially and erotically.[40]

For the erotic man is also spoken of in two senses: in one sense with regard to virtue as a type of worthwhile person, in the other with regard to vice as a reproach, as in the case of a person mad with erotic love. <Worthwhile> erotic love is <for friendship>.[41] The man worthy of erotic love is spoken of in the same way as the man worthy of friendship and not as the man worth erotically loving. So this is the man worth loving erotically: the man who is worthy of worthwhile erotic love.

As with the erotic virtue, they also accept the convivial virtue among the virtues. First, dealing with what is appropriate at a drinking party, it is a knowledge of how one needs to carry out drinking parties and how one needs to drink in company. Then it is the knowledge of the hunt for young men of natural ability, encouraging them toward the things which are in accord with virtue,[42] and, overall, a knowledge of nobly loving.[43] Hence they also say that the person who has good sense will fall in love. To love by itself is merely indifferent, since it sometimes occurs in the

εἶναι, ἐπειδὴ γίνεταί ποτε καὶ περὶ φαύλους.
Τὸν δὲ ἔρωτα οὔτε ἐπιθυμίαν εἶναι οὔτε τινὸς
φαύλου πράγματος, ἀλλ' ἐπιβολὴν φιλοποιίας
διὰ κάλλους ἔμφασιν.

5b10 Λέγουσι δὲ καὶ πάντ' εὖ ποιεῖν τὸν σοφόν, ἃ ποιεῖ· δῆλον. Ὃν τρόπον γὰρ λέγομεν πάντ' εὖ ποιεῖν τὸν αὐλητὴν ἢ κιθαρῳδόν, συνυπακουομένου τοῦ ὅτι τὰ μὲν κατὰ τὴν αὔλησιν, τὰ δὲ κατὰ τὴν κιθαρῳδίαν, τὸν αὐτὸν τρόπον πάντ' εὖ ποιεῖν τὸν φρόνιμον, καθ' ὅσα ποιεῖ καὶ οὐ μὰ Δία, καθ' ἃ μὴ ποιεῖ. Τῷ γὰρ κατὰ λόγον ὀρθὸν ἐπιτελεῖν πάντα καὶ οἷον κατ' ἀρετήν, περὶ ὅλον οὖσαν τὸν βίον τέχνην, ἀκόλουθον ᾠήθησαν τὸ περὶ τοῦ πάντ' εὖ ποιεῖν τὸν σοφὸν δόγμα. Κατὰ τὸ ἀνάλογον δὲ καὶ τὸν φαῦλον πάντα ὅσα ποιεῖ κακῶς ποιεῖν καὶ κατὰ πάσας τὰς κακίας.

5b11 Φιλομουσίαν δὲ καὶ φιλογραμματίαν καὶ φιλιππίαν καὶ φιλοκυνηγίαν καὶ καθόλου ἐγκυκλίους λεγομένας τέχνας ἐπιτηδεύματα μὲν καλοῦσιν, ἐπιστήμας δ' οὔ, ἕν ⟨τε⟩ ταῖς σπουδαίαις ἕξεσι ταῦτα καταλείπουσι, καὶ ἀκολούθως μόνον τὸν σοφὸν φιλόμουσον εἶναι λέγουσι καὶ φιλογράμματον, καὶ ἐπὶ τῶν ἄλλων κατὰ τὸ ἀνάλογον. Τό τε ἐπιτήδευμα τοῦτον ὑπογράφουσι τὸν τρόπον· ὁδὸν διὰ τέχνης ἢ μέρους ἄγουσαν ἐπὶ ⟨τὰ⟩ κατ' ἀρετήν.

5b12 Μόνον δέ φασι τὸν σοφὸν καὶ μάντιν ἀγαθὸν εἶναι καὶ ποιητὴν καὶ ῥήτορα καὶ διαλεκτικὸν καὶ κριτικόν, οὐ πάντα δέ, διὰ τὸ προσδεῖσθαι ἔτι τινὰ τούτων καὶ θεωρημάτων τινῶν ἀναλήψεως. Εἶναι δὲ τὴν μαντικὴν φασιν ἐπιστήμην θεωρητικὴν σημείων τῶν ἀπὸ θεῶν

---

6 δῆλον: FP; δηλονότι: Mullach   11 καθ': Sedley (twice); καὶ: FP   11 καὶ οὐ μὰ Δία: FP; ναὶ μὰ Δία: Hense, deleting οὐ   12 Τῷ γὰρ ... τὸ περὶ: Canter; Τὸ γὰρ ... τῷ περὶ: FP   13 οἷον: Sedley marks as corrupt   18 δὲ καὶ: Heeren; τὴν: FP   19 καὶ καθόλου [καὶ κατὰ] ἐγκυκλίους: FP; καὶ κατὰ: del. Wachsmuth; καὶ καθόλου τὰς ἐγκυκλίους: Usener   21 τε: suppl. Heeren; δὲ: Valckenaar   26 ὑπογράφουσι: Wyttenbach; ἐπιγράφουσι: FP   27 ἢ μέρους: Usener; ἡμέρου: FP   27 ἐπὶ ⟨τὰ⟩ κατ': Wachsmuth; ἐπὶ κατ': FP   31 ἔτι: Meineke; εἴ: FP   33 θεωρητικήν: Wachsmuth; θεωρηματικήν: FP

case of the worthless as well. But erotic love is not an appetite nor is it directed at any worthless thing; rather it is an inclination to forming an attachment arising from the impression of beauty.[44]

5b10 They say that the wise man also does everything he does well. This is obvious: in the way that we say that the flute-player or the lyre-player does everything well (it being understood by this, in the first case, what is concerned with flute-playing and, in the second, what is concerned with lyre-playing), so in the same way the sensible person does everything well with respect to whatever he does, and not, by Zeus, with respect to what he does not do. For they have thought that the belief that the wise man does everything well is consistent with his completing everything in accord with correct reasoning and in a fashion which is in accord with virtue, which is the expertise which deals with life as a whole.[45] Analogously, the worthless man does everything he does badly and in accord with all the vices.

5b11 They call fondness of music, fondness of literature, fondness of horse-riding, fondness of hunting with dogs, and, overall, what are called the everyday expertises,[46] pursuits, but not types of knowledge, and they admit these among the worthwhile conditions.[47] Consistent with this they say that only the wise man is fond of music, fond of literature, and analogously with regard to the other pursuits. They describe a pursuit this way: it is a path through expertise (or through a part of an expertise) which leads to what is in accord with virtue.[48]

5b12 They say that only the wise man is a good prophet, poet, and orator, and capable of dialectic and literary criticism, although not in all respects, since each of the above also needs in addition the acquisition of particular rules. They say that the prophetic art is a rule-based knowledge of signs from the gods or

ἢ δαιμόνων πρὸς ἀνθρώπινον βίον συντεινόντων. Ὁμοίως δὲ καὶ τὰ εἴδη τῆς μαντικῆς.
Λέγουσι δὲ καὶ ἱερέα μόνον εἶναι τὸν σοφόν, φαῦλον δὲ μηδένα. Τὸν γὰρ ἱερέα εἶναι δεῖν ἔμπειρον νόμων τῶν περὶ θυσίας καὶ εὐχὰς καὶ καθαρμοὺς καὶ ἱδρύσεις | καὶ πάντα τὰ τοιαῦτα, πρὸς δὲ τούτοις καὶ ἁγιστείας τε καὶ εὐσεβείας δεῖσθαι καὶ ἐμπειρίας τῆς τῶν θεῶν θεραπείας, καὶ ⟨τοῦ⟩ ἐντὸς εἶναι τῆς φύσεως τῆς θείας. Μηδ' ἓν ⟨δέ τ⟩ι τούτων ὑπάρχειν τῷ φαύλῳ, διὸ καὶ πάντας εἶναι τοὺς ἄφρονας ἀσεβεῖς. Τὴν γὰρ ἀσέβειαν κακίαν οὖσαν, ἄγνοιαν εἶναι θεῶν θεραπείας, τὴν δ' εὐσέβειαν, ὡς εἴπομεν, ἐπιστήμην θεῶν θεραπείας.

Ὁμοίως δὲ μηδ' ὁσίους εἶναί φασι τοὺς φαύλους. Τὴν γὰρ ὁσιότητα ὑπογράφεσθαι δικαιοσύνην πρὸς θεούς· τοὺς δὲ φαύλους παρεκβαίνειν πολλὰ τῶν πρὸς θεοὺς δικαίων, παρ' ὃ καὶ ἀνοσίους εἶναι καὶ ἀκαθάρους καὶ ἀνάγνους καὶ μιαροὺς καὶ ἀνεορτάστους.

Τὸ γὰρ ἑορτάζειν ἀστείου φασὶν εἶναι, τῆς ἑορτῆς οὔσης χρόνου τινὸς ἐν ᾧ χρὴ περὶ τὸ θεῖον γίγνεσθαι τιμῆς χάριν καὶ καθηκούσης ἐπισημασίας, ὅθεν καὶ τὸν ἑορτάζοντα συγκαθεικέναι δεῖ μετ' εὐσεβείας εἰς τὴν τοιαύτην τάξιν.

5b13 Ἔτι δὲ λέγουσι πάντα φαῦλον μαίνεσθαι, ἄγνοιαν ἔχοντα αὐτοῦ καὶ τῶν καθ' αὑτόν, ὅπερ ἐστὶ μανία. Τὴν δ' ἄγνοιαν εἶναι ἐναντίαν κακίαν τῇ σωφροσύνῃ· ταύτην δὲ πρός τί πως ἔχουσαν ἀκαταστάτους καὶ πτοιώδεις παρεχομένην τὰς ὁρμὰς μανίαν εἶναι· διὸ καὶ

SVF 3.604

W 2.68

3.660

3.663
LS 41I

---

8 ἁγιστείας: Usener; ἄλλους διά: FP   8 τε καί: Usener; τε τό: FP   10 τοῦ: suppl. Usener   11 μηδ' ἕν ⟨δέ τ⟩ι: Wachsmuth; μηδενί: FP   11 τῷ φαύλῳ: Meineke; τῶν φαύλων: FP   19 τῶν ... δικαίων: Meineke; τῷ ... δικαίῳ: FP   28 Ἔτι: Canter; ἐπεί: FP   29 αὑτοῦ: Heeren; αὐτοῦ: FP   31 σωφροσύνῃ: FP; φρονήσει: Usener (cf. 5b2) — but it is the virtue which controls the ὁρμαί which is required (5b5): LS 2.259 (=42I)   32 πτοιώδεις ... πτοιώδη: Canter; ποιώδεις ... ποιώδη: FP

spirits which apply to human life. They say the same about the species of the prophetic art.[49]

They also say that only the wise man can be a priest, while no worthless person can be one. For the priest needs to be experienced in the laws concerning sacrifices, prayers, purifications, foundations,[50] and the like. In addition to this, he needs ritual, piety, and experience in the service of the gods, and to be inside the divine nature.[51] Not one of these things belongs to the worthless; hence, also all the stupid are impious. For impiety as a vice is ignorance of the service of the gods, while piety, as we said,[52] is knowledge of the service of the gods.

Likewise they say that the worthless are not holy. For holiness is described as justice with respect to the gods. The worthless transgress many of the just customs pertaining to the gods, on account of which they are unholy, impure, unclean, defiled, and barred from festive rites.[53]

For carrying out festive rites is, they say, the mark of a civilised man,[54] since a festival is a time when one ought to be concerned with the divine for the sake of honour and appropriate celebration. So the person who carries out festive rites needs to have humbly entered with piety into this post.

5b13 Furthermore they say that every worthless person is mad, as he is in a state of ignorance about himself and his affairs, which is madness. But ignorance is the opposite vice to self-restraint. And this, when providing unstable and agitated impulses in relation to something else, is madness. Hence they also describe madness in this manner: as agitated ignorance.

ὑπογράφουσι τὴν μανίαν οὕτως· ἄγνοιαν πτοιώδη.

5c Ἔτι δὲ τῶν ἀγαθῶν τὰ μὲν πᾶσι τοῖς φρονίμοις ὑπάρχειν καὶ αἰεί, τὰ δὲ οὔ. Ἀρετὴν μὲν | πᾶσαν καὶ φρονίμην αἴσθησιν καὶ φρονίμην ὁρμὴν καὶ τὰ ὅμοια πᾶσι τοῖς φρονίμοις ὑπάρχειν καὶ ἐν παντὶ καιρῷ· χαρὰν δὲ καὶ εὐφροσύνην καὶ φρονίμην περιπάτησιν οὔτε πᾶσι τοῖς φρονίμοις ὑπάρχειν οὔτε αἰεί. Ἀνάλογον δὲ καὶ τῶν κακῶν τὰ μὲν πᾶσι τοῖς ἄφροσιν ὑπάρχειν καὶ αἰεί, τὰ δ' οὔ. Κακίαν μὲν οὖν πᾶσαν καὶ ἄφρονα αἴσθησιν καὶ ἄφρονα ὁρμὴν καὶ τὰ παραπλήσια πᾶσι τοῖς ἄφροσιν ὑπάρχειν ⟨καὶ⟩ αἰεί· λύπην δὲ καὶ φόβον καὶ ἄφρονα ἀπόκρισιν οὔτε πᾶσι τοῖς ἄφροσιν ὑπάρχειν οὔτ' ἐν παντὶ καιρῷ.

SVF
3.103

W
2.69

5d Πάντα δὲ τἀγαθὰ ὠφέλιμα εἶναι καὶ εὔχρηστα καὶ συμφέροντα καὶ λυσιτελῆ καὶ σπουδαῖα καὶ πρέποντα καὶ καλὰ καὶ οἰκεῖα· τὰ δὲ κακὰ ἐκ τῶν ἐναντίων πάντα βλαβερὰ καὶ δύσχρηστα καὶ ἀσύμφορα καὶ ἀλυσιτελῆ καὶ φαῦλα καὶ ἀπρεπῆ καὶ αἰσχρὰ καὶ ἀνοίκεια.

3.86

Τὸ δ' ἀγαθὸν λέγεσθαί φασι πλεοναχῶς, τὸ μὲν πρῶτον, οἷον πηγῆς ἔχον χώραν, ὅπερ οὕτως ἀποδίδοσθαι· ἀφ' οὗ συμβαίνει ὠφελεῖσθαι ἢ ὑφ' οὗ (τὸ δὲ | πρώτως εἶναι αἴτιον)· τὸ ⟨δὲ⟩ δεύτερον, καθ' ὃ συμβαίνει ὠφελεῖσθαι· κοινότερον δὲ καὶ διατεῖνον καὶ ἐπὶ τὰ προειρημένα, τὸ οἷον ὠφελεῖν. Ὁμοίως δὲ καὶ τὸ κακὸν κατὰ τὴν τοῦ ἀγαθοῦ ἀναλογίαν ὑπογράφεσθαι. Τὸ μὲν οὖν ἀφ' οὗ συμβαίνει βλάπτεσθαι ἢ ὑφ' οὗ· τὸ δὲ καθ' ὃ συμβαίνει βλάπτεσθαι· κοινότερον δὲ τούτων τὸ οἷον βλάπτειν.

3.74

2.70

14 καὶ: suppl. Heeren   18 εὔχρηστα: Meineke; χρηστὰ: FP   26 ὠφελεῖσθαι ἢ ὑφ' οὗ (τὸ δὲ πρώτως εἶναι αἴτιον): Wachsmuth; ὠφελεῖσθαι τὸ δὲ πρώτως εἶναι αἴτιον καὶ ὑφ' οὗ: FP; ὠφελεῖσθαι τῷ δὲ πρώτον εἶναι αἴτιον ἢ ὑφ' οὗ: Heine   27 δὲ: suppl. Meineke   28 κοινότερον: scholia on Lucian; κοινότατον: F; κονότατον: P   30 τοῦ ἀγαθοῦ: Meineke; τῶν ἀγαθῶν: FP

5c Furthermore of good things, some belong to all the intelligent at all times, others do not. Every virtue, intelligent perception, intelligent impulse, and the like belongs to all the intelligent and on every occasion. Joy, cheerfulness, and intelligent walking do not belong to all the intelligent, nor at all times. Likewise some bad things belong to all the stupid and at all times, others not. So every vice, stupid perception, stupid impulse, and the like belongs to all the stupid at all times. But pain, fear, and stupid answering do not belong to all the stupid, nor on every occasion.

5d All good things are beneficial, useful, advantageous, profitable, worthwhile, suitable, fine, and fitting. Conversely all bad things are harmful, useless, disadvantageous, unprofitable, worthless, unsuitable, shameful, and unfitting.

They say that the good is spoken of in various ways. First as having the role of a source, which is interpreted as follows — that from which or by whose agency being benefitted occurs (in this first sense it is causative). Second, it is that in respect of which being benefitted occurs. More generally, extending to the above explanations as well, whatever benefits.[55] Likewise the bad too is described analogously with the good. It is that from which or by whose agency being harmed occurs. Then, that in respect of which being harmed occurs. More generally than this, whatever harms.

5e Τῶν δ' ἀγαθῶν τὰ μὲν εἶναι περὶ ψυχήν, τὰ δ' ἐκτός, τὰ δ' οὔτε περὶ ψυχὴν οὔτ' ἐκτός. Περὶ ψυχὴν μὲν τὰς ἀρετὰς καὶ ⟨τὰς⟩ σπουδαίας ἕξεις καὶ καθόλου τὰς ἐπαινετὰς ἐνεργείας· ἐκτὸς δὲ τούς τε φίλους καὶ τοὺς γνωρίμους καὶ τὰ παραπλήσια· οὔτε δὲ περὶ ψυχὴν οὔτ' ἐκτός, τοὺς σπουδαίους καὶ καθόλου ⟨τοὺς⟩ τὰς ἀρετὰς ἔχοντας. Ὁμοίως δὲ καὶ τῶν κακῶν τὰ μὲν περὶ ψυχήν, τὰ δ' ἐκτός, τὰ δ' οὔτε περὶ ψυχὴν οὔτ' ἐκτός· περὶ ψυχὴν μὲν τάς τε κακίας σὺν ταῖς μοχθηραῖς ἕξεσι καὶ καθόλου τὰς ψεκτὰς ἐνεργείας· ἐκτὸς δὲ τοὺς ἐχθροὺς σὺν τοῖς εἴδεσιν· οὔτε ⟨δὲ⟩ περὶ ψυχὴν οὔτ' ἐκτὸς τοὺς φαύλους καὶ πάντας τοὺς τὰς κακίας ἔχοντας.

SVF 3.97

5f Τῶν δὲ περὶ ψυχὴν ἀγαθῶν τὰ μὲν εἶναι διαθέσεις, τὰ δὲ ἕξεις μὲν διαθέσεις δ' οὔ, τὰ δ' οὔτε ἕξεις οὔτε διαθέσεις. Διαθέσεις μὲν τὰς ἀρετὰς πάσας, ἕξεις δὲ μόνον καὶ οὐ διαθέσεις τὰ ἐπιτηδεύματα, ὡς τὴν μαντικὴν καὶ τὰ παραπλήσια· οὔτε δὲ ἕξεις οὔτε διαθέσεις τὰς κατ' ἀρετὰς ἐνεργείας, οἷον φρονίμευμα καὶ τὴν τῆς σωφροσύνης χρῆσιν καὶ τὰ παραπλήσια. Ὁμοίως δὲ καὶ τῶν περὶ ψυχὴν κακῶν τὰ μὲν εἶναι διαθέσεις, τὰ δ' ἕξεις μὲν διαθέσεις δ' οὔ, τὰ δὲ οὔτε ἕξεις οὔτε διαθέσεις. Διαθέσεις μὲν τὰς κακίας πάσας, ἕξεις δὲ μόνον τὰς εὐκαταφορίας, οἷον τὴν φθονερίαν, τὴν ἐπιλυπίαν καὶ τὰ ὅμοια καὶ ἔτι τὰ νοσήματα καὶ ἀρρωστήματα, οἷον φιλαργυρίαν, οἰνοφλυγίαν καὶ τὰ παραπλήσια. Οὔτε ⟨δ'⟩ ἕξεις οὔτε διαθέσεις τὰς κατὰ κακίας ἐνεργείας, οἷον ἀφρόνευσιν, ἀδίκευσιν καὶ τὰ ταύταις παραπλήσια.

3.104
W 2.71
LS 60L

---

3 τὰς: suppl. Wachsmuth   8 τοὺς: suppl. Heeren   8 Ὁμοίως: Canter; ὅμως: FP
20 ὡς: Heeren; καὶ: FP   22 κατ' ἀρετὰς: Meineke; κατ' αὐτὰς: FP
22 φρονίμευμα: Wachsmuth (cf. 11e); φρονίμευσιν: scholia on Lucian; φρόνησιν: FP
23 χρῆσιν: Heine; κτῆσιν: FP; ἄσκησιν: Wachsmuth   31 δ': suppl. Meineke

5e Of good things, some concern the soul, others concern externals, while others concern neither the soul nor externals. Concerned with the soul are the virtues, the worthwhile conditions, and, overall, the praiseworthy activities. Externals are friends, acquaintances, and the like. Neither concerned with the soul nor externals are the worthwhile and, overall, those who have the virtues.[56] Likewise of bad things too, some are concerned with the soul, others externals, and others neither concerned with the soul nor externals. Concerned with the soul are the vices together with base dispositions and, overall, the blameworthy activities. Externals are enemies along with their manifestations. Neither concerned with the soul nor externals are the worthless and all those who possess vices.

5f Of the good things to do with the soul, some are dispositions, some are conditions but not dispositions, and others are neither conditions nor dispositions.[57] All the virtues are dispositions, but the pursuits, such as expertise in prophecy and the like, are only conditions and not dispositions. Neither conditions nor dispositions are the activities in respect of the virtues, such as exercise of intelligence and the use of self-restraint and the like. Likewise with regard to the bad things to do with the soul, some are dispositions, others are conditions but not dispositions, and others are neither conditions nor dispositions. All the vices are dispositions, but propensities, such as enviousness, taking offence, and the like, and in addition the illnesses and frailties, such as fondness for money, drunkenness and the like, are only conditions.[58] Neither conditions nor dispositions are the activities in respect of the vices, such as acting with stupidity and acting with injustice, and things like these.

5g Τῶν τε ἀγαθῶν τὰ μὲν εἶναι τελικά, τὰ δὲ ποιητικά, τὰ δὲ ἀμφοτέρως ἔχοντα. Ὁ μὲν οὖν φρόνιμος ἄνθρωπος καὶ ὁ φίλος ποιητικὰ μόνον ἐστὶν ἀγαθά· χαρὰ δὲ καὶ εὐφροσύνη καὶ θάρρος καὶ φρονίμη περιπάτησις τελικὰ μόνον ἐστὶν ἀγαθά· αἱ δ᾽ ἀρεταὶ πᾶσαι καὶ ποιητικά ἐστιν ἀγαθὰ καὶ τελικά, καὶ γὰρ ἀπογεννῶσι τὴν εὐδαιμονίαν καὶ συμπληροῦσι, μέρη αὐτῆς γινόμεναι. Ἀνάλογον δὲ καὶ τῶν κακῶν τὰ μέν ἐστι ποιητικὰ τῆς κακοδαιμονίας, τὰ δὲ τελικά, τὰ δὲ ἀμφοτέρως ἔχοντα. Ὁ μὲν οὖν ἄφρων ἄνθρωπος καὶ ὁ ἐχθρὸς ποιητικὰ μόνον ἐστὶ κακά· λύπη δὲ καὶ φόβος καὶ κλοπὴ καὶ ἄφρων ἐρώτησις καὶ τὰ ὅμοια τελικά ⟨μόνον ἐστὶ κακά⟩· αἱ δὲ κακίαι καὶ ποιητικὰ καὶ τελικά ἐστι κακά· ἀπογεννῶσι γὰρ τὴν κακοδαιμονίαν καὶ συμπληροῦσι, μέρη αὐτῆς γινόμεναι.

5h Ἔτι δὲ τῶν ἀγαθῶν τὰ μὲν εἶναι δι᾽ αὑτὰ αἱρετά, τὰ δὲ ποιητικά. Ὁπόσα μὲν οὖν οὐδενὸς ἄλλου ἕνεκεν εἰς εὔλογον αἵρεσιν ἔρχεται, δι᾽ αὑτὰ αἱρετά· ὁπόσα δὲ τῷ ἑτέρων τινῶν παρασκευαστικὰ γίνεσθαι, κατὰ τὸ ποιητικὸν λέγεσθαι.

5i Καὶ πᾶν μὲν ἀγαθὸν αἱρετὸν εἶναι· ἀρεστὸν γὰρ καὶ δοκιμαστὸν καὶ ἐπαινετὸν ὑπάρχειν· πᾶν δὲ κακὸν φευκτόν. Τὸ γὰρ ἀγαθὸν καθ᾽ ὃ μὲν αἵρεσιν εὔλογον κινεῖ, αἱρετόν ἐστι· καθ᾽ ὃ δὲ ἀνυπόπτως εἰς αἵρεσιν ἔρχεται, ἀρεστόν· καθ᾽ ὃ δὲ πάλιν εὐλόγως ἄν τις περὶ αὐτοῦ καθυπολαμβάνοι τῶν ἀπ᾽ ἀρετῆς εἶναι, ⟨ἐπαινετόν⟩.

5k Ἔτι δὲ τῶν ἀγαθῶν τὰ μὲν εἶναι ἐν κινήσει, τὰ δὲ ἐν σχέσει. Ἐν κινήσει μὲν τὰ

---

9 γινόμεναι: Usener; γινόμενα: FP   15 μόνον ἐστὶ κακά: Wachsmuth, Meineke
19 Περὶ αἱρετῶν καὶ φευκτῶν: FP; deleted by Wachsmuth   22 δὲ τῷ: Heeren;
δὲ τῶν: FP   30 Heeren supplemented ⟨καθ᾽ ὃ δὲ ... , δοκιμαστόν⟩ after ἀρεστόν
31 καθυπολαμβάνοι: FP; ὑπολαμβάνοι: Mullach   31 ἐπαινετόν: suppl. Wachsmuth

5g Of good things, some are final, others are productive, while others are both. Thus the intelligent man and the friend are only productive goods; but joy, cheerfulness, confidence, and intelligent walking[59] are only final goods.[60] All the virtues are both productive and final goods, for they both help to create happiness and make it complete, being parts of it.[61] Analogously, of bad things, some are productive of unhappiness, others are final, while others are both. Thus the stupid man and the enemy are only productive evils. But pain, fear, theft, stupid questioning, and the like <are only> final <evils>. The vices are both productive and final evils, for they help to create unhappiness and make it complete, being parts of it.

5h[62] In addition, some of the good things are worth choosing for themselves, others are productive. So whatever things result in a reasonable choice[63] for the sake of nothing else are worth choosing for themselves; but those which are preparative of something else are spoken of in respect of their productivity.

5i Also, everything good is worth choosing, as it is satisfying, is prized, and is praiseworthy. But everything bad is worth avoiding. For the good, inasmuch as it sets moving a reasonable choice, is worth choosing. Inasmuch as it unhesitatingly results in a choice, it is satisfying. Again, inasmuch as one would reasonably surmise with regard to it that it is one of the things that derive from virtue, <it is praiseworthy>.

5k Furthermore, of good things some are in motion, while others are in a state.[64] In motion are things like these: joy, cheerfulness, and intelligent association. In a state are things like these: orderly

τοιαῦτα, χαράν, εὐφροσύνην, σώφρονα
ὁμιλίαν· ἐν σχέσει δὲ τὰ τοιαῦτα, εὔτακτον
ἡσυχίαν, μονὴν ἀτάραχον, προσοχὴν
ἔπανδρον. Τῶν δὲ ἐν σχέσει τὰ μὲν καὶ ἐν ἕξει
εἶναι, οἷον τὰς ἀρετάς· τὰ δ' ἐν σχέσει μόνον, 5
ὡς τὰ ῥηθέντα. Ἐν ἕξει δὲ οὐ μόνας εἶναι τὰς
ἀρετάς, ἀλλὰ καὶ τὰς ἄλλας τέχνας τὰς ἐν
τῷ σπουδαίῳ ἀνδρὶ ἀλλοιωθείσας ὑπὸ τῆς
ἀρετῆς καὶ γενομένας ἀμεταπτώτους, οἱονεὶ
γὰρ ἀρετὰς γίνεσθαι. Φασὶ δὲ καὶ τῶν ἐν ἕξει 10
ἀγαθῶν εἶναι καὶ τὰ ἐπιτηδεύματα καλούμενα,
οἷον φιλομουσίαν, φιλογραμματίαν,
φιλογεωμετρίαν καὶ τὰ παραπλήσια. Εἶναι
γὰρ ὁδόν τινα ἐκλεκτικὴν τῶν ἐν ταύταις ταῖς
τέχναις οἰκείων πρὸς ἀρετήν, ἀναφέρουσαν 15
αὐτὰ ἐπὶ τὸ τοῦ βίου τέλος.
Ἔτι δὲ τῶν ἀγαθῶν τὰ μὲν εἶναι καθ'
ἑαυτά, τὰ δὲ πρός τί πως ἔχειν. Καθ' ἑαυτὰ
μὲν ἐπιστήμην, δικαιοπραγίαν καὶ τὰ ὅμοια·
πρός τι δὲ τιμήν, εὔνοιαν, φιλίαν, ⟨συμφωνίαν⟩. 20
Εἶναι δὲ τὴν ἐπιστήμην κατάληψιν ἀσφαλῆ καὶ
ἀμετάπτωτον ὑπὸ λόγου· ἑτέραν δὲ
ἐπιστήμην σύστημα ἐκ ἐπιστημῶν τοιούτων,
οἷον ἡ τῶν κατὰ μέρος, λογικὴ ἐν τῷ
σπουδαίῳ ὑπάρχουσα· ἄλλην δὲ σύστημα ἐξ 25
ἐπιστημῶν τεχνικῶν | ἐξ αὑτοῦ ἔχον τὸ
βέβαιον, ὡς ἔχουσιν αἱ ἀρεταί· ἄλλην δὲ ἕξιν
φαντασιῶν δεκτικὴν ἀμετάπτωτον ὑπὸ
λόγου, ἥν τινά φασιν ἐν τόνῳ καὶ δυνάμει
κεῖσθαι. Φιλίαν δ' εἶναι κοινωνίαν βίου· 30
συμφωνίαν δὲ ὁμοδογματίαν περὶ τῶν κατὰ
τὸν βίον. Τῆς δὲ φιλίας εἶναι γνωριμότητα μὲν
φιλίαν ἐγνωσμένων· συνήθειαν δὲ φιλίαν
συνειθισμένων· ἑταιρίαν δὲ φιλίαν καθ' αἵρεσιν,

---

4 τὰ ... τὰ: Reith; τὰς ... τὰς: FP   7 τὰς ἄλλας τέχνας: P; τὰς ἀλλὰ καὶ τὰς τέχνας: F;
τὰς τέχνας: Wachsmuth   14 ἐκλεκτικὴν: Meurer; ἐκλεκτὴν: FP
17 Ἔτι: Canter; ἐπεὶ: FP   20 συμφωνωνίαν: Wachsmuth, from 51 below
22 ἑτέραν ... ἄλλην ... ἄλλην: emended by Wachsmuth to ἑτέρως ... ἄλλως ... ἄλλως;
but see LS 2.258 (=41H) for a defence of the manuscript text
23 ἐπιστημῶν: FP; καταλήψεων: Wachsmuth   25 ὑπάρχουσα: Heeren;
ὑπάρχουσαν: FP   26 αὑτοῦ: Meineke; αὐτοῦ: P; αὐτῶν: F   27 ἔχουσιν: Canter; ἔχουσαν: FP

rest, calm persistence, manly attention. Of things in a state, some are also in a condition, such as the virtues,[65] while some are only in a state, such as the things named above. Not only are the virtues in a condition but also the other expertises in a worthwhile man which have been altered by virtue and have become unchangeable, for they become like virtues. They say that among the good things which are in a condition are also what are called the pursuits, such as fondness for music, fondness for literature, fondness for geometry, and the suchlike. For there is a selective path of the things in these expertises which have an affinity with virtue, referring them to the goal of life.

51   Furthermore, of good things, some are good in themselves, while others are good being related in a certain way to something. Good in themselves are knowledge, acting justly, and the like. Good in relation to something are honour, good-will, friendship, <and harmony>.[66]

Knowledge is an apprehension which is secure and irreversible by reason.[67] In a different sense knowledge is a composite of such kinds of knowledge, such as the knowledge of particulars, which is rational[68] in a worthwhile person. In another sense it is a composite of expert types of knowledge, possessing a solidness out of itself as do the virtues. In another sense, knowledge is a condition which is receptive of impressions and irreversible by reason[69] — this, they say, is something which consists in tension and capacity.

Friendship is a partnership in life. Harmony is an agreement in beliefs concerning matters in life. Of friendships, acquaintance is friendship of those known to one another; intimacy is the friendship of people grown accustomed to one another; comradeship is friendship by choice, as, for example, with those of

ὡς ἂν ὁμηλίκων· ξενίαν δὲ φιλίαν ἀλλοδαπῶν.
Εἶναι δὲ καὶ συγγενικήν τινα φιλίαν ἐκ
συγγενῶν· καὶ ἐρωτικὴν ἐξ ἔρωτος. Ἀλυπίαν
δὲ καὶ εὐταξίαν τὰς αὐτὰς εἶναι τῇ
σωφροσύνῃ, νοῦν δὲ καὶ φρένας φρονήσει, 5
μεταδοτικὴν δὲ καὶ ἐπιδοτικὴν χρηστότητι· τῷ
μέντοι γε πρός τί πως ἔχειν ὠνομάσθησαν·
ὅπερ καθήκει καὶ ἐπὶ τῶν ἄλλων ἀρετῶν
παρατηρεῖν.

5m   Ἔτι δὲ τῶν ἀγαθῶν τὰ μὲν εἶναι ἄμικτα, 10   SVF
οἷον ἐπιστήμην, τὰ δὲ μεμιγμένα, οἷον   3.101
εὐτεκνίαν, εὐγηρίαν, εὐζωίαν. Ἔστι δ' ἡ μὲν
εὐτεκνία χρῆσις τέκνοις κατὰ φύσιν ἔχουσι
σπουδαία, ἡ δὲ εὐγηρία χρῆσις σπουδαία γήρᾳ
κατὰ φύσιν ἔχοντι, καὶ ὁμοίως ἡ εὐζωία.   15

5n   Φανερὸν δὲ αἰεὶ ἐπὶ τούτων, ὅτι καὶ τῶν
κακῶν αἱ ὅμοιαι διαιρέσεις ἔσονται. | W

5o   Διαφέρειν δὲ λέγουσιν αἱρετὸν καὶ ληπτόν.   2.75
Αἱρετὸν μὲν γὰρ εἶναι τὸ ὁρμῆς αὐτοτελοῦς
κινητικόν, ⟨ληπτὸν δὲ ὃ εὐλογίστως 20   3.131
ἐκλεγόμεθα⟩. Ὅσῳ δὲ διαφέρει τὸ αἱρετὸν τοῦ
ληπτοῦ, τοσούτῳ καὶ τὸ ⟨καθ'⟩ αὕθ' αἱρετὸν
τοῦ καθ' αὑτὸ ληπτοῦ, καὶ καθόλου τὸ ἀγαθὸν
τοῦ ἀξίαν ἔχοντος.

6   Τοῦ δὲ ἀνθρώπου ὄντος ζῴου λογικοῦ 25
θνητοῦ, φύσει πολιτικοῦ, φασὶ καὶ τὴν ἀρετὴν
πᾶσαν τὴν περὶ ἄνθρωπον καὶ τὴν
εὐδαιμονίαν ζωὴν ἀκόλουθον ὑπάρχειν καὶ
ὁμολογουμένην φύσει.

6a   Τὸ δὲ τέλος ὁ μὲν Ζήνων οὕτως ἀπέδωκε· 30   1.179
'τὸ ὁμολογουμένως ζῆν'· τοῦτο δ' ἐστὶ καθ' ἕνα   LS
λόγον καὶ σύμφωνον ζῆν, ὡς τῶν μαχομένως   63B
ζώντων κακοδαιμονούντων. | Οἱ δὲ μετὰ   2.76
τοῦτον προσδιαρθροῦντες οὕτως ἐξέφερον

3 Ἀλυπίαν ...παρατηρεῖν: transposed from the end of 5m by Wachsmuth   13 χρῆσις: FP;
κτῆσις: Wachsmuth   13 τέκνοις: F; τέχνοις: P; τέκνων: Heeren   13 ἔχουσι: FP;
ἔχουσα: Heeren   14 γήρᾳ: FP; γήρως: Mullach   15 ἔχοντι: FP; ἔχουσα: Heeren
16 ἐπὶ τούτων: Wachsmuth; τι τούτων: FP   20 κινητικόν: Canter; νικητικόν: FP
20 ληπτὸν δὲ ὃ εὐλογίστως ἐκλεγόμεθα: Wachsmuth; cf. Plut. de comm. not. 20, 23, 26 (=Mor.
1068a, 1070a ,1071a)   22 καθ' αὕθ' αἱρετὸν: Wachsmuth; αὐθαίρετον: FP   32 τῶν μαχομένως
ζώντων: scholiast on Lucian (4 p.210,22 Jacobitz); τῶν μαχομένων ζῴων: FP

the same age group; hospitality is friendship with strangers. There is also a kin friendship of kinsmen, and an erotic friendship from erotic love.[70]

Not feeling distress and orderliness are the same as self-restraint, good sense and brains are the same as intelligence, the skill of sharing and the skill of giving are the same as kindness — however, they have been named by being in a certain condition with respect to something. It is appropriate to observe carefully this distinction with regard to the other virtues as well.

5m Furthermore, of good things, some are unmixed, such as knowledge, while others are mixed, such as being fortunate with children, a fortunate old age, and a fortunate life. Being fortunate with children is a worthwhile usage in the case of children in accord with nature, being fortunate in old age is a worthwhile usage in the case of old age in accord with nature, and being fortunate in life is defined similarly.[71]

5n It is always clear with regard to these goods that there will be the same divisions of bad things as well.

5o They also say there is a difference between what is worth choosing and what is worth acquiring. What is worth choosing is stimulative of an impulse which is complete in itself, <while what is worth acquiring is what we select circumspectly>. In the same degree as what is worth choosing differs from what is worth acquiring, so what is worth choosing for itself differs from what is worth acquiring for itself, and, overall, the good differs from what has value.[72]

6 As man is a rational mortal creature, political by nature, they also say that every virtue which is associated with man and the happy life is consistent with and in agreement with nature.

6a Zeno interpreted the goal thus: "To live in agreement"[73] — that is to live according to a single line of reason and in harmony, as those who live in conflict are unhappy.[74] Those after him,

'ὁμολογουμένως τῇ φύσει ζῆν' ὑπολαβόντες ἔλαττον εἶναι ⟨ἢ⟩ κατηγόρημα τὸ ὑπὸ τοῦ Ζήνωνος ῥηθέν. Κλεάνθης γὰρ πρῶτος διαδεξάμενος αὐτοῦ τὴν αἵρεσιν προσέθηκε 'τῇ φύσει' καὶ οὕτως ἀπέδωκε· 'τέλος ἐστὶ τὸ ὁμολογουμένως τῇ φύσει ζῆν'. Ὅπερ ὁ Χρύσιππος σαφέστερον βουλόμενος ποιῆσαι, ἐξήνεγκε τὸν τρόπον τοῦτον· 'ζῆν κατ' ἐμπειρίαν τῶν φύσει συμβαινόντων'. Διογένης δέ· 'εὐλογιστεῖν ἐν τῇ τῶν κατὰ φύσιν ἐκλογῇ καὶ ἀπεκλογῇ'. Ἀρχέδημος δέ· 'πάντα τὰ καθήκοντα ἐπιτελοῦντας ζῆν'. Ἀντίπατρος δέ· 'ζῆν ἐκλεγομένους μὲν τὰ κατὰ φύσιν, ἀπεκλεγομένους δὲ τὰ παρὰ φύσιν διηνεκῶς". Πολλάκις δὲ καὶ οὕτως ἀπεδίδου· 'πᾶν τὸ καθ' αὑτὸν ποιεῖν διηνεκῶς καὶ ἀπαραβάτως πρὸς τὸ τυγχάνειν τῶν προηγουμένων κατὰ φύσιν'.

SVF 1.552
3.12
3.44 Diog. LS 58K
3.20 Arch.
3.57 Ant.

6b Τὸ δὲ τέλος λέγεσθαι τριχῶς ὑπὸ τῶν ἐκ τῆς αἱρέσεως ταύτης· τό τε γὰρ τελικὸν ἀγαθὸν λέγεσθαι τέλος ἐν τῇ φιλολόγῳ συνηθείᾳ, ὡς τὴν ὁμολογίαν λέγουσι τέλος εἶναι· λέγουσι δὲ καὶ τὸν σκοπὸν τέλος, οἷον τὸν ὁμολογούμενον βίον ἀναφορικῶς λέγοντες ἐπὶ τὸ παρακείμενον κατηγόρημα· κατὰ δὲ τὸ τρίτον σημαινόμενον λέγουσι τέλος τὸ ἔσχατον τῶν ὀρεκτῶν, ἐφ' ὃ πάντα τὰ ἄλλα ἀναφέρεσθαι. |

3.3

6c Διαφέρειν δὲ τέλος καὶ σκοπὸν ἡγοῦνται· σκοπὸν μὲν γὰρ εἶναι τὸ ἐκκείμενον σῶμα, οὗ τυχεῖν ἐφίεσθαι * * * τοὺς τῆς εὐδαιμονίας στοχαζομένους, διὰ τὸ πάντα μὲν σπουδαῖον εὐδαιμονεῖν, πάντα δὲ φαῦλον ἐκ τῶν ἐναντίων κακοδαιμονεῖν.

W 2.77

6d Καὶ τῶν ἀγαθῶν τὰ μὲν ἀναγκαῖα εἶναι πρὸς εὐδαιμονίαν, τὰ δὲ μή. Καὶ ἀναγκαῖα μὲν

3.113

2 ἢ: suppl. Sedley   10 εὐλογιστεῖν: Davisius on Cicero, de Finibus 2.11; εὐλογιστίαν: FP; εὐλόγιστον ζωήν: scholia on Lucian p.209, 22-24 vol iv ed Jacobitz   13 ἐκλεγομένους ... ἀπεκλεγομένους: cod. Aug.; ἐκλεγόμενος ... ἀπεκλεγόμενος: FP   21 συνηθείᾳ: FP; συνθεσίᾳ: Meineke, after scholia on Lucian   30 Wachsmuth indicates a lacuna here on the basis of 2.7. 3c   31 στοχαζομένους: Wyttenbach; σκεπτομένους: FP

adding further detail, expressed it thus: "To live in agreement with nature", assuming that Zeno's statement was insufficient as a predicate.[75] So Cleanthes, the first to take over the sect after him, added "with nature" and interpreted it thus: "The goal is living in agreement with nature".[76] Chrysippus, wanting to make this clearer, expressed it in this way: "To live in accord with experience of what happens naturally".[77] Diogenes offered this: "To be circumspect in the selection and rejection of things in accord with nature."[78] Archedemus: "To live completing everything appropriate".[79] But Antipater interpreted it as: "To live continually selecting what is in accordance with nature and rejecting what is contrary to nature." And on many occasions he also used to interpret it thus: "To do everything in one's power continually and unerringly with regard to obtaining the things which are preferentially in accord with nature."[80]

6b The goal is spoken of in three ways by the members of this sect. The final good is spoken of as the goal in scholarly usage, when they say agreement is the goal. They also say that the target is the goal, such as speaking of the life which is in agreement with reference to the associated predicate.[81] In relation to the third meaning they say that the last of the desired objects, to which all the others are referred, is the goal.

6c They think that the goal and the target are different things. For the target is the body set forth, which they set their sights on hitting; [but] those aiming at happiness [have as their goal the striking of this target] because every worthwhile person is happy and every worthless person conversely is unhappy.[82]

6d Of good things, some are necessary for happiness, others are not. Necessary are all the virtues and the activities making use of

τάς τε ἀρετὰς πάσας καὶ τὰς ἐνεργείας τὰς χρηστικὰς αὐτῶν· οὐκ ἀναγκαῖα δὲ χαράν τε καὶ εὐφροσύνην καὶ τὰ ἐπιτηδεύματα. Παραπλησίως δὲ καὶ τῶν κακῶν τὰ μὲν ἀναγκαῖα ὡς ἂν κακὰ πρὸς κακοδαιμονίαν εἶναι, τὰ δ' οὐκ ἀναγκαῖα· ἀναγκαῖα μὲν τάς τε κακίας πάσας καὶ τὰς ἐνεργείας τὰς ἐπ' αὐτῶν· οὐκ ἀναγκαῖα δὲ τά τε πάθη πάντα καὶ τὰ ἀρρωστήματα καὶ τὰ τούτοις παραπλήσια.

6e Τέλος δέ φασιν εἶναι τὸ εὐδαιμονεῖν, οὗ ἕνεκα πάντα πράττεται, αὐτὸ δὲ πράττεται μὲν οὐδενὸς δὲ ἕνεκα· τοῦτο δὲ ὑπάρχειν ἐν τῷ κατ' ἀρετὴν ζῆν, ἐν τῷ ὁμολογουμένως ζῆν, ἔτι, ταὐτοῦ ὄντος, ἐν τῷ κατὰ φύσιν ζῆν. Τὴν δὲ εὐδαιμονίαν ὁ Ζήνων ὡρίσατο τὸν τρόπον τοῦτον· εὐδαιμονία δ' ἐστὶν εὔροια βίου. Κέχρηται δὲ καὶ Κλεάνθης τῷ ὅρῳ τούτῳ ἐν τοῖς ἑαυτοῦ συγγράμμασι καὶ ὁ Χρύσιππος καὶ οἱ ἀπὸ τούτων πάντες, τὴν εὐδαιμονίαν εἶναι λέγοντες οὐχ ἑτέραν τοῦ εὐδαίμονος βίου, καίτοι γε λέγοντες, τὴν μὲν εὐδαιμονίαν σκοπὸν ἐκκεῖσθαι, τέλος δ' εἶναι τὸ τυχεῖν τῆς εὐδαιμονίας, ὅπερ ταυτὸν εἶναι τῷ εὐδαιμονεῖν. |

Δῆλον οὖν ἐκ τούτων, ὅτι ἰσοδυναμεῖ 'τὸ κατὰ φύσιν ζῆν' καὶ 'τὸ καλῶς ζῆν' καὶ 'τὸ εὖ ζῆν' καὶ πάλιν 'τὸ καλὸν κἀγαθόν' καὶ 'ἡ ἀρετὴ καὶ τὸ μέτοχον ἀρετῆς'· καὶ ὅτι πᾶν ἀγαθὸν καλόν, ὁμοίως δὲ καὶ πᾶν αἰσχρὸν κακόν· δι' ὃ καὶ τὸ Στωικὸν τέλος ἴσον δύνασθαι τῷ κατ' ἀρετὴν βίῳ.

6f Διαφέρειν δὲ λέγουσι τὸ αἱρετὸν καὶ τὸ αἱρετέον. Αἱρετὸν μὲν εἶναι ⟨ἀγαθὸν⟩ πᾶν, αἱρετέον δὲ ὠφέλημα πᾶν, ὃ θεωρεῖται παρὰ τὸ ἔχειν τὸ ἀγαθόν. Δι' ὃ αἱρούμεθα μὲν τὸ αἱρετέον, οἷον τὸ φρονεῖν, ὃ θεωρεῖται παρὰ

---

5 κακοδαιμονίαν: Heeren; δυσδαιμονίαν: Meineke; εὐδαιμονίαν: FP 7 ἐπ': Usener; ἀπ': FP
15 ταὐτοῦ: Heeren; τοῦ: FP 28 πάλιν: Meineke; πᾶν: FP 34 ἀγαθὸν: suppl. Heeren

them.[83] Not necessary are joy, cheerfulness, and the pursuits. In a similar fashion, some bad things are necessary, as much as bad things can be necessary, for unhappiness, others are not necessary. Necessary are all the vices and the activities in respect of[84] them. Not necessary are all passions, frailties, and things similar to these.

6e They say that happiness is the goal: everything is produced for its sake, while it is not produced for the sake of anything else.[85] It consists in living according to virtue, in living in agreement, and in addition, this being the same thing, in living in accordance with nature. Zeno defined happiness in this way: happiness is a smooth flow of life.[86] Cleanthes also used this definition in his treatises, as did Chrysippus and all their followers, saying that happiness was nothing other than the happy life, but saying that happiness was set up as the target, while the goal was to achieve happiness, which is the same as being happy.[87]

So it is clear from this that "living in accord with nature", "living the good life", "living well" are equivalent, as are also "the fine and good" and "virtue and what participates in virtue".[88] And that every good thing is fine, and likewise every shameful thing is bad. Because of this the Stoic goal is equivalent to life in accord with virtue.

6f They say that what is worth choosing and what must be chosen are different. Thus "worth-choosing" is every <good>, but "must-be-chosen" is every benefit: this is viewed in relation to possessing the good. Hence we choose what must be chosen, such as being intelligent, which is considered in relation to

τὸ ἔχειν φρόνησιν· τὸ δὲ αἱρετὸν οὐχ
αἱρούμεθα, ἀλλ' εἰ ἄρα, ἔχειν αὐτὸ αἱρούμεθα.
Ὁμοίως δὲ καὶ τὰ μὲν ἀγαθὰ πάντα ἐστὶν
ὑπομενετὰ καὶ ἐμμενετὰ καὶ ἀνάλογον ἐπὶ τῶν
ἄλλων ἀρετῶν ἐστιν, εἰ καὶ μὴ κατωνόμασται· 5
τὰ δὲ ὠφελήματα πάντα ὑπομενετέα καὶ
ἐμμενετέα. Καὶ κατὰ τὸν αὐτὸν λόγον ἐπὶ τῶν
ἄλλων τῶν κατὰ τὰς κακίας. |

7 Διεληλυθότες δ' ἱκανῶς περὶ ἀγαθῶν καὶ
κακῶν καὶ αἱρετῶν καὶ φευκτῶν καὶ περὶ 10
τέλους καὶ εὐδαιμονίας, ἀναγκαῖον ἡγησάμεθα
καὶ τὰ περὶ τῶν ἀδιαφόρων λεγόμενα κατὰ
τὴν οἰκείαν τάξιν ἐπελθεῖν. Ἀδιάφορα δ' εἶναι
λέγουσι τὰ μεταξὺ τῶν ἀγαθῶν καὶ τῶν
κακῶν, διχῶς τὸ ἀδιάφορον νοεῖσθαι φάμενοι, 15
καθ' ἕνα μὲν τρόπον τὸ μήτε ἀγαθὸν μήτε
κακὸν καὶ τὸ μήτε αἱρετὸν μήτε φευκτόν· καθ'
ἕτερον δὲ τὸ μήτε ὁρμῆς μήτε ἀφορμῆς
κινητικόν, καθ' ὃ καὶ λέγεσθαί τινα καθάπαξ
ἀδιάφορα εἶναι, οἷον τὸ ⟨ἀρτίας ἔχειν ἐπὶ τῆς 20
κεφαλῆς τρίχας ἢ περιττάς, ἢ τὸ⟩ προτεῖναι
τὸν δάκτυλον ὡδὶ ἢ ὡδί, ἢ τὸ ἀνελέσθαι τι
τῶν ἐμποδών, κάρφος ἢ φύλλον. Κατὰ τὸ
πρότερον δὴ λεκτέον τὰ μεταξὺ ἀρετῆς καὶ
κακίας ἀδιάφορα λέγεσθαι κατὰ τοὺς ἀπὸ τῆς 25
αἱρέσεως ταύτης, οὐ μὴν πρὸς ἐκλογὴν καὶ
ἀπεκλογήν· δι' ὃ καὶ τὰ μὲν ἀξίαν ἐκλεκτικὴν
ἔχειν, τὰ δ' ἀπαξίαν ἀπεκλεκτικήν,
συμβλητικὴν δ' οὐδαμῶς πρὸς τὸν εὐδαίμονα
βίον. 30

7a Καὶ τὰ μὲν εἶναι κατὰ φύσιν, τὰ δὲ παρὰ
φύσιν, τὰ δὲ οὔτε παρὰ φύσιν οὔτε κατὰ φύσιν.
Κατὰ φύσιν μὲν οὖν τὰ τοιαῦτα· ὑγίειαν, ἰσχύν,
αἰσθητηρίων | ἀρτιότητα, καὶ τὰ
παραπλήσια τούτοις· παρὰ φύσιν δὲ τὰ 35
τοιαῦτα· νόσον, ἀσθένειαν, πήρωσιν καὶ τὰ

---

4 καὶ ἀνάλογον: Meurer; κατὰ λόγον: FP; κατὰ τὸν αὐτὸν λόγον: Meineke
5 ἀρετῶν: Wachsmuth; αἱρετῶν: FP   6 ὠφελήματα: Hirzel; ὠφέλημα: FP
8 τὰς κακίας: Hirzel, Wachsmuth; τὰς οἰκείας: FP; τὰς οἰκείας τάξεις: Meineke; τὰ οἰκεία: Heeren   20 Wachsmuth supplements from Diogenes Laertius 7.104, comparing the scholia on Lucian here: ὡς τὸ τὸ περιττάς ἢ ἀρτίους ἔχειν τὰς τρίχας and Sext. Emp. math. 11.59

possessing intelligence.[89] However, we do not choose what is worth choosing, but rather we choose to possess it.

Likewise all good things are worth maintaining and persisting in, and the case is analogous for the other virtues, even if they have not been given names. But all benefits must be maintained and persisted in. The same reasoning applies to the other things which are in accord with vice.[90]

7 Having given an adequate account of the good and the bad, and what is worth choosing and what is to be avoided, and about the goal and happiness, we have thought it necessary also to give an account of what they say about indifferents in suitable order. They say that the things between good and bad are indifferents, saying that the indifferent is thought of in two ways: in one way as the neither good nor bad, and as what is neither worth choosing nor to be avoided;[91] in the other, as stimulative of neither impulse nor repulsion. In accord with the latter[92] some things are said to be utterly indifferent, such as <having an even or odd number of hairs on one's head, or> pointing a finger in this direction or that, or picking up something in the way, such as a twig or leaf. It is according to the first sense that the things in between virtue and vice are called indifferent by the adherents of this sect, not in view of selection and rejection. Hence as well some things have a selective value, but others have a rejective lack of value, as contributing nothing to the happy life.

7a Of indifferent things, some are in accord with nature, others contrary to nature, while others are neither contrary to nor in accord with nature. In accord with nature then are things like these: health, strength, soundness of the organs of sensation, and those things similar to these. But contrary to nature are such: sickness, feebleness, disability and the like. Neither contrary to nor in

τοιαῦτα· οὔτε δὲ παρὰ φύσιν οὔτε κατὰ φύσιν·
ψυχῆς κατάστασιν καὶ σώματος, καθ' ἃς ἡ μὲν
ἐστι φαντασιῶν ψευδῶν δεκτική, τὸ δὲ
τραυμάτων καὶ πηρώσεων δεκτικόν, καὶ τὰ
τούτοις ὅμοια. Ποιεῖσθαι δὲ λέγουσι τὸν περὶ 5
τούτων λόγον ⟨ἀπὸ⟩ τῶν πρώτων κατὰ
φύσιν καὶ παρὰ φύσιν. Τὸ γὰρ διαφέρον καὶ
τὸ ἀδιάφορον τῶν πρός τι λεγομένων εἶναι.
Διότι κἄν, φασί, λέγωμεν ἀδιάφορα τὰ
σωματικὰ καὶ τὰ ἐκτός, πρὸς τὸ εὐσχημόνως 10
ζῆν (ἐν ᾧπέρ ἐστι τὸ εὐδαιμόνως) ἀδιάφορά
φαμεν αὐτὰ εἶναι, οὐ μὰ Δία πρὸς τὸ κατὰ
φύσιν ἔχειν οὐδὲ πρὸς ὁρμὴν καὶ ἀφορμήν.   SVF
7b Ἔτι δὲ τῶν ἀδιαφόρων τὰ μὲν πλείω   3.133
ἀξίαν ἔχειν, τὰ δ' ἐλάττω· καὶ τὰ μὲν καθ' 15
αὑτά, τὰ δὲ ποιητικά· καὶ τὰ μὲν προηγμένα,
τὰ δ' ἀποπροηγμένα, τὰ δ' οὐδετέρως ἔχοντα.
Προηγμένα μέν, ὅσα ἀδιάφορα ὄντα πολλὴν
ἔχει ἀξίαν, ὡς ἐν ἀδιαφόροις· ἀποπροηγμένα
δέ, ὅσα πολλὴν ἔχει ἀπαξίαν ὁμοίως· οὔτε δὲ 20
προηγμένα οὔτε ἀποπροηγμένα, ὅσα μήτε
πολλὴν ἔχει ⟨ἀξίαν μήτε⟩ ἀπαξίαν.
Τῶν δὲ προηγμένων τὰ μὲν εἶναι περὶ   3.136
ψυχήν, τὰ δὲ περὶ σῶμα, τὰ δ' ἐκτός. Περὶ   W
ψυχὴν μὲν εἶναι | τὰ τοιαῦτα· εὐφυίαν, 25 2.81
προκοπήν, μνήμην, ὀξύτητα διανοίας, ἕξιν καθ'
ἣν ἐπίμονοί εἰσιν ἐπὶ τῶν καθηκόντων καὶ
τέχνας ὅσαι δύνανται συνεργεῖν ἐπιπλεῖον
πρὸς τὸν κατὰ φύσιν βίον· περὶ σῶμα δ' εἶναι
προηγμένα ὑγίειαν, εὐαισθησίαν καὶ τὰ 30
παραπλήσια τούτοις· τῶν δ' ἐκτὸς γονεῖς,
τέκνα, κτῆσιν σύμμετρον, ἀποδοχὴν παρὰ
ἀνθρώπων.
  Τῶν δ' ἀποπροηγμένων περὶ ψυχὴν μὲν
εἶναι τὰ ἐναντία τοῖς εἰρημένοις· περὶ σῶμα δὲ 35
καὶ ἐκτὸς τὰ ὁμοίως ἀντιτιθέμενα τοῖς

2 καθ' ἃς: FP; καθ' ἣν: Heeren   4 τραυμάτων: Wachsmuth; τρωμάτων: FP; τρώτον: scholia on Lucian   5 Ποιεῖσθαι: FP; προηγεῖσθαι: Hirzel   6 ἀπὸ: auppl. Wachsmuth   11 ἐν ᾧπέρ ἐστι: Meineke; ἐν ᾧ παρέστι: FP   22 ἀξίαν μήτε: suppl. Heeren

accord with nature are: the state of the soul and the state of the body, in accord with which the soul is receptive of false impressions, while the body is receptive of wounds and disabilities, and things like these.[93] They say that they reason about these things from the first things in accord with and contrary to nature.[94] For the differing and the indifferent are among the things spoken of as being in relation to something. Hence, they say, even if we say that bodily things and externals are indifferent, we are saying that they are indifferent in relation to living with dignity (in which living happily consists), but not, by Zeus, in relation to being in accord with nature nor in relation to impulse and repulsion.[95]

7b Furthermore, of indifferent things, some have more value, others have less. Some have their value in themselves, others as productive.[96] And some are preferred, others dispreferred, while others are neither. Preferred are whatever indifferent things have much value — to the extent this exists among indifferent things. Likewise dispreferred are whatever have much lack of value. Neither preferred nor dispreferred are whatever have neither much <value nor> much lack of value.

Of the preferred, some concern the soul, others the body, others externals. Concerning the soul are such things: natural ability, progress, memory, quickness of the mind, a condition in accord with which people are steadfast in the case of the appropriate acts, and all expertises that are able, for the most part, to work in partnership for the life in accord with nature. Concerning the body, the preferred are health, keen perception,[97] and things like these. Of externals, the preferred are parents, children, moderate possessions, and acceptance by one's fellow men.

Of the dispreferred, those concerning the soul are the opposite to the those which have been stated. Concerning the body and

εἰρημένοις περί τε σῶμα καὶ τοῖς ἐκτὸς προηγμένοις. Οὔτε δὲ προηγμένα οὔτ' ἀποπροηγμένα περὶ ψυχὴν ⟨μὲν⟩ φαντασίαν καὶ συγκατάθεσιν καὶ ὅσα τοιαῦτα· περὶ δὲ σῶμα λευκότητα καὶ μελανότητα καὶ χαροπότητα καὶ ἡδονὴν πᾶσαν καὶ πόνον καὶ εἴ τι ἄλλο τοιοῦτο. Τῶν δ' ἐκτὸς οὔτε προηγμένα ⟨οὔτε ἀποπροηγμένα⟩ εἶναι τὰ τοιαῦτα, ὅσα εὐτελῆ ὄντα καὶ μηδὲν χρήσιμον προσφερόμενα μικρὰν παντελῶς ἔχει τὴν ἀφ' αὑτῶν χρείαν. Τῆς δὲ ψυχῆς οὔσης κυριωτέρας τοῦ σώματος καὶ πρὸς τὸ κατὰ φύσιν ζῆν φασὶ τὰ περὶ τὴν ψυχὴν κατὰ | φύσιν ὄντα καὶ προηγμένα πλείονα τὴν ἀξίαν ἔχειν τῶν περὶ σῶμα καὶ τῶν ἐκτός, οἷον εὐφυίαν ψυχῆς πρὸς ἀρετὴν ὑπεράγειν τῆς τοῦ σώματος εὐφυίας καὶ ὁμοίως ἐπὶ τῶν ἄλλων ἔχειν.

W 2.82

7c Ἔτι δὲ τῶν ἀδιαφόρων φασὶ τὰ μὲν εἶναι ὁρμῆς κινητικά, τὰ δὲ ἀφορμῆς, τὰ δὲ οὔτε ὁρμῆς οὔτε ἀφορμῆς. Ὁρμῆς μὲν οὖν κινητικά, ἅπερ ἐλέγομεν εἶναι κατὰ φύσιν· ἀφορμῆς δὲ ὅσα παρὰ φύσιν· οὔτε δὲ ὁρμῆς οὔτε ἀφορμῆς τὰ μηδετέρως ἔχοντα, οἷά ἐστι τὸ περιττὰς ἢ ἀρτίας ἔχειν τὰς τρίχας.

SVF 3.121

7d Τῶν δὲ κατὰ φύσιν ἀδιαφόρων ὄντων τὰ μέν ἐστι πρῶτα κατὰ φύσιν, τὰ δὲ κατὰ μετοχήν. Πρῶτα μέν ἐστι κατὰ φύσιν κίνησις ἢ σχέσις κατὰ τοὺς σπερματικοὺς λόγους γινομένη, οἷον ⟨ἀρτιότης καὶ⟩ ὑγίεια καὶ αἴσθησις (λέγω δὲ τὴν κατάληψιν) καὶ ἰσχύς. Κατὰ μετοχὴν δέ, ὅσα μετέχει κινήσεως καὶ σχέσεως κατὰ τοὺς σπερματικοὺς λόγους, οἷον χεὶρ ἀρτία καὶ σῶμα ὑγιεινὸν καὶ αἰσθήσεις μὴ πεπηρωμέναι. Ὁμοίως δὲ καὶ τῶν παρὰ φύσιν κατὰ τὸ ἀνάλογον.

3.141

---

1 περί τε σῶμα καὶ τοῖς ἐκτὸς προηγμένοις: del. Hirzel 3 μέν: suppl. Meineke 6 Wachsmuth suggests adding καὶ γλαυκότητα 6 ἡδονὴν πᾶσαν: scholia on Lucian; ἡδονήν τις ἂν: FP 8 οὔτε ἀποπροηγμένα: suppl. Heeren 14 τὴν ἀξίαν: scholia on Lucian; τὴν εὐεξίαν: FP 30 ἀρτιότης καὶ: suppl. Wachsmuth, comparing ἀρτία below

externals, they are similarly opposed to those stated concerning the body and the preferred externals.

Neither preferred nor dispreferred concerning the soul are impression and assent and the like. And concerning the body, neither preferred nor dispreferred are pale or dark skin, the brightness of the eyes,[98] every pleasure and toil, and anything else of this type. Of externals, neither preferred nor dispreferred are all things for which, being cheap and bringing nothing useful, there is overall little need deriving from themselves.

Since the soul is more in control than the body, they say that, with respect to living in accord with nature, things concerning the soul which are in accord with nature and preferable also have more value than things concerning the body and externals. Thus, in relation to virtue, natural ability of the mind surpasses the natural ability of the body and they say that the same holds for the other things.[99]

7c Furthermore, they say that some of the indifferents are stimulative of impulse, others of repulsion, others of neither impulse nor repulsion. So whatever things we have said to be in accord with nature are stimulative of impulse; and whatever we have said to be contrary to nature are stimulative of repulsion.[100] Things which are neither are not stimulative of either impulse or repulsion, such as having an odd or even number of hairs on the head.

7d Of the indifferent things which are in accord with nature, some are first things in accord with nature, others are so by participation. First things in accord with nature are a motion or a state in accord with generative principles,[101] such as <soundness and> health and perception (I'm referring to apprehension)[102] and strength. In accord with nature through participation are what participate in motion and state in accordance with generative principles, such as a sound hand and a healthy body and senses which have not been injured.[103] The argument follows likewise by analogy with regard to the things which are contrary to nature.

7e Πάντα δὲ ⟨τὰ⟩ κατὰ φύσιν ληπτὰ εἶναι καὶ πάντα τὰ ⟨παρὰ⟩ φύσιν ἄληπτα. Τῶν δὲ κατὰ φύσιν τὰ μὲν | καθ' αὑτὰ ληπτὰ εἶναι, τὰ δὲ δι' ἕτερα. Καθ' αὑτὰ μέν, ὅσα ἐστὶν ὁρμῆς κινητικὰ καταστρεπτικῶς ἐφ' ἑαυτὰ ἢ ἐπὶ τὸ 5 ἀντέχεσθαι αὐτῶν, οἷον ὑγίειαν, εὐαισθησίαν, ἀπονίαν καὶ κάλλος σώματος. Ποιητικὰ ⟨δὲ⟩, ὅσα ἐστὶν ὁρμῆς κινητικὰ ἀν⟨εν⟩εκτικῶς ἐφ' ἕτερα καὶ μὴ κατατρεπτικῶς ⟨ἐφ' ἑαυτά⟩, οἷον πλοῦτον, δόξαν καὶ τὰ τούτοις ὅμοια. 10 Παραπλησίως δὲ καὶ τῶν παρὰ φύσιν τὰ μὲν εἶναι καθ' αὑτὰ ἄληπτα, τὰ δὲ τῷ ποιητικὰ εἶναι τῶν καθ' αὑτὰ ἀλήπτων.

SVF 3.142

W 2.83

LS 58C

7f Πάντα δὲ τὰ κατὰ φύσιν ἀξίαν ἔχειν καὶ πάντα τὰ παρὰ φύσιν ἀπαξίαν. Τὴν δὲ ἀξίαν 15 λέγεσθαι τριχῶς, τήν τε δόσιν καὶ τιμὴν καθ' αὑτὸ καὶ τὴν ἀμοιβὴν τοῦ δοκιμαστοῦ· καὶ τὴν τρίτην, ἣν ὁ Ἀντίπατρος ἐκλεκτικὴν προσαγορεύει, καθ' ἣν διδόντων τῶν πραγμάτων τάδε τινὰ μᾶλλον ἀντὶ τῶνδε 20 αἱρούμεθα, οἷον ὑγίειαν ἀντὶ νόσου καὶ ζωὴν ἀντὶ θανάτου καὶ πλοῦτον | ἀντὶ πενίας. Κατὰ τὸ ἀνάλογον δὲ καὶ τὴν ἀπαξίαν τριχῶς φασὶ λέγεσθαι, ἀντιτιθεμένων τῶν σημαινομένων τοῖς ἐπὶ τῆς τριττῆς ἀξίας εἰρημένοις. 25

3.124 58D 3.52 Ant.

2.84

Τὴν δὲ δόσιν φησὶν ὁ Διογένης κρίσιν εἶναι, ἐφ' ὅσον κατὰ φύσιν ἐστὶν ἢ ἐφ' ὅσον χρείαν τῇ φύσει παρέχεται. Τὸ δὲ δοκιμαστόν, οὐχ ὡς λέγεται τὰ πράγματα δοκιμαστὰ παραλαμβάνεσθαι, ἀλλ' ὡς δοκιμαστὴν φαμεν 30 εἶναι τὸν τὰ πράγματα δοκιμάζοντα· τῆς οὖν ἀμοιβῆς τὸν τοιοῦτόν φησι δοκιμαστὴν εἶναι.

3.125 3.47 Diog.

---

1 τὰ: suppl. Meineke   2 τὰ ⟨παρὰ⟩ φύσιν: scholia on Lucian, omitting καὶ πάντα; τὰ φύσιν: P, omitting παρὰ   5 καταστρεπτικῶς: scholia on Lucian, here and below, where F has παρατρεπτικῶς; κατατρεπτικῶς: P; προτρεπτικῶς: Wachsmuth and also below 7 δὲ: suppl. Heeren   8 ἀν⟨εν⟩εκτικῶς: von Arnim; ἀνετικῶς: cod. Escur.; ἀνεκτικῶς: F; ἀνεκτῶς: P   9 ἐφ' ἑαυτά: suppl. Meineke   13 εἶναι τῶν καθ' αὑτὰ ἀλήπτων: Wachsmuth; εἶναι, τῶν δὲ καθ' αὑτὰ ἀλήπτων: FP, which requires a lacuna to be proposed after ἀλήπτων 15 τε: F; δὲ: P   16 τήν τε δόσιν καὶ τιμήν: Meineke; τήν τε δόσιν καὶ τὴν: FP; τήν τε δόσιν τὴν καθ' αὑτήν: Wachsmuth   25 τριττῆς: Wachsmuth; πρώτης:FP 28 δοκιμαστόν: F; δοκιμαστικόν: P; δοκιμαστοῦ: Meineke   32 φησι: Wachsmuth; φασι: FP

7e All that is in accord with nature is worth acquiring and all which is contrary to nature is worth shunning. Some of the things in accord with nature are worth acquiring for their own sake, others for the sake of other things.[104] For their own sake are those things which in a self-referential fashion are stimulative of an impulse toward themselves or toward the laying hold of themselves, such as health, good perception, lack of pain, and the beauty of the body. Worth acquiring as productive are those things which by reference[105] to something else are stimulative of an impulse toward other things rather than in self-referential fashion <toward themselves>, such as wealth, reputation, and things like these. Similarly of those things contrary to nature some are worth shunning for their own sake, others by being productive of other things which are worth shunning for their own sake.

7f All the things which are in accord with nature have value and all the things contrary to nature have lack-of-value. Value is spoken of in three ways: its contribution and esteem in itself; the price set by the appraiser; and the third type, which Antipater calls selective, through which, when things allow, we rather choose these particular things instead of those, such as health instead of sickness, life instead of death, and riches instead of poverty.[106] Similarly, they say that lack of value is also spoken of in three ways, such that the meanings are opposed to those previously stated with respect to the three types of value.

Diogenes says "contribution" is a judgement of the extent to which something is in accord with nature or the extent to which it provides a need to nature.[107] The "prized" is not spoken of as things priced to be used, but in the way we say the man appraising things is an appraiser. So he says such a man is the appraiser of the price.[108]

Καὶ ταύτας μὲν τὰς δύο ἀξίας καθ' ἃς λέγομέν τινα τῇ ἀξίᾳ προῆχθαι, τρίτην δέ φησιν εἶναι, καθ' ἣν φαμεν ἀξίωμά τινα ἔχειν καὶ ἀξίαν, ἥπερ περὶ ἀδιάφορα οὐ γίνεται, ἀλλὰ περὶ μόνα τὰ σπουδαῖα. Χρῆσθαι δ' ἡμᾶς φησιν ἐνίοτε τῷ ὀνόματι τῆς ἀξίας ἀντὶ τοῦ ἐπιβάλλοντος· ὡς ἐν τῷ τῆς δικαιοσύνης ὅρῳ παρείληπται, ὅταν λέγηται εἶναι ἕξις ἀπονεμητικὴ τοῦ κατ' ἀξίαν ἑκάστῳ· ἔστι γὰρ οἷον τοῦ ἐπιβάλλοντος ἑκάστῳ.

7g Τῶν δ' ἀξίαν ἐχόντων τὰ μὲν ἔχειν πολλὴν ἀξίαν, τὰ δὲ βραχεῖαν. Ὁμοίως δὲ καὶ τῶν ἀπαξίαν ἐχόντων ἃ μὲν ἔχειν πολλὴν ἀπαξίαν, ἃ δὲ βραχεῖαν. Τὰ μὲν ⟨οὖν⟩ πολλὴν ἔχοντα ἀξίαν προηγμένα λέγεσθαι, τὰ δὲ πολλὴν ἀπαξίαν ἀποπροηγμένα, Ζήνωνος ταύτας τὰς ὀνομασίας θεμένου πρώτου τοῖς πράγμασι. Προηγμένον δ' εἶναι λέγουσιν, ὃ ἀδιάφορον ⟨ὂν⟩ ἐκλεγόμεθα κατὰ προηγούμενον λόγον. Τὸν δ' ὅμοιον λόγον ἐπὶ τῷ ἀποπροηγμένῳ εἶναι, καὶ τὰ παραδείγματα κατὰ τὴν ἀναλογίαν ταὐτά. Οὐδὲν δὲ τῶν ἀγαθῶν εἶναι προηγμένον διὰ τὸ τὴν μεγίστην ἀξίαν αὐτὰ ἔχειν. Τὸ δὲ προηγμένον, τὴν δευτέραν χώραν καὶ ἀξίαν ἔχον, συνεγγίζειν πως τῇ τῶν ἀγαθῶν φύσει· οὐδὲ γὰρ ἐν αὐλῇ τῶν προηγμένων εἶναι τὸν βασιλέα, ἀλλὰ τοὺς μετ' αὐτὸν τεταγμένους. Προηγμένα δὲ λέγεσθαι, οὐ τῷ πρὸς εὐδαιμονίαν τινὰ συμβάλλεσθαι συνεργεῖν τε πρὸς αὐτήν, ἀλλὰ τῷ ἀναγκαῖον εἶναι τούτων τὴν ἐκλογὴν ποιεῖσθαι παρὰ τὰ ἀποπροηγμένα.

8 Ἀκόλουθος δ' ἐστὶ τῷ λόγῳ τῷ περὶ τῶν προηγμένων ὁ περὶ τοῦ καθήκοντος τόπος. Ὁρίζεται δὲ τὸ καθῆκον· τὸ ἀκόλουθον ἐν ζωῇ,

SVF
3.128
1.192
LS
58E

W
2.85

3.494

1.230

14 οὖν: suppl. Heeren   19 ὂν: suppl. Heeren   20 λόγον: Mullach; ἀνάλογον: FP
21 τῷ ἀποπροηγμένῳ: Wachsmuth; τὸ ἀποπροηγμένον, F, τὸ ἀποπροηγμένος: P
27 ἐν αὐλῇ τῶν: Canter; ἂν αὐλητῶν; FP   27 προηγμένων: Madvig; προαγόμενον: FP

These are the two values according to which we say that particular things are preferred in value; they say the third is the value according to which we say particular things have dignity[109] and value, which does not occur in the case of indifferents, but only in the case of things which are worthwhile. They say that we sometimes use the term "value" instead of "the befitting", as is employed in the definition of justice, whenever it is said to be a condition apportioning to each according to its value. For it is the same as the befitting for each.

7g Of things which have value, some have much value, others little. Likewise of those things having lack-of-value, some have much lack-of-value, others little. So those things which have much value are called preferred, those which have much lack-of-value are called dispreferred — Zeno was the first to give these nomenclatures to things.[110] They say that the preferred is an indifferent thing which we select in accord with preferential reasoning. There is the same reasoning about the dispreferred and the examples are correspondingly similar. No good thing is a preferred, because they have the greatest value in themselves. But the preferred, having the second rank and value, to some extent come close to the nature of the good. The king is not in the court of the preferred, but rather those ranked after him.[111] The preferred are so called, not because they contribute some things to happiness and work in partnership towards it,[112] but because it is necessary to make the selection from these things instead of the dispreferred.

8 Consistent with the account of the preferred is the topic of the appropriate.[113] The appropriate is defined as "what is consistent in

ὃ πραχθὲν εὔλογον ἀπολογίαν ἔχει· παρὰ τὸ καθῆκον δὲ τὸ ἐναντίως. Τοῦτο διατείνει καὶ εἰς τὰ ἄλογα τῶν ζῴων, ἐνεργεῖ γάρ τι κἀκεῖνα ἀκολούθως τῇ ἑαυτῶν φύσει· ἐπὶ ⟨δὲ⟩ τῶν λογικῶν ζῴων οὕτως ἀποδίδοται· 'τὸ ἀκόλουθον ἐν βίῳ'. Τῶν δὲ καθηκόντων τὰ μὲν εἶναί φασι τέλεια, ἃ δὴ καὶ κατορθώματα λέγεσθαι. Κατορθώματα δ' εἶναι τὰ κατ' ἀρετὴν ἐνεργήματα, οἷον τὸ φρονεῖν, τὸ δικαιοπραγεῖν. Οὐκ εἶναι δὲ κατορθώματα τὰ μὴ οὕτως ἔχοντα, ἃ δὴ οὐδὲ τέλεια καθήκοντα προσαγορεύουσιν, ἀλλὰ μέσα, οἷον τὸ γαμεῖν, τὸ πρεσβεύειν, τὸ διαλέγεσθαι, τὰ τούτοις ὅμοια.

8a Τῶν δὲ κατορθωμάτων τὰ μὲν εἶναι ὧν χρή, τὰ δ' οὔ. Ὧν χρὴ μὲν εἶναι ⟨τὰ⟩ κατηγορούμενα ὠφελήματα, οἷον τὸ φρονεῖν, τὸ σωφρονεῖν· οὐκ εἶναι δὲ ὧν χρὴ τὰ μὴ οὕτως ἔχοντα. Ὁμοίως δὲ καὶ τῶν παρὰ τὸ καθῆκον τὴν αὐτὴν γίνεσθαι τεχνολογίαν.

Πᾶν δὲ τὸ παρὰ τὸ καθῆκον ἐν λογικῷ ⟨ζῴῳ⟩ γινόμενον ἁμάρτημα εἶναι· τὸ δὲ καθῆκον τελειωθὲν κατόρθωμα γίνεσθαι. Παραμετρεῖσθαι δὲ τὸ μέσον καθῆκον ἀδιαφόροις τισί, ἐκλεγομένοις δὲ παρὰ φύσιν καὶ κατὰ φύσιν, τοιαύτην δ' εὔροιαν προσφερομένοις, ὥστ' εἰ μὴ λαμβάνοιμεν αὐτὰ ἢ διωθοίμεθα ἀπεριστάτως, μὴ ἂν εὐδαιμονεῖν.

9 Τὸ δὲ κινοῦν τὴν ὁρμὴν οὐδὲν ἕτερον εἶναι λέγουσιν ἀλλ' ἢ φαντασίαν ὁρμητικὴν τοῦ καθήκοντος αὐτόθεν, τὴν δὲ ὁρμὴν εἶναι φορὰν ψυχῆς ἐπί τι κατὰ τὸ γένος. ταύτης δ' ἐν εἴδει θεωρεῖσθαι τήν τε ἐν τοῖς λογικοῖς γιγνομένην ὁρμὴν καὶ τὴν ἐν τοῖς ἀλόγοις

---

1 πραχθὲν: Ménage; παραχθὲν: FP   4 δὲ: suppl. Lynden   8 τὰ ... ἐνεργήματα: Davies; τὸ ... ἐνέργημα: FP   16 τὰ: suppl. von Arnim; κατηγορούμενα ὠφελήματα: Wachsmuth, κατηγόρημα ὠφέλημα: FP   22 ζῴῳ: suppl. Wachsmuth, comparing 11a   25 ἀδιαφόροις: Heeren; διαφόροις: FP   26 εὔροιαν: Hense; εὐφυίαν: F, ἐφυίαν: P; εὐθηνίαν: Wachsmuth; εὐποιίαν: Meineke; εὐεξίαν: Heine   28 ἀπεριστάτως: Wachsmuth; ἀπεριστάστως: FP; ἀπερισκέπτως: Wachsmuth   30 ἀλλ' ἢ: Meurer; ἀλλὰ: FP   32 ταύτης δ' ἐν εἴδει: Hirzel; ταύτης δ' ἐνι ἀεὶ: F, ταύτης δ' ἄγι ἀεὶ: P

life, which, when carried out, has a reasonable defence." The inappropriate is defined oppositely. This extends even to the irrational among creatures, for they also act in a particular respect consistently with their nature.[114] But with regard to rational creatures, it is interpreted thus: "what is consistent in life". Of appropriate acts, they say that some are complete — these are also spoken of as right acts. Right acts are activations in accord with virtue, such as being intelligent and acting justly.[115] Acts which are not such are not right acts and they do not call them complete appropriate acts either, but intermediates: for example, marrying, serving as an ambassador, discussing matters, and the like.[116]

8a Of right acts, some are obligatory, others are not. Obligatory are the predicative benefits, such as being intelligent and showing self-restraint. Whatever is not such is not obligatory.[117] Likewise there is also the same prescription of rules regarding the inappropriate.

Every inappropriate act occurring in a rational <creature> is a wrong act, while an appropriate act that has been made complete is a right act. The intermediate appropriate is measured by certain indifferent things, selected in accord with or contrary to nature, which bring such a smooth flow that if we did not acquire them or reject them, except in special circumstances, we would not be happy.[118]

9 They say that what sets impulse moving is nothing other than a spontaneously impulsive impression of what is appropriate,[119] while in genus impulse is a motion of the soul towards something. The impulse which occurs in rational creatures is viewed as a species of this, as well as that which occurs in irrational creatures

ζῴοις· οὐ κατωνομασμέναι δ' εἰσίν. ἡ γὰρ ὄρεξις οὐκ ἔστι λογικὴ ὁρμή, ἀλλὰ λογικῆς ὁρμῆς εἶδος. Τὴν δὲ λογικὴν ὁρμὴν δεόντως ἄν τις ἀφορίζοιτο, λέγων εἶναι φορὰν διανοίας ἐπί τι τῶν ἐν τῷ πράττειν· ταύτῃ δ' 5 ἀντιτίθεσθαι ἀφορμήν, φοράν τινα ⟨διανοίας ἀπό τινος τῶν ἐν τῷ πράττειν⟩. Ἰδίως δὲ καὶ τὴν ὅρουσιν ὁρμὴν λέγουσι τῆς πρακτικῆς ὁρμῆς οὖσαν εἶδος. εἶναι δὲ τὴν ὅρουσιν φορὰν διανοίας ἐπί τι μέλλον. "Ὥστε μέχρι μὲν 10 τούτων τετραχῶς ὁρμὴν λέγεσθαι, διχῶς δ' ἀφορμήν· προστεθείσης δὲ καὶ τῆς ἕξεως τῆς ὁρμητικῆς, ἣν δὴ καὶ ἰδίως ὁρμὴν λέγουσιν, ἀφ' ἧς συμβαίνει ὁρμᾶν, ⟨ὁρμὴν⟩ πενταχῶς.

9a Τῆς δὲ πρακτικῆς ὁρμῆς εἴδη πλείονα εἶναι, 15   SVF
ἐν οἷς καὶ ταῦτα· πρόθεσιν, ἐπιβολήν,   3.173
παρασκευήν, ἐγχείρησιν, ⟨αἵρεσιν,⟩ προαίρεσιν,
βούλησιν, θέλησιν. Πρόθεσιν μὲν οὖν εἶναι
λέγουσι σημείωσιν ἐπιτελέσεως· ἐπιβολὴν δὲ
ὁρμὴν πρὸ ὁρμῆς· παρασκευὴν δὲ πρᾶξιν πρὸ 20
πράξεως· ἐγχείρησιν δὲ ὁρμὴν ἐπί τινος ἐν
χερσὶν ἤδη ὄντος· αἵρεσιν δὲ βούλησιν ἐξ
ἀναλογισμοῦ· προαίρεσιν δὲ αἵρεσιν πρὸ
αἱρέσεως· βούλησιν δὲ εὔλογον ὄρεξιν· θέλησιν
δὲ ἑκούσιον βούλησιν. | 25 W   LS
9b Πάσας δὲ τὰς ὁρμὰς συγκαταθέσεις εἶναι,   2.88   33I
τὰς δὲ πρακτικὰς καὶ τὸ κινητικὸν περιέχειν.
Ἤδη δὲ ἄλλων μὲν εἶναι συγκαταθέσεις, ἐπ'   3.171
ἄλλο δὲ ὁρμάς· καὶ συγκαταθέσεις μὲν
ἀξιώμασί τισιν, ὁρμὰς δὲ ἐπὶ κατηγορήματα, 30
τὰ περιεχόμενά πως ἐν τοῖς ἀξιώμασιν, οἷς
συγκαταθέσεις. Ἐπεὶ δ' ἐν εἴδει τὸ πάθος τῆς
ὁρμῆς ἐστι, λέγωμεν ἑξῆς περὶ παθῶν.   3.378

4 ἄν τις ἀφορίζοιτο: Salmasius; ἀνταφορίζοιτο: FP   6 διανοίας ἀπό τινος τῶν ἐν τῷ πράττειν: suppl. Wachsmuth from Galen de Hippocr. et Plat. 4.2, following Salmasius; Wachsmuth, however, adds μή before πράττειν. This is rejected by von Arnim (SVF 3.169) and Inwood, Ethics 227   9 εἶναι δὲ τὴν ὅρουσιν: Canter; εἰδέναι δὲ τὴν ὅρουσιν: P, τὴν δὲ ὅρουσιν εἰδέναι δὲ: F   14 ὁρμὴν: suppl. Wachsmuth   17 αἵρεσιν: suppl. Salmasius   21 ἐν χερσὶν: Salmasius; ἐγχείρησιν: FP   28 ἄλλων: FP; ἄλλῳ: Wachsmuth   31 οἷς συγκαταθέσεις: Madvig; οἷς συγκατατίθεσθαι: Wachsmuth; αἱ συγκαταθέσεις: FP; καὶ συγκαταθέσεσι: Usener

(although the impulses have not been given corresponding names).[120] Thus desire is not the same as rational impulse, but a species of rational impulse. You would rightly define rational impulse, if you said it was a motion of the mind toward something in the field of action. Opposed to this is repulsion, a motion <of the mind away from something in the field of action>. In a special sense they also call impulsion an impulse as a species of practical impulse. Impulsion is a motion of the mind towards what is going to occur. As a result, up till here, impulse is spoken of in four ways, repulsion in two ways. When we add on the condition which is able to impel, which they also in a particular sense call a impulse (that from which impelling occurs), impulse is defined in five ways.[121]

9a There are numerous species of practical impulse, including these: proposal, inclination, preparation, undertaking,[122] <choice>, policy, wish, and willingness.[123] They say that proposal is an indication of completion; inclination is an impulse before an impulse; preparation is an action before an action; undertaking is an impulse towards something that is now in hand; choice is a wish from comparison; policy is a choice before a choice; wish is reasonable desire; willingness is a voluntary wish.

9b All impulses are assents and practical impulses also include that which is stimulative. At the same time there are assents "for" things and impulses "toward" something else: assents are "for" certain propositions, while impulses are "toward" predicates, included somehow in the propositions for which there is assent.[124] Since in species passion is an impulse, let's speak next about passions.

10 Πάθος δ' εἶναί φασιν ὁρμὴν πλεονάζουσαν καὶ ἀπειθῆ τῷ αἱροῦντι λόγῳ ἢ κίνησιν ψυχῆς ⟨ἄλογον⟩ παρὰ φύσιν (εἶναι δὲ πάθη πάντα τοῦ ἡγεμονικοῦ τῆς ψυχῆς), διὸ καὶ πᾶσαν πτοίαν πάθος εἶναι, ⟨καὶ⟩ πάλιν ⟨πᾶν⟩ πάθος 5 πτοίαν. Τοῦ δὲ πάθους τοιούτου ὄντος ὑποληπτέον, τὰ μὲν πρῶτα εἶναι καὶ ἀρχηγά, τὰ δ' εἰς ταῦτα τὴν ἀναφορὰν ἔχειν. Πρῶτα δ' εἶναι τῷ γένει ταῦτα τὰ τέσσαρα, ἐπιθυμίαν, φόβον, λύπην, ἡδονήν. Ἐπιθυμίαν μὲν οὖν καὶ 10 φόβον προηγεῖσθαι, τὴν μὲν πρὸς τὸ φαινόμενον ἀγαθόν, τὸν δὲ πρὸς τὸ φαινόμενον κακόν. Ἐπιγίγνεσθαι δὲ τούτοις ἡδονὴν καὶ λύπην, ἡδονὴν μὲν ὅταν τυγχάνωμεν ὧν ἐπεθυμοῦμεν ἢ ἐκφύγωμεν ἃ 15 ἐφοβούμεθα· λύπην δέ, ὅταν ἀποτυγχάνωμεν ὧν ἐπεθυμοῦμεν ἢ περιπέσωμεν οἷς ἐφοβούμεθα. Ἐπὶ πάντων δὲ τῶν τῆς ψυχῆς παθῶν, ἐπεὶ δόξας | αὐτὰ λέγουσιν εἶναι, παραλαμβάνεσθαι τὴν δόξαν ἀντὶ τῆς 20 ἀσθενοῦς ὑπολήψεως, τὸ δὲ πρόσφατον ἀντὶ τοῦ κινητικοῦ συστολῆς ἀλόγου ⟨ἢ⟩ ἐπάρσεως.

10a Τὸ δὲ 'ἄλογον' καὶ τὸ 'παρὰ φύσιν' οὐ κοινῶς, ἀλλὰ τὸ μὲν 'ἄλογον' ἴσον τῷ ἀπειθὲς τῷ λόγῳ. Πᾶν γὰρ πάθος βιαστικόν ἐστι, ὡς 25 πολλάκις ὁρῶντας τοὺς ἐν τοῖς πάθεσιν ὄντας ὅτι συμφέρει τόδε οὐ ποιεῖν, ὑπὸ τῆς σφοδρότητος ἐκφερομένους, καθάπερ ὑπό τινος ἀπειθοῦς ἵππου, ἀνάγεσθαι πρὸς τὸ ποιεῖν αὐτό, παρ' ὃ καὶ πολλάκις τινὰς 30 ἐξομολογεῖσθαι λέγοντας τὸ θρυλούμενον τοῦτο·

Γνώμην δ' ἔχοντά μ' ἡ φύσις βιάζεται·

SVF 1.205
LS 65A
1.206

1.211

W 2.89
65C

3.389

---

3 ἄλογον: suppl. Wachsmuth, comparing 10a and Diogenes Laertius 7.110   4 τοῦ ἡγεμονικοῦ: Wachsmuth; τῷ γένει ἦ: FP   5 ⟨καὶ⟩: suppl. Heeren; ⟨πᾶν⟩ : suppl. Meineke   15 ἐπεθυμοῦμεν: (also immediately below) Meurer; ἐπιθυμοῦμεν: FP   19 ἐπεὶ: Usener; ἐπὶ: FP; περὶ : Meineke   22 ἤ: suppl. Salmasius   24 ἴσον: Usener; ὅσον: FP   24 τῷ ἀπειθὲς: Usener; τῷ ἀπειθῶς: FP   25 ὡς: Meineke; καὶ: FP   27 τόδε οὐ: Canter; τόδε εὖ: FP

10 They say a passion is an impulse which is excessive, disobedient to the choosing reason or an <irrational> motion of the soul contrary to nature (all passions belong to the controlling part of the soul).[125] Hence also every agitation is a passion, <and> again <every> passion is an agitation.[126] As passion is like this, it must be assumed that some passions are primary and fundamental, while others have reference to these. First in genus are these four: appetite, fear, pain, and pleasure. Appetite and fear lead the way, the former toward the apparently good, the other toward the apparently evil. Pleasure and pain come after them: pleasure whenever we obtain that for which we had an appetite or escape from that which we feared; pain whenever we fail to get that for which we had an appetite or encounter that which we feared. With regard to all the passions of the soul, when they say they are opinions, "opinion" is employed for "feeble assumption" and "fresh" for "that which is stimulative of an irrational contraction <or> elation".[127]

10a The terms "irrational" and "contrary to nature" are not used in the usual sense, but "irrational" as equivalent of "disobedient to reason"[128]. For every passion is overpowering, just as when those in the grips of passion often see that it would be useful not to do this, but carried away by its violence, as if by some disobedient horse, are led to doing this.[129] As a result, often people even confess to this, uttering this commonly repeated line:[130]

"Although I have (better) judgement, nature forces me to do this".[131]

γνώμην γὰρ λέγει νῦν τὴν εἴδησιν καὶ γνῶσιν τῶν ὀρθῶν πραγμάτων. Καὶ τὸ 'παρὰ φύσιν' δ' εἴληπται ἐν τῇ τοῦ πάθους ὑπογραφῇ, ὡς συμβαίνοντος παρὰ τὸν ὀρθὸν καὶ κατὰ φύσιν λόγον. Πάντες δ' οἱ ἐν τοῖς πάθεσιν ὄντες 5 ἀποστρέφονται τὸν λόγον, οὐ παραπλησίως δὲ τοῖς ἐξηπατημένοις ἐν ὁτῳοῦν, ἀλλ' ἰδιαζόντως. Οἱ μὲν γὰρ ἠπατημένοι, λόγου χάριν περὶ ⟨τοῦ⟩ τὰς ἀτόμους ἀρχὰς | εἶναι, διδαχθέντες ὅτι οὐκ εἰσιν, ἀφίστανται τῆς 10 κρίσεως· οἱ δ' ἐν τοῖς πάθεσιν ὄντες, κἂν μάθωσι, κἂν μεταδιδαχθῶσιν ὅτι οὐ δεῖ λυπεῖσθαι ἢ φοβεῖσθαι, ἢ ὅλως ἐν τοῖς πάθεσιν εἶναι τῆς ψυχῆς, ὅμως οὐκ ἀφίστανται τούτων, ἀλλ' ἄγονται ὑπὸ τῶν παθῶν εἰς τὸ ὑπὸ τῆς 15 τούτων κρατεῖσθαι τυραννίδος.

10b Τὴν μὲν οὖν ἐπιθυμίαν λέγουσιν ὄρεξιν εἶναι ἀπειθῆ λόγῳ· αἴτιον δ' αὐτῆς τὸ δοξάζειν ἀγαθὸν ἐπιφέρεσθαι, οὗ παρόντος εὖ ἀπαλλάξομεν, τῆς δόξης αὐτῆς ἐχούσης τὸ 20 ἀτάκτως κινητικὸν ⟨πρόσφατον τοῦ ὄντως αὐτὸ ὀρεκτὸν εἶναι⟩. Φόβον δ' εἶναι ἔκκλισιν ἀπειθῆ λόγῳ, αἴτιον δ' αὐτοῦ τὸ δοξάζειν κακὸν ἐπιφέρεσθαι, τῆς δόξης τὸ κινητικὸν [καὶ] πρόσφατον ἐχούσης τοῦ ὄντως αὐτὸ φευκτὸν 25 εἶναι. Λύπην δ' εἶναι συστολὴν ψυχῆς ἀπειθῆ λόγῳ, αἴτιον δ' αὐτῆς τὸ δοξάζειν πρόσφατον κακὸν παρεῖναι, ἐφ' ᾧ καθήκει ⟨συστέλλεσθαι. Ἡδονὴν δ' εἶναι ἔπαρσιν ψυχῆς ἀπειθῆ λόγῳ, αἴτιον δ' αὐτῆς τὸ δοξάζειν πρόσφατον 30 ἀγαθὸν παρεῖναι, ἐφ' ᾧ καθήκει⟩ ἐπαίρεσθαι.

Ὑπὸ μὲν οὖν τὴν ἐπιθυμίαν ὑπάγεται τὰ τοιαῦτα· | ὀργὴ καὶ τὰ εἴδη αὐτῆς, (θυμὸς καὶ χόλος καὶ μῆνις καὶ κότος καὶ πικρίαι καὶ τὰ τοιαῦτα,) ἔρωτες σφοδροὶ καὶ πόθοι καὶ ἵμεροι 35 καὶ φιληδονίαι καὶ φιλοπλουτίαι καὶ φιλοδοξίαι

---

9 τοῦ: suppl. Wachsmuth   21 πρόσφατον τοῦ ὄντως αὐτὸ ὀρεκτὸν εἶναι: suppl. Wachsmuth, after Meineke and Salmasius   24 καὶ: del. Wachsmuth   28 συστέλλεσθαι....ἐφ' ᾧ καθήκει: suppl. Salmasius, comparing Diogenes Laertius 7.114   34 κότος: Canter; σκότος: P

Here "judgement" means the awareness and recognition of right things. "Contrary to nature" in the description of passion is taken as something which occurs contrary to correct and natural reasoning. All those in the grips of passion turn their backs on reason, not in the same way as those who have been thoroughly deceived in any matter, but in a special way. For those who have been fooled, for example, that there are indivisible first elements, when taught that they do not exist,[132] abandon this judgement. But those in the grips of passion, even if they know or have been taught that they need not feel pain or be afraid or be involved at all in the passions of the soul, nevertheless do not abandon them, but are led by their passions to being governed by their tyranny.

10b They say that appetite is a desire which is disobedient to reason. The cause of this is forming an opinion that something good is approaching and if that were present we would be getting away fine, when the opinion itself has the unruly, <fresh> stimulation <that it is really something worth desiring>.[133] Fear is an avoidance which is disobedient to reason, its cause being forming an opinion that something bad is approaching, when the belief has the fresh stimulation that it is really something worth avoiding. Pain is a contraction of the soul which is disobedient to reason. The cause of it is forming a fresh opinion that an evil is present, in the face of which it is appropriate <to contract.[134] Pleasure is an elation of the soul disobedient to reason. The cause of it is forming a fresh opinion that a good is present, in the face of which it is appropriate> to be elated.

Under appetite[135] are subsumed things like these: anger and its species (temper, rage, wrath, rancour, cases of ire, and such), violent cases of erotic love, cravings, yearnings, cases of fondness for pleasure, cases of fondness for wealth, cases of fondness for

καὶ τὰ ὅμοια· ὑπὸ δὲ τὴν ἡδονὴν ἐπιχαιρεκακίαι
καὶ ἀσμενισμοὶ καὶ γοητεῖαι καὶ τὰ ὅμοια· ὑπὸ
δὲ τὸν φόβον ὄκνοι καὶ ἀγωνίαι καὶ ἔκπληξις
καὶ αἰσχύναι καὶ θόρυβοι καὶ δεισιδαιμονίαι καὶ
δέος καὶ δείματα· ὑπὸ δὲ τὴν λύπην φθόνος, 5
ζῆλος, ζηλοτυπία, ἔλεος, πένθος, ἄχθος, ἄχος,
ἀνία, ὀδύνη, ἄση.

10c Ὀργὴ μὲν οὖν ἐστιν ἐπιθυμία
τιμωρήσασθαι τὸν δοκοῦντα ἠδικηκέναι παρὰ
τὸ προσῆκον· θυμὸς δὲ ὀργὴ ἐναρχομένη· 10
χόλος δὲ ὀργὴ διοιδοῦσα· μῆνις δὲ ὀργὴ εἰς
παλαίωσιν ἀποτεθειμένη ἢ ἐναποκειμένη·
κότος δὲ ὀργὴ ἐπιτηροῦσα καιρὸν εἰς τιμωρίαν·
πικρία δὲ ὀργὴ παραχρῆμα ἐκρηγνυμένη· ἔρως
δὲ ἐπιβολὴ φιλοποιίας διὰ κάλλος 15
ἐμφαινόμενον· πόθος δὲ ἐπιθυμία κατ' ἔρωτα
ἀπόντος· ἵμερος δὲ ἐπιθυμία φίλου ἀπόντος
ὁμιλίας· φιληδονία δὲ ἐπιθυμία ἡδονῶν·
φιλοπλουτία δὲ πλούτου· φιλοδοξία δὲ δόξης.

Ἐπιχαιρεκακία δὲ ἡδονὴ ἐπ' ἀλλοτρίοις 20
κακοῖς· ἀσμενισμὸς δὲ ἡδονὴ ἐπὶ
ἀπροσδοκήτοις· γοητεία δὲ ἡδονὴ δι' ὄψεως
κατὰ ἀπάτην. |

Ὄκνος δὲ φόβος μελλούσης ἐνεργείας·
ἀγωνία δὲ φόβος διαπτώσεως καὶ ἑτέρως 25
φόβος ἥττης· ἔκπληξις δὲ φόβος ἐξ ἀσυνήθους
φαντασίας· αἰσχύνη δὲ φόβος ἀδοξίας·
θόρυβος δὲ φόβος μετὰ φωνῆς κατεπείγων·
δεισιδαιμονία δὲ φόβος θεῶν ἢ δαιμόνων· δέος
δὲ φόβος δεινοῦ· δεῖμα δὲ φόβος ἐκ λόγου. 30

Φθόνος δὲ λύπη ἐπ' ἀλλοτρίοις ἀγαθοῖς·
ζῆλος δὲ λύπη ἐπὶ τῷ ἕτερον ἐπιτυγχάνειν ὧν
αὐτὸς ἐπιθυμεῖ, αὐτὸν δὲ μή· λέγεσθαι δὲ καὶ
ἑτέρως ζῆλον, μακαρισμὸν ἐνδεοῦς καὶ ἔτι
ἄλλως μίμησιν ὡς ἂν κρείττονος· ζηλοτυπίαν 35

SVF
3.395

3.402

W
2.92
3.408

3.413

---

3 καὶ ἔκπληξις: transposed by Wachsmuth from after θόρυβοι, comparing 10c
9 τιμωρήσασθαι: FP; τοῦ τιμωρήσασθαι: von Arnim   12 ἀποτεθειμένη:
Meineke; ἀποτιθεμένη: FP   16 κατ' ἔρωτα ἀπόντος: Andronicus, *Peri Pathôn*;
τοῦ ἔρωτι ἀπόντος: FP;   τοῦ ἐρωτικοῦ ἀπόντος: Meurer;
τοῦ ἐρωμένου ἀπόντος: Meineke   22 ἡδονὴ: Heeren; δι' ἡδονῆς: FP

esteem, and the like. Under pleasure are subsumed cases of joy at others' misfortunes, cases of self-gratification, cases of charlatanry, and the like. Under fear are subsumed cases of hesitancy, cases of anguish, astonishment, feelings of shame, commotions, superstitions, dread, and terrors. Under pain are subsumed distress, envy, jealousy, pity, grief, worry, sorrow, annoyance, mental pain, and vexation.

10c Anger is an appetite to take vengeance on a person who seems to have acted unjustly contrary to what is fitting. Temper is anger starting up; rage is anger boiling over; wrath is anger set aside or stored up to mature; rancour is anger keeping watch for an opportunity for revenge; ire is anger breaking out on the spot. Erotic love is an inclination for forming an attachment arising from the display of beauty;[136] craving is an appetite in accord with erotic love for one who is absent; yearning is an appetite for the company of an absent friend; fondness for pleasure is an appetite for pleasures; fondness for wealth is an appetite for wealth; fondness for esteem is an appetite for opinion.[137]

Joy at others' misfortunes is pleasure at the evils suffered by others.[138] Self-gratification is taking pleasure in the unexpected. Charlatanry is taking pleasure in visual deception.[139]

Hesitancy is fear about a future activity. Anguish is fear of failure and, in another sense, fear of defeat. Astonishment is fear arising from an unaccustomed impression. Shame is fear of loss of reputation. Commotion is fear together with noise urging us on. Superstition is fear of the gods or spirits.[140] Dread is fear of the terrible. Terror is fear from reasoning.

Distress is pain at good occurring to others.[141] Envy is pain at another getting what you yourself have an appetite for, but you do not yourself get. Envy is spoken of in another sense as well, as a benediction of what is lacking, and, in another sense as well, as the imitation of another as being superior to oneself.[142] Jealousy is pain

δὲ λύπην ἐπὶ τῷ ⟨καὶ⟩ ἕτερον ἐπιτυγχάνειν ὧν
αὐτὸς ἐπεθύμει· ἔλεον δὲ λύπην ἐπὶ τῷ δοκοῦντι
ἀναξίως κακοπαθεῖν· πένθος δὲ λύπην ἐπὶ
θανάτῳ ἀώρῳ· ἄχθος δὲ λύπην βαρύνουσαν·
ἄχος δὲ λύπην ἀφωνίαν ἐμποιοῦσαν· ἀνίαν δὲ 5
λύπην κατὰ διαλογισμόν· ὀδύνην δὲ λύπην
εἰσδύνουσαν καὶ καθικνουμένην· ἄσην δὲ λύπην
μετὰ ῥιπτασμοῦ.

10d Τούτων δὲ τῶν παθῶν τὰ μὲν ἐμφαίνειν
τὸ ἐφ' ᾧ γίγνεται, οἷον ἔλεον, φθόνον, 10
ἐπιχαιρεκακίαν, αἰσχύνην· τὰ δὲ τὴν ἰδιότητα
τῆς κινήσεως, οἷον ὀδύνην, δεῖμα. |

10e Εὐεμπτωσίαν δ' εἶναι εὐκαταφορίαν εἰς
πάθος, ὥς τι τῶν παρὰ φύσιν ἔργων, οἷον
ἐπιλυπίαν, ὀργιλότητα, φθονερίαν, 15
ἀκροχολίαν καὶ τὰ ὅμοια. Γίγνεσθαι δὲ
εὐεμπτωσίας καὶ εἰς ἄλλα ἔργα τῶν παρὰ
φύσιν, οἷον εἰς κλοπὰς καὶ μοιχείας καὶ ὕβρεις,
καθ' ἃς κλέπται τε καὶ μοιχοὶ καὶ ὑβρισταὶ
λέγονται. Νόσημα δ' εἶναι δόξαν ἐπιθυμίας 20
ἐρρυηκυῖαν εἰς ἕξιν καὶ ἐνεσκιρωμένην, καθ' ἣν
ὑπολαμβάνουσι τὰ μὴ αἱρετὰ σφόδρα αἱρετὰ
εἶναι, οἷον φιλογυνίαν, φιλοινίαν, φιλαργυρίαν·
εἶναι δέ τινα καὶ ἐναντία ⟨τούτοις⟩ τοῖς
νοσήμασι κατὰ προσκοπὴν γινόμενα, οἷον 25
μισογυνίαν, μισοινίαν, μισανθρωπίαν. Τὰ δὲ
νοσήματα μετ' ἀσθενείας συμβαίνοντα
ἀρρωστήματα καλεῖσθαι.

11a Κατόρθωμα δ' εἶναι λέγουσι καθῆκον
πάντας ἀπέχον τοὺς ἀριθμούς, ἢ καθάπερ 30
προείπομεν, τέλειον καθῆκον· ἁμάρτημά τε τὸ
παρὰ τὸν ὀρθὸν λόγον πραττόμενον, ἢ ἐν ᾧ
παραλέλειπταί τι καθῆκον ὑπὸ λογικοῦ ζῴου.

SVF
3.394

W
2.93
3.421
LS
65S

3.500
59K

---

1 καὶ: suppl. Heine, comparing Diogenes Laertius 7.111 2 ἐπεθύμει: Davisius; ἐπιθυμεῖ: FP
14 ὥς τι: Meineke; ἤ τι: von Arnim; εἴς τι: FP 24 τούτοις: suppl. Heeren 30 ἀπέχον: FP
— cf LSJ ἀπέχω, IV; ἐπέχον: Canter 31 ἁμάρτημά τε: Heeren; ἁμαρτήματα: FP

at another also getting what you yourself had an appetite for. Pity is pain at someone appearing to suffer harm undeservedly.[143] Grief is pain at a premature death. Worry is pain becoming burdensome. Sorrow is pain which produces speechlessness. Annoyance is pain in accordance with calculation. Mental pain is pain which burrows into a person and takes up home there. Vexation is pain with thrashing around.

10d Of these passions, some display the occcasion which prompts them, such as pity, distress, joy at others' misfortunes, and shame. Others show the specific type of motion, such as mental pain and terror.[144]

10e A proclivity is a propensity to a passion, as[145] a particular deed contrary to nature, such as taking offence, irascibility, enviousness, outbursts of rage, and the like. There are also proclivities to other deeds contrary to nature, such as acts of theft, acts of adultery, and acts of violence, through which they are called thieves, adulterers, and hooligans.[146] An illness is an opinion about an appetite which has inclined into a condition and become ingrained,[147] through which they assume that things that are not worth choosing are especially worth choosing, such as fondness for women, fondness for wine, and fondness for money. There are also some things opposite to these illnesses which occur by aversion, such as the hatred of women, the hatred of wine, and the hatred of mankind. Those illnesses which occur together with weakness are called frailties.[148]

11a They say that a right act is an appropriate act having in full all its features,[149] or as we said earlier,[150] a complete appropriate act. A wrong act is something done contrary to correct reason or where some appropriate act has been omitted by a rational creature.[151]

11b Τά τε ἀγαθὰ πάντα τῶν σπουδαίων εἶναι ⟨κοινὰ⟩ λέγουσι, καθ' ὃ καὶ τὸν ὠφελοῦντά τινα τῶν | πλησίον καὶ ἑαυτὸν ὠφελεῖν. Τήν τε ὁμόνοιαν ἐπιστήμην εἶναι κοινῶν ἀγαθῶν, δι' ὃ καὶ τοὺς σπουδαίους πάντας ὁμονοεῖν ἀλλήλοις διὰ τὸ συμφωνεῖν ἐν τοῖς κατὰ τὸν βίον· τοὺς δὲ φαύλους διαφωνοῦντας πρὸς ἀλλήλους ἐχθροὺς εἶναι καὶ κακοποιητικοὺς ἀλλήλων καὶ πολεμίους.

Τό τε δίκαιόν φασι φύσει εἶναι καὶ μὴ θέσει. Ἑπόμενον δὲ τούτοις ὑπάρχειν καὶ τὸ πολιτεύεσθαι τὸν σοφὸν καὶ μάλιστ' ἐν ταῖς τοιαύταις πολιτείαις ταῖς ἐμφαινούσαις τινὰ προκοπὴν πρὸς τὰς τελείας πολιτείας· καὶ τὸ νομοθετεῖν δὲ καὶ τὸ παιδεύειν ἀνθρώπους, ἔτι δὲ συγγράφειν τὰ δυνάμενα ὠφελεῖν τοὺς ἐντυγχάνοντας τοῖς γράμμασιν οἰκεῖον εἶναι τοῖς σπουδαίοις καὶ τὸ συγκαταβαίνειν καὶ εἰς γάμον καὶ εἰς τεκνογονίαν καὶ αὐτοῦ χάριν καὶ τῆς πατρίδος καὶ ὑπομένειν περὶ ταύτης, ἐὰν ᾖ μετρία, καὶ πόνους καὶ θάνατον. Παρακεῖσθαι δὲ τούτοις φαῦλα, τό τε δημοκοπεῖν καὶ τὸ σοφιστεύειν καὶ τὸ συγγράφειν ἐπιβλαβῆ τοῖς ἐντυγχάνουσιν, ἅπερ εἰς σπουδαίους οὐκ ἂν πέσοι.

11c Τριχῶς δὲ λεγομένης τῆς φιλίας, καθ' ἕνα μὲν τρόπον τῆς κοινῆς ἕνεκ' ὠφελείας, καθ' ἣν φίλοι εἶναι λέγονται, ταύτην μὲν οὔ φασι τῶν ἀγαθῶν εἶναι, διὰ τὸ μηδὲν ἐκ διεστηκότων ἀγαθὸν εἶναι κατ' αὐτούς· τὴν δὲ κατὰ τὸ δεύτερον σημαινόμενον λεγομένην φιλίαν, κατάσχεσιν οὖσαν φιλικὴν πρὸς τῶν πέλας, τῶν ἐκτὸς λέγουσιν ἀγαθῶν· τὴν δὲ περὶ αὐτὸν φιλίαν, καθ' | ἣν φίλος ἐστὶ τῶν πέλας, τῶν περὶ ψυχὴν ἀποφαίνουσιν ἀγαθῶν.

SVF
W 3.625
2.94

3.611

3.98

2.95

---

2 κοινὰ: suppl. Wachsmuth   15 ἔτι: Heeren; ἔστι: FP   21 μετρία: Meineke; μέτρια: FP
27 ἕνεκ' ὠφελείας: Meineke; ἕνεκα φιλίας: FP   32 κατάσχεσιν: Madvig; κατὰ σχέσιν: FP

11b They say that all good things are common to the worthwhile — hence, in addition, the man who benefits any of his neighbours also benefits himself. Concord is a knowledge of common goods. Hence also all the worthwhile are in concord with one another, because they are in harmony in the affairs of life. But the worthless, being in disharmony with one another, are enemies of one another, are ready to do harm to each other, and are at war with one another.

They say justice is by nature and not by convention. Following on from this, it is the case that the wise man takes part in politics, especially in such political systems as display some progress toward being complete political systems.[152] It is also the case that he makes laws and educates his fellow men; furthermore, it is fitting for the worthwhile to write down what is able to benefit those who happen upon their writings, as is also to stoop to marriage and the raising of children, both for his own and his country's sake, and also to endure for its sake, if it is moderate, toils and death.[153] Opposed to these are worthless things: courting the mob, being a sophist, and writing works which are harmful to those who happen upon them, things which would not befall the worthwhile.

11c Friendship is spoken of in three ways: in one way, for the sake of common benefit, according to which people are called friends — but they say that this is not one of the good things, since according to them nothing which is made up of separate parts is a good. What is called friendship according to the second definition, a friendly relationship with one's neighbours, they say is one of the external goods. But the friendship which pertains to oneself, in accord with which one is a friend of one's neighbours, they declare to be one of the good things of the soul.[154]

11d Εἶναι δὲ καὶ θάτερον τρόπον κοινὰ τὰ ἀγαθά. Πάντα γὰρ τὸν ὁντινοῦν ὠφελοῦντα ἴσην ὠφέλειαν ἀπολαμβάνειν νομίζουσι παρ' αὐτὸ τοῦτο, μηδένα δὲ φαῦλον μήτε ὠφελεῖσθαι μήτε ὠφελεῖν. Εἶναι γὰρ τὸ ὠφελεῖν ἴσχειν κατ' ἀρετὴν καὶ τὸ ὠφελεῖσθαι κινεῖσθαι κατ' ἀρετήν.
    Οἰκονομικὸν δ' εἶναι μόνον λέγουσι τὸν σπουδαῖον καὶ ἀγαθὸν οἰκονόμον, ἔτι δὲ χρηματιστικόν. Τὴν μὲν γὰρ οἰκονομικὴν εἶναι θεωρητικὴν ἕξιν καὶ πρακτικὴν τῶν οἴκῳ συμφερόντων· τὴν δ' οἰκονομίαν διάταξιν περὶ ἀναλωμάτων καὶ ἔργων καὶ κτήσεως ἐπιμέλειαν καὶ τῶν κατ' ἀγρὸν ἐργαζομένων· τὴν δὲ χρηματιστικὴν ἐμπειρίαν περιποιήσεως χρημάτων ἀφ' ὧν δέον καὶ ἕξιν ὁμολογουμένως ἀναστρέφεσθαι ποιοῦσαν ἐν συναγωγῇ χρημάτων καὶ τηρήσει καὶ ἀναλώσει πρὸς εὐπορίαν· τὸ δὲ χρηματίζεσθαί τινες μὲν μέσον εἶπον εἶναι, τινὲς δὲ ἀστεῖον. Φαῦλον δὲ μηδένα προστάτην ἀγαθὸν οἴκου γίνεσθαι, μηδὲ δύνασθαι οἰκίαν εὖ οἰκονουμένην παρασχεῖν. Μόνον δὲ τὸν σπουδαῖον ἄνδρα χρηματιστικὸν εἶναι, γινώσκοντα ἀφ' ὧν χρηματιστέον καὶ πότε καὶ πῶς καὶ μέχρι πότε.
    Φασὶ ⟨δὲ⟩ μηδὲ συγγνώμην ἔχειν ⟨μηδενὶ τὸν νοῦν ἔχοντα· τοῦ γὰρ αὐτοῦ συγγνώμην τε ἔχειν⟩ καὶ νομίζειν | τὸν ἡμαρτηκότα μὴ παρ' αὐτὸν ἡμαρτηκέναι, πάντων ἁμαρτανόντων παρὰ τὴν ἰδίαν κακίαν· διὸ καὶ δεόντως λέγεσθαι τὸ μηδὲ συγγνώμην ἔχειν τοῖς ἁμαρτάνουσιν. Οὐκ ἐπιεικῆ δέ φασιν εἶναι τὸν ἀγαθὸν ἄνδρα, τὸν γὰρ ἐπιεικῆ παραιτητικὸν εἶναι τῆς κατ' ἀξίαν κολάσεως καὶ τοῦ αὐτοῦ εἶναι ἐπιεικῆ τε εἶναι καὶ ὑπολαμβάνειν τὰς ἐκ τοῦ νόμου τεταγμένας κολάσεις τοῖς ἀδικοῦσι σκληροτέρας εἶναι καὶ τὸ ἡγεῖσθαι παρὰ τὴν ἀξίαν ἀπονέμειν τὰς κολάσεις τὸν νομοθέτην.

SVF
3.94

3.623

3.640
W
2.96

16 δέον: Meineke; δέος: FP   17 ὁμολογουμένως: Heeren; ὁμολογοῦμεν ὡς: FP
26 δὲ: suppl. Heeren   26 μηδενὶ ... τε ἔχειν: suppl. *Florilegia* 46.50, τε suppl. Wachsmuth

11d Goods are common in another way. For they believe that everyone who benefits anyone else gains an equal advantage by the act itself,[155] while no worthless man can either benefit someone else or receive a benefit. For to confer a benefit is to be in accord with virtue and to be benefitted is to be moved in accord with virtue.[156]

They say that only the worthwhile man is skilled in household management and a good manager of his household, and, in addition, skilled at making money.[157] For the skill of managing a household is a rule-based and practical condition with regard to what is useful for the household; household management is the organisation of expenses and deeds, and the care of acquisitions and the produce from the fields. The money-making skill is experience in the acquisition of money from appropriate sources and a condition which creates conduct in agreement (with nature) in the collecting, preservation, and expenditure of money to produce affluence. Some say that making money is an intermediate, others that it is something civilised. But no worthless man can be a good head of his household, nor is he able to provide for a well-managed house. Only the worthwhile man is skilled at making money, knowing from what sources money must be gained, and when, how, and for how long.

They also say that <the man with good sense does not forgive anyone. For it is characteristic of the same person both to forgive> someone and to believe that he did not do wrong through his own fault, when all do wrong through their own evil. Accordingly it is rightly said that he does not forgive those who are doing wrong. They say that the good man is not tolerant, since the tolerant can be begged off the punishment in accord with what is due, and that it is the mark of the same man to be tolerant and to assume that the punishments set out by law for the unjust are too harsh and to consider that the lawmaker apportions punishments contrary to what is due.

Τόν τε νόμον σπουδαῖον εἶναί φασι, λόγον ὀρθὸν ὄντα, προστακτικὸν μὲν ὧν ποιητέον, ἀπαγορευτικὸν δὲ ὧν οὐ ποιητέον. Τοῦ δὲ νόμου ἀστείου ὄντος καὶ ὁ νόμιμος ἀστεῖος ἂν ⟨εἴη⟩· νόμιμον μὲν γὰρ εἶναι ἄνδρα καὶ 5 ἀκολουθητικὸν τῷ νόμῳ καὶ πρακτικὸν τῶν ὑπ' αὐτοῦ προσταττομένων· νομικὸν δὲ τὸν ἐξηγητικὸν τοῦ νόμου. Μηδένα δὲ τῶν φαύλων μήτε νόμιμον εἶναι μήτε νομικόν.

SVF 3.613

11e Ἔτι δὲ τῶν ἐνεργημάτων φασὶ τὰ μὲν 10 εἶναι κατορθώματα, τὰ δὲ ἁμαρτήματα, τὰ δ' οὐδέτερα. Κατορθώματα μὲν τὰ τοιαῦτα· φρονεῖν, σωφρονεῖν, δικαιοπραγεῖν, χαίρειν, εὐεργετεῖν, εὐφραίνεσθαι, φρονίμως περιπατεῖν, πάνθ' ὅσα κατὰ τὸν ὀρθὸν λόγον 15 πράττεται· ἁμαρτήματα δ' εἶναι, τό τε ἀφραίνειν καὶ τὸ ἀκολασταίνειν | καὶ τὸ ἀδικεῖν καὶ τὸ λυπεῖσθαι καὶ τὸ φοβεῖσθαι καὶ τὸ κλέπτειν καὶ καθόλου ὅσα παρὰ τὸν ὀρθὸν λόγον πράττεται· οὔτε δὲ κατορθώματα οὔτε 20 ἁμαρτήματα τὰ τοιαῦτα· λέγειν, ἐρωτᾶν, ἀποκρίνεσθαι, περιπατεῖν, ἀποδημεῖν καὶ τὰ τούτοις παραπλήσια. Πάντα δὲ τὰ κατορθώματα δικαιοπραγήματα εἶναι καὶ εὐνομήματα καὶ εὐτακτήματα καὶ 25 εὐεπιτηδεύματα καὶ εὐτυχήματα καὶ εὐδαιμονήματα καὶ εὐκαιρήματα καὶ εὐσχημονήματα· οὐκ ἔτι μέντοι γε φρονιμεύματα, ἀλλὰ μόνα τὰ ἀπὸ φρονήσεως καὶ ὁμοίως ἐπὶ τῶν ἄλλων ἀρετῶν, εἰ καὶ μὴ 30 ὠνόμασται, οἷον σωφρονήματα μὲν τὰ ἀπὸ σωφροσύνης, δικαιώματα δὲ τὰ ἀπὸ δικαιοσύνης. Τὰ δὲ ἁμαρτήματα ἐκ τῶν ἀντικειμένων ἀδικοπραγήματα καὶ ἀνομήματα καὶ ἀτακτήματα. 35

3.501 LS 59M

W 2.97

3.502

---

5 εἴη: suppl. *Florilegia* 44.11   25 εὐνομήματα: Dindorf (cf. Plut. *Stoic. rep.* 15); εὐνοήματα: FP   26 εὐεπιτηδεύματα: Heeren; ἐπιτηδεύματα: FP   31 σωφρονήματα: Canter; σωφρονημεύματα: P; σωφρονικεύματα: F

They say that the law is worthwhile, since it is correct reasoning, ordering what must be done, but forbidding what must not be done. And as the law is civilised, the law-abiding citizen <would be> civilised too. For the man is law-abiding who is able both to follow the law and to carry out the things ordered by it, while the man is learned in the law who is able to interpret the law. But no worthless man is either law-abiding or learned in the law.

11e In addition, they say that some activations are right acts, while others are wrong acts, while others are neither. Right acts are such as these: to be intelligent, to show self-restraint, to act justly, to be joyful, to be benevolent, to be cheerful, to walk around intelligently, and everything else which is done in accord with correct reasoning. Wrong acts include to act stupidly, to show lack of restraint, to act unjustly, to feel pain, to be afraid, to steal, and, overall, whatever is done contrary to correct reasoning. Neither right nor wrong acts are such: to talk, to pose a question, to answer, to walk around, to live abroad, and things like these.[158] All right acts are justly performed acts, lawfully performed acts, orderly acts, properly pursued acts, prosperous acts, successful acts, opportune acts, and dignified acts. However, they are not intelligent acts, but only those which derive from intelligence are such — and the same is true in relation to the other virtues (even if they have not been named), such as restrained acts derived from self-restraint and just acts from justice.[159] Wrong acts derived from the opposing vices are unjust acts, lawless acts, and unruly acts.

11f Διαφέρειν δὲ λέγουσιν, ὥσπερ αἱρετὸν καὶ αἱρετέον, οὕτω καὶ ὀρεκτὸν καὶ ὀρεκτέον καὶ βουλητὸν καὶ βουλητέον καὶ ἀποδεκτὸν καὶ ἀποδεκτέον. Αἱρετὰ μὲν γὰρ εἶναι καὶ βουλητὰ καὶ ὀρεκτὰ ⟨καὶ ἀποδεκτὰ τἀγαθά· τὰ δ' ὠφελήματα αἱρετέα καὶ βουλητέα καὶ ὀρεκτέα⟩ καὶ ἀποδεκτέα, κατηγορήματα ὄντα, παρακείμενα δ' ἀγαθοῖς. Αἱρεῖσθαι μὲν γὰρ ἡμᾶς τὰ αἱρετέα καὶ βούλεσθαι τὰ βουλητέα καὶ ὀρέγεσθαι τὰ ὀρεκτέα. Κατηγορημάτων γὰρ αἵ τε αἱρέσεις καὶ ὀρέξεις καὶ βουλήσεις γίνονται, ὥσπερ καὶ αἱ ὁρμαί· ἔχειν μέντοι αἱρούμεθα καὶ βουλόμεθα καὶ ὁμοίως ὀρεγόμεθα τἀγαθά, διὸ καὶ αἱρετὰ καὶ βουλητὰ καὶ ὀρεκτὰ τἀγαθά ἐστι. Τὴν γὰρ φρόνησιν αἱρούμεθα ἔχειν καὶ τὴν σωφροσύνην, οὐ μὰ Δία τὸ φρονεῖν καὶ σωφρονεῖν, ἀσώματα ὄντα καὶ κατηγορήματα.

Λέγουσι δὲ ὁμοίως καὶ τἀγαθὰ πάντα εἶναι ὑπομενετὰ καὶ ἐμμενετὰ καὶ ἀνάλογον ἐπὶ τῶν ἄλλων ἀρετῶν, εἰ καὶ μὴ κατωνόμασται· τὰ δὲ ὠφελήματα πάντα ὑπομενετέα καὶ ἐμμενετέα καὶ τὰ ὅμοια. Ὡσαύτως δὲ διαφέρειν ὑπολαμβάνουσι καὶ τὰ εὐλαβητὰ καὶ τὰ εὐλαβητέα καὶ ἀνυπομενετὰ καὶ ἀνυπομενετέα. Τῶν δ' ἄλλων τῶν κατὰ τὰς κακίας ὁ αὐτὸς λόγος.

11g Πάντα δὲ τὸν καλὸν καὶ ἀγαθὸν ἄνδρα τέλειον εἶναι λέγουσι διὰ τὸ μηδεμιᾶς ἀπολείπεσθαι ἀρετῆς· τὸν δὲ φαῦλον τοὐναντίον ἀτελῆ διὰ τὸ μηδεμιᾶς μετέχειν ἀρετῆς. Δι' ὃ καὶ πάντως εὐδαιμονεῖν ἀεὶ τῶν ἀνθρώπων τοὺς ἀγαθούς, τοὺς δὲ φαύλους κακοδαιμονεῖν. καὶ ⟨ἐκείνων⟩ τὴν εὐδαιμονίαν μὴ διαφέρειν τῆς θείας εὐδαιμονίας, μηδὲ τὴν ἀμεριαίαν ὁ Χρύσιππός φησι διαφέρειν τῆς τοῦ

---

5 καὶ ἀποδεκτὰ ... καὶ ὀρεκτέα: suppl. Heine from 11i   14 τἀγαθά: Usener; ἀγαθά:FP   21 καὶ ἀνάλογον: Heeren; κατ' ἀνάλογον: FP
35 ἐκείνων: suppl. Usener   37 ἀμεριαίαν: Madvig; ἀμεριμνίαν: FP

11f They say that just as what is worth choosing and what must be chosen differ, so too do what is worth desiring and what must be desired, what is worth wanting and what must be wanted, and what is worth accepting and what must be accepted. For good things are worth choosing, being wanted, desired, <and accepted, while benefits must be chosen, wanted, desired,> and accepted, as they are predicates, associated with good things.[160] They say that we choose what must be chosen, wish for what must be wanted, and desire what must be desired. For choices, desires, and wishes are for predicates, as with the impulses.[161] However, we choose, want, and likewise desire to have good things. Hence good things are worth choosing, worth wanting, and worth desiring. We choose to have intelligence and self-restraint, not, by Zeus, to have "being sensible" and "being self-restrained", which are incorporeals and predicates.[162]

Likewise they say that all goods are worth maintaining and worth persisting in and that the case is analogous for the other virtues, even if they have not been given names.[163] All benefits must be maintained and persisted in and so forth. Similarly they assume that there is a difference between what is worth avoiding and what must be avoided and what is not worth sustaining and what must be sustained. There is the same account of other matters which are associated with vices.

11g They say that every fine and good man is complete because he is lacking in no virtue. Conversely, every worthless man is incomplete because he participates in no virtue. Hence also the good among men always live an absolutely happy life, while the worthless are unhappy, and the happiness <of the former> is in no way different from the happiness of the gods. Chrysippus says

Διὸς εὐδαιμονίας, ⟨καὶ⟩ κατὰ | μηδὲν
αἱρετωτέραν εἶναι μήτε καλλίω μήτε
σεμνοτέραν τὴν τοῦ Διὸς εὐδαιμονίαν τῆς τῶν
σοφῶν ἀνδρῶν.
 Ἀρέσκει γὰρ τῷ τε Ζήνωνι καὶ τοῖς ἀπ' 5
αὐτοῦ Στωικοῖς φιλοσόφοις δύο γένη τῶν
ἀνθρώπων εἶναι, τὸ μὲν τῶν σπουδαίων, τὸ
δὲ τῶν φαύλων· καὶ τὸ μὲν τῶν σπουδαίων
διὰ παντὸς τοῦ βίου χρῆσθαι ταῖς ἀρεταῖς, τὸ
δὲ τῶν φαύλων ταῖς κακίαις· ὅθεν τὸ μὲν ἀεὶ 10
κατορθοῦν ἐν ἅπασιν οἷς προστίθεται, τὸ δὲ
ἁμαρτάνειν. Καὶ τὸν μὲν σπουδαῖον ταῖς περὶ
τὸν βίον ἐμπειρίαις χρώμενον ἐν τοῖς
πραττομένοις ὑπ' αὐτοῦ πάντ' εὖ ποιεῖν,
καθάπερ φρονίμως καὶ σωφρόνως καὶ κατὰ 15
τὰς ἄλλας ἀρετάς· τὸν δὲ φαῦλον κατὰ
τοὐναντίον κακῶς. Καὶ τὸν μὲν σπουδαῖον
μέγαν εἶναι καὶ ἁδρὸν καὶ ὑψηλὸν καὶ ἰσχυρόν.
Μέγαν μέν, ὅτι δύναται ἐφικνεῖσθαι τῶν κατὰ
προαίρεσιν ὄντων αὐτῷ καὶ προκειμένων· 20
ἁδρὸν δέ, ὅτι ἐστὶν ηὐξημένος πάντοθεν·
ὑψηλὸν δ', ὅτι μετείληφε τοῦ ἐπιβάλλοντος
ὕψους ἀνδρὶ γενναίῳ καὶ σοφῷ· καὶ ἰσχυρὸν
δ', ὅτι τὴν ἐπιβάλλουσαν ἰσχὺν περιπεποίηται,
ἀήττητος ὢν καὶ ἀκαταγώνιστος. Παρ' ὃ καὶ 25
οὔτε ἀναγκάζεται ὑπό τινος οὔτε ἀναγκάζει
τινά, οὔτε κωλύεται οὔτε κωλύει, οὔτε
βιάζεται ὑπό τινος οὔτ' αὐτὸς βιάζει τινά, οὔτε
δεσπόζει οὔτε δεσπόζεται, οὔτε κακοποιεῖ τινα
οὔτ' αὐτὸς κακοποιεῖται, οὔτε κακοῖς 30
περιπίπτει ⟨οὔτ' ἄλλον ποιεῖ κακοῖς
περιπίπτειν⟩, οὔτ' ἐξαπατᾶται οὔτε |
ἐξαπατᾷ ἄλλον, οὔτε διαψεύδεται οὔτε ἀγνοεῖ
οὔτε λανθάνει ἑαυτὸν οὔτε καθόλου ψεῦδος
ὑπολαμβάνει· εὐδαίμων δ' ἐστὶ μάλιστα καὶ 35
εὐτυχὴς καὶ μακάριος καὶ ὄλβιος καὶ εὐσεβὴς

1 καὶ: suppl. Wachsmuth   5 ἀπ': Heeren; ὑπ': FP.   12 τὸν: Wachsmuth; τὸ: FP
16 τὸν: Wachsmuth; τὸ: FP   30 κακοῖς: Gaisford; κακῶς: FP
32 οὔτ' ἄλλον ποιεῖ κακοῖς περιπίπτειν: suppl. Meineke

that their momentary happiness is no different from the happiness of Zeus <and> that the happiness of Zeus is in no respect more worth choosing, nor finer, nor more majestic than that of wise men.[164]

It is the view of Zeno and his Stoic followers that there are two races of men, that of the worthwhile, and that of the worthless. The race of the worthwhile employ the virtues through all their lives, while the race of the worthless employ the vices. Hence the worthwhile always do right in everything on which they embark, while the worthless do wrong. The worthwhile man, using his practical experiences with regard to life in the things done by him, does all things well, just as he does them sensibly, with self-restraint, and in accord with the other virtues. The worthless man, conversely, does badly. The worthwhile man is also great, powerful, eminent, and strong.[165] Great because he is able to accomplish the things which accord with his policy and are proposed.[166] Powerful, because he is extolled on all sides. Eminent, because he has gained a share in the eminence which befalls a noble and wise man. And strong, because he has possession of the strength which befalls such a man, being invincible and unconquerable. Consequently, he is neither compelled by anyone nor does he compel another, neither prevented by nor preventing anyone else, neither forced by another nor forcing anyone else, neither lording it over others nor being lorded over, neither doing harm to another nor suffering harm from anyone else, neither encountering evils <nor causing anyone else to encounter evil>, neither deceived nor deceiving another, neither subjected to falsehood nor failing to understand nor unaware of what he is doing nor, overall, does he assume a falsehood. He is particularly happy, prosperous, blessed, fortunate, pious, dear to

καὶ θεοφιλὴς καὶ ἀξιωματικός, βασιλικός τε καὶ
στρατηγικὸς καὶ πολιτικὸς καὶ οἰκονομικὸς καὶ
χρηματιστικός. Τοὺς δὲ φαύλους ἅπαντα
τούτοις ἐναντία ἔχειν.

Καθόλου δὲ τοῖς μὲν σπουδαίοις πάντα τἀγαθὰ ὑπάρχειν, τοῖς δὲ φαύλοις πάντα τὰ κακά. Οὐ νομιστέον δὲ λέγειν αὐτοὺς οὕτως, ὡς εἴ τινά ἐστιν ἀγαθά, ἐκεῖνα ὑπάρχει τοῖς σπουδαίοις, ὁμοίως δὲ καὶ ἐπὶ τῶν κακῶν· ἀλλά τοι τοὺς μὲν τοσαῦτα ἔχειν ἀγαθὰ ὥστε μηδὲν ἐλλείπειν εἰς τὸ τέλειον αὐτοῖς εἶναι τὸν βίον ⟨καὶ εὐδαίμονα⟩, τοὺς δὲ τοσαῦτα κακά, ὥστε τὸν βίον ἀτελῆ εἶναι καὶ κακοδαίμονα.

11h Τὴν δ' ἀρετὴν πολλοῖς ὀνόμασι προσαγορεύουσιν. Ἀγαθόν τε γὰρ λέγουσιν αὐτήν, ὅτι ἄγει ἡμᾶς ἐπὶ τὸν ὀρθὸν βίον· καὶ ἀρεστόν, ὅτι δοκιμαστόν ἐστιν ἀνυπόπτως· καὶ πολλοῦ ἄξιον, ⟨ὅτι⟩ ἀνυπέρβλητον ἔχει τὴν ἀξίαν· καὶ σπουδαῖον, ἄξιον γὰρ εἶναι πολλῆς σπουδῆς· καὶ ἐπαινετόν, εὐλόγως γὰρ ἄν τις αὐτὴν ἐπαινοίη· καὶ καλόν, ὅτι πρὸς ἑαυτὴν καλεῖν πέφυκε τοὺς ὀρεγομένους αὐτῆς· καὶ συμφέρον, φέρειν γὰρ τοιαῦτα ἃ συντείνει πρὸς τὸ εὖ ζῆν· καὶ χρήσιμον, ὅτι ἐν τῇ χρείᾳ ὠφέλιμόν ἐστι· καὶ αἱρετόν, συμβαίνειν γὰρ ἀπ' αὐτῆς ἃ εὐλόγως ἔστιν αἱρεῖσθαι· καὶ ἀναγκαῖον, ὅτι παροῦσά τε ὠφελεῖ καὶ μὴ παρούσης οὐκ ἔστιν ὠφελεῖσθαι· καὶ λυσιτελές, τὰς γὰρ ἀπ' αὐτῆς ὠφελείας κρείττους εἶναι τῆς πραγματείας τῆς εἰς ταύτας συντεινούσης· καὶ αὔταρκες, ἐξαρκεῖν γὰρ τῷ ἔχοντι· καὶ ἀνενδεές, ὅτι ἐνδείας ἀπαλλάττει πάσης· καὶ ἀποχρῶν διὰ τὸ ἐν τῇ χρήσει ἱκανὸν εἶναι καὶ διατείνειν εἰς πᾶσαν τὴν κατὰ τὸν βίον χρείαν.

11i Τῶν τε ἀγαθῶν μηδενὸς μετέχειν τοὺς φαύλους, ἐπειδὴ τὸ ἀγαθὸν ἀρετή ἐστιν ἢ τὸ μετέχον ἀρετῆς· τά τε παρακείμενα τοῖς ἀγαθοῖς, ἅπερ ἐστὶν ὧν χρή, ὠφελήματα

---

10 ἀλλά τοι: Hense; ἀλλ' οὕτω: Heeren; ἀλλὰ τῷ: FP
12 καὶ εὐδαίμονα: suppl. Meineke   18 ὅτι: suppl. Heeren

the gods, meritorious, kingly, fit for command, political, good at managing the household and at making money. The worthless have everything opposite to this.

Overall, all good things belong to the worthwhile, all evils to the worthless. It should not be thought that they are saying this: that if particular good things exist, these belong to the worthwhile, and that it is also the same case regarding evils. But rather they have so many good things that there is nothing lacking for their life to be complete <and happy>, while the other group has so many evils that their life is incomplete and unhappy.[167]

11h They describe virtue by numerous terms.[168] They say it is good, because it leads us to the correct life;[169] pleasing, because it is prized unhesitatingly; highly valued, because it has unsurpassable value; worthwhile, as being deserving of the utmost regard; praiseworthy, because someone would reasonably praise it; beautiful, because it naturally calls to itself those desiring it; advantageous, because it produces the sort of things that contribute to the good life; useful, because it is beneficial in use; worth choosing, because what can reasonably be chosen occur as a result of it; necessary, because when it is present it benefits and, if it is not present, it is not possible to be benefitted; profitable, for its benefits are greater than the effort which contributes to them; self-sufficient, as it suffices for the person who has it; free from want, because it removes any want; and enough, because it is adequate for our usage and extends to every need in life.

11i The worthless participate in none of the good things, since the good is a virtue or something which participates in virtue. The things associated with the goods — whatever things exist which are needed, that is, benefits — occur only to the

ὄντα, μόνοις τοῖς σπουδαίοις συμβαίνειν·
καθάπερ καὶ τὰ παρακείμενα τοῖς κακοῖς, ἅπερ
ἐστὶν ὧν οὐ χρή, μόνοις τοῖς κακοῖς· βλάμματα
γὰρ εἶναι, καὶ διὰ τοῦτο τοὺς μὲν ἀγαθοὺς
ἀβλαβεῖς πάντας εἶναι κατ' ἀμφότερα, οὔτε 5
βλάπτειν οἵους τε ὄντας οὔτε βλάπτεσθαι,
τοὺς δὲ φαύλους κατὰ τοὐναντίον.

SVF
Τὸν δὲ κατ' ἀλήθειαν πλοῦτον ἀγαθὸν 3.593
εἶναι λέγουσι, καὶ τὴν κατ' ἀλήθειαν πενίαν
κακόν. Καὶ τὴν μὲν κατ' ἀλήθειαν ἐλευθερίαν 10
ἀγαθόν, τὴν δὲ κατ' ἀλήθειαν δουλείαν κακόν.
Δι' ὃ δὴ καὶ τὸν σπουδαῖον εἶναι μόνον
πλούσιον καὶ ἐλεύθερον, τὸν δὲ φαῦλον
τοὐναντίον πένητα, τῶν εἰς τὸ πλουτεῖν
ἀφορμῶν ὑστερημένον καὶ δοῦλον διὰ τὴν 15
ὑποπτωτικὴν ἐν αὐτῷ διάθεσιν.

Τὰ δ' ἀγαθὰ πάντα κοινὰ εἶναι τῶν 3.626
σπουδαίων, τῶν δὲ φαύλων τὰ κακά. Δι' ὃ LS
καὶ τὸν ὠφελοῦντά τινα καὶ αὐτὸν ὠφελεῖσθαι, 60P
τὸν δὲ βλάπτοντα καὶ ἑαυτὸν βλάπτειν. 20
Πάντας δὲ τοὺς σπουδαίους ὠφελεῖν
ἀλλήλους, οὔτε φίλους ὄντας ἀλλήλων
πάντως οὔτε εὔνους ⟨οὔτε⟩ εὐδοκίμους οὔτε
ἀποδεχομένους παρὰ τὸ μήτε καταλαμβάνεσθαι W
μήτ' ἐν ταὐτῷ κατοικεῖν τόπῳ, εὐνοητικῶς | 25 2.102
μέντοι γε πρὸς ἀλλήλους διακεῖσθαι καὶ
φιλικῶς καὶ δοκιμαστικῶς καὶ ἀποδεκτικῶς·
τοὺς δὲ ἄφρονας ἐν τοῖς ἐναντίοις τούτων
ὑπάρχειν.

Τοῦ δὲ νόμου ὄντος σπουδαίου, καθάπερ 30 3.614
εἴπομεν, ἐπειδὴ λόγος ὀρθός ἐστι προστακτικὸς
μὲν ὧν ποιητέον, ἀπαγορευτικὸς δὲ ὧν οὐ
ποιητέον, μόνον τὸν σοφὸν εἶναι λέγουσι
νόμιμον, πρακτικὸν ὄντα τῶν ὑπὸ τοῦ νόμου
προσταττομένων καὶ μόνον ἐξηγητικὸν 35
τούτου, δι' ὃ καὶ νομικὸν εἶναι· τοὺς δ' ἠλιθίους
ἐναντίως ἔχειν.

15 ὑστερημένον: F; ἐστερημένον: P   23 οὔτε: suppl. Heeren
31 προστακτικὸς   μὲν: Meineke;   μὲν   προστακτικὸς: FP

worthwhile, just as the things associated with the evils — that is, whatever things exist which are not needed — occur only to the bad, as they are harmful things. Because of this the good are all free from harm in both respects, neither being able to harm nor to be harmed; while the worthless are in the opposite position.[170]

They say that true riches are a good and true poverty an evil. True freedom is a good, true slavery an evil.[171] Because of this they also say that the worthwhile man is the only rich and free man, and, conversely, the worthless man is poor, deprived of the impulses towards being rich, and a slave because of his submissive disposition.[172]

All goods are common to the worthwhile, all evils to the worthless.[173] Because of this, whoever benefits someone also is himself benefitted, and the person who harms another also harms himself. All the worthwhile benefit one another. They are not totally friends of one another, nor well-disposed to each other, <nor> highly prized nor accepted by each other because they are not aware of each other and do not live together in the same place. However, they are in attitude well-disposed and friendly to each other, and prized and accepted by one another. The stupid are the opposite of this.

As the law is worthwhile, as we have said[174] (since it is correct reason ordering what must be done and forbidding what must not be done),[175] they say that only the wise man is law-abiding, as he is able to do what is ordered by the law, and that he alone is able to interpret it — hence, he is also learned in the law. The silly are the opposite of this.

Ἀστείοις δ' ἔτι καὶ τὴν ἀρχικὴν κατανέμουσιν ἐπιστασίαν καὶ τὰ ταύτης εἴδη, βασιλείαν, στρατηγίαν, ναυαρχίαν καὶ τὰς ταύταις παραπλησίους. Κατὰ τοῦτο δὴ καὶ μόνος ὁ σπουδαῖος ἄρχει καὶ εἰ μὴ πάντως κατ' ἐνέργειαν, κατὰ διάθεσιν δὲ καὶ πάντως. Καὶ πειθαρχικὸς μόνος ὁ σπουδαῖός ἐστιν, ἀκολουθητικὸς ὢν ἄρχοντι. Τῶν δ' ἀφρόνων οὐδεὶς τοιοῦτος· οὔτε γὰρ ἄρχειν οὔτ' ἄρχεσθαι οἷός ⟨τ'⟩ ἐστιν ὁ ἄφρων, αὐθάδης τις ὢν καὶ ἀνάγωγος.

Πάντα τε εὖ ποιεῖ ὁ νοῦν ἔχων, καὶ γὰρ φρονίμως καὶ ἐγκρατῶς καὶ κοσμίως καὶ εὐτάκτως ταῖς περὶ τὸν βίον ἐμπειρίαις χρώμενος συνεχῶς. ὁ δὲ φαῦλος, ἄπειρος ὢν τῆς ὀρθῆς χρήσεως, πάντα κακῶς ποιεῖ καθ' ἣν ἔχει διάθεσιν ἐνεργῶν, εὐμετάπτωτος ὢν καὶ παρ' ἕκαστα μεταμελείᾳ συνεχόμενος. Εἶναι δὲ τὴν μεταμέλειαν λύπην ἐπὶ πεπραγμένοις ὡς παρ' αὐτοῦ ἡμαρτημένοις, κακοδαιμονικόν τι πάθος ψυχῆς καὶ στασιῶδες· ἐφ' ὅσον γὰρ ἄχθεται τοῖς συμβεβηκόσιν ὁ ἐν ταῖς μεταμελείαις ὤν, ἐπὶ τοσοῦτον ἀγανακτεῖ πρὸς ἑαυτὸν ὡς αἴτιον γεγονότα τούτων· δι' ὃ καὶ ἄτιμον εἶναι πάντα φαῦλον, μήτε τιμῆς ἄξιον ὄντα μήτε τίμιον ὑπάρχοντα. Τὴν γὰρ τιμὴν εἶναι γέρως ἀξίωσιν, τὸ δὲ γέρας ἆθλον ἀρετῆς εὐεργετικῆς. Τὸ οὖν ἀρετῆς ἀμέτοχον ἄτιμον δικαίως λέγεσθαι.

Λέγουσι δὲ καὶ φυγάδα πάντα φαῦλον εἶναι, καθ' ὅσον στέρεται νόμου καὶ πολιτείας κατὰ φύσιν ἐπιβαλλούσης. Τὸν γὰρ νόμον εἶναι, καθάπερ εἴπομεν, σπουδαῖον, ὁμοίως δὲ καὶ τὴν πόλιν. Ἱκανῶς δὲ καὶ Κλεάνθης περὶ τὸ σπουδαῖον εἶναι τὴν πόλιν λόγον ἠρώτησε τοιοῦτον· Πόλις μὲν ⟨εἰ⟩ ἔστιν οἰκητήριον

SVF 3.615

3.563, 3.567

W 2.103

3.328
LS 67I

1.587

1 ἀστείοις δ' ἔτι: Heeren; ἀστείοις δ' εἶναι: FP; ἀστείων δ' εἶναι: Meineke   1 ἀρχικὴν: Usener; ἀρχὴν: FP   3 κατανέμουσιν: Usener; κατανέμουσαν: FP   6 πάντως: Heeren; πάντες: FP   10 τ': suppl. Usener   18 μεταμελείᾳ: Heeren; μεταμελείας: FP   20 αὑτοῦ: Meineke; αὐτὸν: F, αὐτῶν: P   36 εἰ: suppl. Heeren; πόλις ⟨εἰ ἔννομόν⟩ ἐστιν: Schofield

Furthermore they assign to the civilised the governing superintendence and its species: kingship, generalship, admiralship, and the like. In accord with this also only the worthwhile man governs and, if he does not do this totally with respect to activity, he governs totally with respect to his disposition.[176] And only the worthwhile man is obedient to command, being ready to follow the man who governs. None of the stupid is such. For the stupid person is neither able to govern nor to be governed, being headstrong and unmanageable.

The person with good sense does everything well, and so intelligently, temperately, modestly, and in orderly fashion continually using his practical experiences with regard to life.[177] The worthless man, however, having no experience of the correct use, does everything badly, acting in accord with his disposition, easily changing his mind and in the grip of regret over every matter. Regret is pain at things that have been done, as having been done wrongly by oneself, a passion of the soul which creates unhappiness and is quarrelsome. To the extent that the person in a state of regret feels some sorrow at the occurrences, he is annoyed with himself as having been responsible for them. Hence, every worthless person is dishonoured, neither being worthy of honour nor being held in honour. For honour is an evaluation (as deserving) of privilege, and privilege is the prize for benevolent virtue. So what is without any participation in virtue is rightly spoken of as dishonoured.

They also say that every worthless person is also an exile, to the extent that he is deprived of law and befitting government in accord with nature.[178] For the law, as we have stated,[179] is worthwhile, and, likewise, so too is the city. With regard to the city being a worthwhile thing, Cleanthes adequately posed the question in this fashion, "If the city is an arrangement for dwelling in a

κατασκεύασμα, εἰς ὃ καταφεύγοντας ἔστι δίκην
δοῦναι καὶ λαβεῖν, οὐκ ἀστεῖον δὴ πόλις ἐστίν;
ἀλλὰ μὴν τοιοῦτόν ἐστιν ἡ πόλις οἰκητήριον·
ἀστεῖον ἄρ' ἔστιν ἡ πόλις. Τριχῶς δὲ λεγομένης
τῆς πόλεως, τῆς τε κατὰ τὸ οἰκητήριον καὶ 5
τῆς κατὰ τὸ σύστημα τῶν ἀνθρώπων καὶ
τρίτον τῆς κατ' ἀμφότερα τούτων, κατὰ δύο
σημαινόμενα λέγεσθαι τὴν πόλιν ἀστείαν,
κατά τε τὸ σύστημα τῶν ἀνθρώπων καὶ κατὰ
τὸ συναμφότερον διὰ ⟨τὴν εἰς⟩ τοὺς 10
ἐνοικοῦντας ἀναφοράν.

11k Φασὶ δὲ καὶ ἄγροικον εἶναι πάντα φαῦλον·
τὴν γὰρ ἀγροικίαν ἀπειρίαν εἶναι τῶν κατὰ
πόλιν ἐθῶν καὶ νόμων· ᾗ πάντα φαῦλον
ἔνοχον ὑπάρχειν. εἶναι δὲ καὶ ἄγριον, 15
ἐναντιωτικὸν ὄντα τῇ κατὰ νόμον διεξαγωγῇ
καὶ θηριώδη καὶ βλαπτικὸν ἄνθρωπον. Τὸν δ'
αὐτὸν τοῦτον καὶ ἀνήμερον ὑπάρχειν καὶ
τυραννικόν, οὕτως διακείμενον ὥστε
δεσποτικὰ ποιεῖν, ἔτι δὲ ὠμὰ καὶ βίαια καὶ 20
παράνομα καιρῶν ἐπιλαβόμενον. Εἶναι δὲ καὶ
ἀχάριστον, οὔτε πρὸς ἀνταπόδοσιν χάριτος
οἰκείως ἔχοντα οὔτε πρὸς μετάδοσιν διὰ τὸ
μήτε κοινῶς τι ποιεῖν μήτε φιλικῶς μήτ'
ἀμελετήτως. 25

Μηδὲ φιλόλογον εἶναι τὸν φαῦλον μηδὲ
φιλήκοον, παρὰ τὸ μηδ' ἀρχὴν παρεσκευάσθαι
πρὸς τὴν τῶν ὀρθῶν λόγων παραδοχὴν διὰ
τὴν ὑπείκουσαν ἐκ τῆς διαστροφῆς ἀφροσύνην,
παρὰ τὸ μήτε προτετράφθαι τινὰ τῶν 30
φαύλων μήτε προτρέπειν πρὸς ἀρετήν· τὸν
γὰρ προτετραμμένον ἢ προτρέποντα ἑτέρους
ἕτοιμον εἶναι δεῖ πρὸς τὸ φιλοσοφεῖν, τὸν δ'
ἕτοιμον ἀνεμποδίστως ἔχειν, μηδένα ⟨δὲ⟩ τῶν
ἀφρόνων εἶναι τοιοῦτον. Οὐ γὰρ τὸν 35
προθύμως ἀκούοντα καὶ ὑπομνηματιζόμενον

SVF
3.677

W
2.104

3.682

---

10 τὴν εἰς: suppl. Wachsmuth   14 ᾗ: Meineke; ἡ: FP   27 ἀρχὴν: Heeren; ἄρχειν: FP
29 ὑπείκουσαν: F; ἀπήκουσαν: P; παρήκουσαν: Usener; ὑπάρχουσαν: von Arnim
32 προτρέποντα: Meineke; προτρεπόμενον: FP   34 δὲ: suppl. Heeren

place[180] and it is possible for people who have taken refuge in this to get and suffer judgement, then isn't the city civilised? But it is in fact such a dwelling place. So the city is civilised." The city is spoken of in three ways: with regard to the dwelling place, with regard to the composite made of men, and thirdly with regard to both of these. The city is spoken of as civilised in respect of two definitions, in regard to the definition "the composite made of men", and, because of the reference to the inhabitants, in regard to the definition "in both respects".[181]

11k They also say that every worthless person is rustic.[182] For rusticity is a lack of experience of the customs and laws of the city to which every worthless person is subject. He is also wild, being hostile to the lifestyle which is in accord with the law, bestial, and a harmful person. This same fellow is savage and despotic, inclined to do tyrannical acts, and furthermore to do cruel, violent, and lawless acts when he gets opportunities. He is also ungrateful, neither having an affinity to the return of a favour nor to the bestowal of one because he does not do anything cooperatively nor amicably nor spontaneously.

The worthless person is neither fond of discussion nor of listening, because he has not been prepared for the reception of correct reasoning because of his stupidity which fails from its distortion,[183] and because none of the worthless is inclined toward nor can incline others to virtue. For the person who is inclined or can incline others needs to be ready for philosophising, and the person who is ready is without impediment, and none of the stupid are such. For it is not the person who eagerly listens to and makes

τὰ λεγόμενα ὑπὸ τῶν φιλοσόφων ἕτοιμον εἶναι πρὸς τὸ φιλοσοφεῖν, ἀλλὰ τὸν ἑτοίμως ἔχοντα πρὸς τὸ τὰ διὰ τῆς φιλοσοφίας παραγγελλόμενα μεταφέρειν ἐπὶ τὰ ἔργα καὶ κατ' αὐτὰ βιοῦν. Οὐδένα δὲ τῶν φαύλων τοιοῦτον εἶναι, προκατειλημμένον τοῖς τῆς κακίας δόγμασιν. Εἰ γὰρ προετέτραπτό τις τῶν φαύλων καὶ ἀπὸ τῆς κακίας ἂν ἐτέτραπτο. Οὐδεὶς δ' ἔχων τὴν κακίαν πρὸς ἀρετὴν τέτραπται, ὡς οὐδὲ νοσῶν πρὸς ὑγίειαν. Μόνον δὲ προτετράφθαι τὸν σοφὸν καὶ μόνον προτρέπειν δύνασθαι, τῶν δ' ἀφρόνων μηδένα· κατὰ γὰρ ⟨ἀρετῆς⟩ παραγγέλματα βιοῦν μηδένα τῶν ἀφρόνων. Μηδ' εἶναι φιλόλογον, λογόφιλον δὲ μᾶλλον, μέχρι λαλιᾶς ἐπιπολαίου προβαίνοντα, μηκέτι δὲ καὶ τοῖς ἔργοις ἐκβεβαιούμενον τὸν τῆς ἀρετῆς λόγον.

Μηδὲ γὰρ φιλόπονόν τινα τῶν φαύλων εἶναι· τὴν γὰρ φιλοπονίαν διάθεσιν ἐξεργαστικὴν εἶναι τῶν ἐπιβαλλόντων ἀνυπόπτως διὰ πόνον, οὐδένα δὲ τῶν φαύλων ἀνυπόπτως ἔχειν πρὸς τὸν πόνον.

Μηδὲ γὰρ τὴν κατ' ἀξίαν ποιεῖσθαι δόσιν τῆς ἀρετῆς τῶν φαύλων τινά, σπουδαῖον μὲν γὰρ εἶναι τὴν δόσιν, ἐπιστήμην οὖσαν, καθ' ἣν ἀξιόλογόν τι ἡγούμεθα περιποιεῖσθαι. Τῶν δὲ σπουδαίων μηδὲν εἰς φαύλους πίπτειν, ὥστε μηδὲ τὴν ἀξίαν τῆς ἀρετῆς δόσιν ποιεῖσθαί τινα τῶν φαύλων. Εἰ γὰρ τὴν κατ' ἀξίαν τις ἐποιεῖτο δόσιν τῶν ἀφρόνων τῆς ἀρετῆς, ἐφ' ὅσον ἐτίμα ταύτην, ἀπῳκονομεῖτο ἂν τὴν κακίαν. Πᾶς δέ τις ἄφρων σύνεστιν ἡδέως τῇ ἑαυτοῦ κακίᾳ. Σκοπεῖν γὰρ δεῖ μὴ τὸν ἐξώφορον αὐτῶν λόγον, φαῦλον ὄντα, ἀλλὰ τὸν τῶν πράξεων. Ἐκ τούτων γὰρ

W
2.105

SVF
3.683

3.684

---

10 νοσῶν: Heine; νόσον: FP   13 ἀρετῆς: suppl. Wachsmuth
19 φαύλων: Canter; σπουδαίων: FP   33 δέ τις: Wachsmuth; δέ τε: FP; δέ: Meineke

notes of what is spoken by the philosophers who is ready for philosophizing, but the person who is ready to transfer the prescriptions of philosophy to his deeds and to live in accord with them. None of the worthless are such, being already prejudiced by the teachings of vice. For if any of the worthless had been so inclined, he would also have turned from vice. But no one who possesses vice is turned toward virtue, just as no one who is sick is turned towards health. Only the wise man is inclined to virtue and only he is able to incline others, while none of the stupid can. For none of the stupid are able to live according to the prescriptions <of virtue>. Nor can they be fond of discussion, but are instead fond of talking, advancing as far as superficial chatter, but not, in addition, strengthening the reasoning of virtue by deeds as well.

None of the worthless are industrious. For industriousness[184] is a disposition able to accomplish unhesitatingly what is befitting through toil, and none of the worthless are unhesitating with regard to toil.

Nor do any of the worthless gain virtue's contribution in accord with their merits,[185] for contribution is something worthwhile, being knowledge in accord with which we think we are acquiring something worthwhile. None of the worthwhile things befall the worthless, so none of the stupid gain virtue's contribution in accord with their merits. If any of the stupid gained virtue's contribution in accord with his merits, to the extent that he honoured it, he would be getting rid of vice. But every stupid person gladly lives with his vice. It is necessary to examine, not the published accounts of these men, which are worthless, but rather the accounts of their deeds. From these they are convicted of being eager, not for the good and

ἀπελέγχονται [καὶ] μὴ περὶ τὰ καλὰ καὶ
σπουδαῖα παρωρμημένοι, ἀλλὰ περὶ τὰς
ἀνδραποδώδεις ἀμέτρους ἀπολαύσεις.
Ἀρέσκει δὲ καὶ πᾶν ἁμάρτημα ἀσέβημα
εἶναι. Τὸ γὰρ παρὰ τὴν βούλησίν τι 5
πράττεσθαι τοῦ θεοῦ, ἀσεβείας εἶναι τεκμήριον.
Τῶν γὰρ θεῶν οἰκειουμένων μὲν τῇ ἀρετῇ καὶ
τοῖς ταύτης ἔργοις, ἀλλοτριουμένων δὲ τῇ
κακίᾳ | καὶ τοῖς ἀπὸ ταύτης συντελουμένοις,
τοῦ δ' ἁμαρτήματος ὄντος ἐνεργήματος κατὰ 10
κακίαν, κατεφαίνετο πᾶν ἁμάρτημα
ἀπαρεστὸν θεοῖς ὑπάρχον (τοῦτο δ' ἐστὶν
ἀσέβημα)· [καὶ] καθ' ἕκαστον γὰρ ἁμάρτημα
ὁ φαῦλος ἀπαρεστόν τι ποιεῖ θεοῖς.
Ἔτι δὲ ἐπεὶ πᾶς φαῦλος ὅσα ποιεῖ κατὰ 15
κακίαν ποιεῖ, καθάπερ ὁ σπουδαῖος κατ'
ἀρετήν, καὶ ὁ μίαν ἔχων κακίαν πάσας ἔχει.
Ἐν δὲ ταύταις ὁρᾶσθαι καὶ τὴν ἀσέβειαν, οὐ
τὴν τεταγμένην κατὰ τὴν ἐνέργειαν, ἀλλὰ τὴν
τῇ εὐσεβείᾳ ἐναντίαν ἕξιν. Τὸ δὲ κατὰ ἀσέβειαν 20
πεπραγμένον ἀσέβημα εἶναι, πᾶν ⟨οὖν⟩
ἁμάρτημα ἀσέβημα εἶναι.
Ἔτι δ' ἀρέσκει αὐτοῖς καὶ πάντ' εἶναι τὸν
ἄφρονα θεοῖς ἐχθρόν· τὴν γὰρ ἔχθραν
ἀσυμφωνίαν εἶναι ⟨περὶ⟩ τῶν κατὰ τὸν βίον 25
καὶ διχόνοιαν, ὥσπερ καὶ τὴν φιλίαν
συμφωνίαν καὶ ὁμόνοιαν. Διαφωνοῦσι δ' οἱ
φαῦλοι πρὸς τοὺς θεοὺς περὶ τῶν κατὰ τὸν
βίον, διόπερ πᾶς ἄφρων θεοῖς ἐχθρός ἐστιν.
Ἔτι εἰ πάντες τοὺς ἐναντίους αὐτοῖς ἐχθροὺς 30
εἶναι νομίζουσι, τῷ δὲ σπουδαίῳ ὁ φαῦλός
ἐστιν ἐναντίος καὶ σπουδαῖός ἐστιν ὁ θεός, ὁ
φαῦλος θεοῖς ἐστιν ἐχθρός.

111 Ἴσα τε πάντα λέγουσιν εἶναι τὰ
ἁμαρτήματα, οὐκέτι δ' ὅμοια. Καθάπερ γὰρ 35
ἀπὸ μιᾶς τινος πηγῆς τῆς κακίας φέρεσθαι
πέφυκε, τῆς κρίσεως οὔσης ἐν πᾶσι τοῖς

SVF
3.661

W
2.106

3.528

1 καὶ: del. Heeren   13 καὶ: del. Wachsmuth   21 οὖν: suppl. Heeren; ἄρ': Wachsmuth
25 περὶ: suppl. Meineke   30 Ἔτι εἰ: Heine; ἐπεὶ: F, ἐπὶ: P   35 οὐκέτι: Heeren; οὐκ ἔστι: FP

worthwhile, but for slavish, immoderate pleasures.

It is their view that every wrong act is an impious act. For to do something against the wish of the god is proof of impiety. As the gods have an affinity with virtue and its deeds, but are alienated from vice and those things which are produced by it, and as a wrong act is an activation in accord with vice, every wrong act is revealed as displeasing to the gods (that is, an impious act): for with every wrong act the worthless man does something displeasing to the gods.

Furthermore, since every worthless man does whatever he does in accord with vice, just as the worthwhile man acts in accord with virtue, the person who has one vice has them all. Among them can also be seen impiety, not the type of impiety which is classified in accord with its activity, but the condition which is opposed to piety.[186] But what is achieved in accord with impiety is an impious act. So every wrong act is an impious act.

Furthermore, it is their view that every stupid person is an enemy of the gods. For enmity is disharmony and discord in matters of life, just as friendship is harmony and concord. But the worthless are in disharmony with the gods in matters of life. Hence, every stupid person is an enemy of the gods. Furthermore if all believe that those opposed to them are their enemies, and the worthless person is hostile to the worthwhile, and god is worthwhile, then the worthless person is an enemy of the gods.

111 They say that all wrong acts are equal, but are not now the same. Inasmuch as they naturally come from, as it were, one source, that of vice, the judgement is the same in the case of every wrong

ἁμαρτήμασι τῆς αὐτῆς· παρὰ δὲ τὴν ἔξωθεν αἰτίαν, τῶν ἐφ' οἷς αἱ κρίσεις ἀποτελοῦνται μέσων διαλλαττόντων, διάφορα κατὰ ποιότητα γίνεσθαι τὰ ἁμαρτήματα. | Λάβοις δ' ἂν εἰκόνα σαφῆ τοῦ δηλουμένου τῷδ' ἐπιστήσας· πᾶν γὰρ τὸ ψεῦδος ἐπ' ἴσης ψεῦδος συμβέβηκεν, οὐ γὰρ εἶναι ἕτερον ἑτέρου μᾶλλον διεψευσμένον· τὸ [τε] γὰρ νύκτ' ⟨ἀεὶ⟩ εἶναι ψεῦδός ἐστι, καθάπερ τὸ ἱπποκένταυρον ζῆν· καὶ οὐ μᾶλλον εἰπεῖν ἔστι ψεῦδος εἶναι θάτερον θατέρου· ἀλλ' οὐχὶ τὸ ψευδὲς ἐπίσης ψευδές ἐστιν, οὐχὶ δὲ καὶ οἱ διεψευσμένοι ἐπίσης εἰσὶ διεψευσμένοι. Καὶ ἁμαρτάνειν δὲ μᾶλλον καὶ ἧττον οὐκ ἔστι, πᾶσαν γὰρ ἁμαρτίαν κατὰ διάψευσιν πράττεσθαι. Ἔτι οὐχὶ κατόρθωμα μὲν μεῖζον καὶ ἔλαττον οὐ γίγνεσθαι, ἁμάρτημα δὲ μεῖζον καὶ ἔλαττον γίγνεσθαι· πάντα γάρ ἐστι τέλεια, διόπερ οὔτ' ἐλλείπειν οὔθ' ὑπερέχειν δύναιτ' ἂν ἀλλήλων. Ἴσα τοίνυν ἐστὶ πάντα τὰ ἁμαρτήματα.

W
2.107

11m Περὶ δὲ εὐφυοῦς, ἔτι δὲ εὐγενοῦς οἱ μὲν τῶν ἐκ τῆς αἱρέσεως ἐπηνέχθησαν ἐπὶ τὸ λέγειν πάντα σοφὸν τοιοῦτον εἶναι, οἱ δ' οὔ. Οἱ μὲν γὰρ οἴονται οὐ μόνον εὐφυεῖς γίγνεσθαι πρὸς ἀρετὴν ἐκ φύσεως, ἀλλὰ καί τινας ἐκ κατασκευῆς, καὶ τὸ ἐν ταῖς παροιμίαις λεγόμενον τοῦτο ἀπεδέξαντο

μελέτη χρονισθεῖσ' εἰς φύσιν καθίσταται.

Τὸ δ' ὅμοιον καὶ περὶ εὐγενείας ὑπέλαβον, ὥστε εὐφυίαν | μὲν εἶναι κοινῶς ἕξιν ἐκ φύσεως ἢ ἐκ κατασκευῆς οἰκείαν πρὸς ἀρετήν, ἢ ἕξιν καθ' ἣν εὐανάληπτοι ἀρετῆς εἰσί τινες· τὴν δ' εὐγένειαν ἕξιν ἐκ γένους ἢ ἐκ κατασκευῆς οἰκείαν πρὸς ἀρετήν.

SVF
3.366

2.108

---

8 τε: del. Meineke   8 ἀεὶ: suppl. Heeren   9 εἶναι: FP; ἐνεστάναι, without Heeren's supplement: Pomeroy   11 ψευδὲς ἐπίσης ψευδές: Wachsmuth; ψεῦδος ἐπίσης ψεῦδος: FP   13 καὶ ἁμαρτάνειν: Meineke; διαμαρτάνειν: FP   17 γίγνεσθαι: Heeren; γίγνεται: FP   19 ἴσα τοίνυν: Meineke; ἴσα τε νῦν: FP   25 καί τινας: Heine; καί τοὺς: FP; Meineke deletes τοὺς   33 ἐκ γένους: Canter; εὐγενοῦς: FP

act. But, in relation to the external cause, since the intermediates vary with regard to which the judgements are completed, wrong acts are different in quality.[187] You would get a clear image of what is being explained by considering it is this way: every falsehood is equally a falsehood, for none are more falsified than the others. So that it is <always>[188] night is a falsehood, just as is saying that centaurs live — to say one is no more a falsehood than the other. (But the false is not equally false, and also those who have been subjected to a falsehood are not equally subjected to a falsehood.)[189] Also to do wrong to a greater or lesser extent is impossible, as every wrong is produced through falsehood. Furthermore, it can't be that a right act cannot occur to a greater or lesser degree, but a wrong act can occur to a greater or lesser degree: all of them are complete things.[190] Hence, they could not lack or have anything more than one another. So, then, all mistaken acts are equal.

11m Concerning natural ability and being well-bred, some of the members of this school have been led to say that every wise man has such qualities, while others do not. For the latter think that people naturally suitable for virtue occur not only by nature, but also as a result of training, and they have agreed with this proverbial saying:

Practice over a long time turns into second nature.[191]

They have come to the same supposition about good breeding as well: so while natural ability is, in normal usage, a condition from nature, or a condition from training which has an affinity with virtue, or a condition in accordance with which people are easily able to gain virtue, good breeding is a condition, inherited or as the result of training, which has an affinity with virtue.

Τὸν δὲ σπουδαῖον, ὁμιλητικὸν ὄντα καὶ ἐπιδέξιον καὶ προτρεπτικὸν καὶ θηρευτικὸν διὰ τῆς ὁμιλίας εἰς εὔνοιαν καὶ φιλίαν, ὡς δυνατὸν εὐάρμοστον εἶναι πρὸς πλῆθος ἀνθρώπων, παρ' ὃ καὶ ἐπαφρόδιτον εἶναι καὶ ἐπίχαριν καὶ πιθανόν, ἔτι δὲ αἱμύλον καὶ εὔστοχον καὶ εὔκαιρον καὶ ἀγχίνουν καὶ ἀφελῆ καὶ ἀπερίεργον καὶ ἁπλοῦν καὶ ἄπλαστον· τὸν δὲ φαῦλον ἔνοχον πᾶσι τοῖς ἐναντίοις. Τὸ δ' εἰρωνεύεσθαι φαύλων εἶναί φασιν, οὐδένα γὰρ ἐλεύθερον καὶ σπουδαῖον εἰρωνεύεσθαι· ὁμοίως δὲ καὶ τὸ σαρκάζειν, ὅ ἐστιν εἰρωνεύεσθαι μετ' ἐπισυρμοῦ τινος. Ἐν μόνοις τε τοῖς σοφοῖς ἀπολείπουσι φιλίαν, ἐπεὶ ἐν μόνοις τούτοις ὁμόνοια γίνεται περὶ τῶν κατὰ τὸν βίον· τὴν δ' ὁμόνοιαν εἶναι κοινῶν ἀγαθῶν ἐπιστήμην. Φιλίαν γὰρ ἀληθινὴν καὶ μὴ ψευδώνυμον ἀδύνατον χωρὶς πίστεως καὶ βεβαιότητος ὑπάρχειν· ἐν δὲ τοῖς φαύλοις, ἀπίστοις καὶ ἀβεβαίοις οὖσι καὶ δόγματα πολεμικὰ κεκτημένοις, οὐκ εἶναι φιλίαν, ἑτέρας δέ τινας ἐπιπλοκὰς καὶ συνδέσεις ἔξωθεν ἀνάγκαις καὶ δόξαις κατεχομένας γίνεσθαι. Φασὶ δὲ καὶ τὸ ἀγαπᾶν καὶ τὸ ἀσπάζεσθαι καὶ τὸ φιλεῖν μόνων εἶναι σπουδαίων.

Καὶ μόνον εἶναι τὸν σοφὸν βασιλέα τε καὶ βασιλικόν, τῶν δὲ φαύλων μηδένα· τὴν γὰρ βασιλείαν ἀρχὴν ἀνυπεύθυνον εἶναι καὶ τὴν ἀνωτάτω καὶ τὴν ἐπὶ πάσαις.

Λέγουσι δὲ καὶ ἄριστον αὐτοῦ ἰατρὸν εἶναι τὸν σπουδαῖον ἄνδρα· ἐπιμελῆ γὰρ ὄντα τῆς ἰδίας φύσεως παρατηρητὴν ὑπάρχειν καὶ τῶν πρὸς ὑγίειαν ἐπιστήμονα συμφερόντων.

Οὐχ οἷον δὲ μεθυσθήσεσθαι τὸν νοῦν ἔχοντα· τὴν γὰρ μέθην ἁμαρτητικὸν περιέχειν, λήρησιν εἶναι ⟨γὰρ⟩ παρὰ τὸν οἶνον, ἐν μηδενὶ δὲ τὸν σπουδαῖον ἁμαρτάνειν, δι' ὃ πάντα κατ' ἀρετὴν ποιεῖν καὶ τὸν ἀπὸ ταύτης ὀρθὸν λόγον.

---

3 ὡς δυνατὸν: Meineke; καὶ δυνατὸν: FP   34 οἷον δὲ: Usener; οἱόντε: FP; οἷόν τε δὲ: Canter

The worthwhile man, being affable, clever, encouraging, and able to hunt for goodwill and friendship through association, is as accommodating as possible to the mass of men, through which he is also charming, gracious, and trustworthy, and, in addition, soothing, keen in aim, opportune, shrewd, guileless, simple, straightforward, and unaffected, while the worthless person is subject to all the opposites. They say to dissemble is a mark of the worthless, since no one who is a free man[192] and worthwhile dissembles. Likewise with sarcasm, which is to dissemble with a type of mockery. They accept friendship only among the wise, since among them alone is there concord regarding the matters of life, as concord is a knowledge of common goods.[193] For true friendship, not that falsely so-named, cannot exist without trust and firmness. In the case of the worthless, as they are unreliable and unstable and in possession of contradictory beliefs, it is not friendship, but different ties and attachments held together externally by their needs and opinions. They also say that being affectionate, embracing, and loving belong to the worthwhile alone.

Only the wise man can be a king and kingly, while none of the worthless can be such, since kingship is an office answerable to none, both being the office above all others and controlling all other offices.

They also say that the worthwhile man is the best doctor of himself. For, being careful about his personal nature, he is a close observer of and knowledgeable about what is useful for his health.

It is not possible for a person with intelligence to get drunk. For drunkenness encompasses the wrongful, since it is raving caused by wine, and the worthwhile man does wrong in nothing. Hence, he does everything in accord with virtue and the correct reasoning derived from it.[194]

Τρεῖς δὲ προηγουμένους εἶναι βίους, τόν τε βασιλικὸν καὶ τὸν πολιτικὸν καὶ τρίτον τὸν ἐπιστημονικόν· ὁμοίως δὲ καὶ χρηματισμοὺς τρεῖς προηγουμένους, τόν τε ἀπὸ τῆς βασιλείας, καθ' ὃν ἢ αὐτὸς βασιλεύσει ἢ μοναρχικῶν χρημάτων εὐπορήσει· δεύτερον δὲ τὸν ἀπὸ τῆς πολιτείας, πολιτεύσεσθαι γὰρ κατὰ τὸν προηγούμενον λόγον· καὶ γὰρ γαμήσειν καὶ παιδοποιήσεσθαι, ἀκολουθεῖν ⟨γὰρ⟩ ταῦτα τῇ τοῦ λογικοῦ ζῴου καὶ κοινωνικοῦ καὶ φιλαλλήλου ⟨φύσει⟩. Χρηματιεῖσθαι οὖν καὶ ἀπὸ τῆς πολιτείας καὶ ἀπὸ τῶν φίλων, τῶν ἐν ὑπεροχαῖς ὄντων. Περὶ δὲ τοῦ σοφιστεύσειν καὶ ἀπὸ σοφιστείας εὐπορήσειν χρημάτων διέστησαν οἱ ἀπὸ τῆς αἱρέσεως κατὰ τὸ σημαινόμενον. Τὸ μὲν γὰρ χρηματιεῖσθαι ἀπὸ τῶν κατὰ τὴν παιδείαν καὶ μισθούς ποτε λήψεσθαι παρὰ τῶν φιλομαθούντων διωμολογήσαντο· περὶ δὲ τὸ σημαινόμενον ἐγένετό τις ἐν αὐτοῖς ἀμφισβήτησις, τῶν μὲν αὐτὸ τοῦτο λεγόντων σοφιστεύειν, τὸ ἐπὶ μισθῷ μεταδιδόναι τῶν τῆς φιλοσοφίας δογμάτων, τῶν δ' ὑποτοπησάντων ἐν τῷ σοφιστεύειν περιέχεσθαί τι φαῦλον, οἱονεὶ λόγους καπηλεύειν, οὐ φαμένων δεῖν ἀπὸ παιδείας παρὰ τῶν ἐπιτυχόντων χρηματίζεσθαι, καταδεέστερον γὰρ εἶναι τὸν τρόπον τοῦτον τοῦ χρηματισμοῦ τοῦ τῆς φιλοσοφίας ἀξιώματος.

Φασὶ δέ ποτε καὶ τὴν ἐξαγωγὴν τὴν ἐκ τοῦ βίου τοῖς σπουδαίοις καθηκόντως ⟨γίγνεσθαι⟩ κατὰ πολλοὺς τρόπους, τοῖς ⟨δὲ⟩ φαύλοις μονὴν ⟨τὴν⟩ ἐν τῷ ζῆν καὶ οἳ μὴ μέλλοιεν ἔσεσθαι σοφοί· οὔτε γὰρ τὴν ἀρετὴν

SVF 3.686
LS 67W

W 2.110

3.758

---

1 προηγουμένους: Heeren; προηγορευμένους: FP   5 ἢ: Heine; καὶ: FP   6 μοναρχικῶν: Heeren; μοναρχικοῖς: FP; μοναρχικῶς: Heeren in his notes; ⟨ἢ συνὼν βασιλεῦσι⟩ καὶ μοναρχικοῖς χρημάτων: Hirzel   7 πολιτεύεσθαι: Meineke; πολιτεύσεσθαι: FP   10 γὰρ: suppl. Heeren   11 φύσει: suppl. Heeren   14 σοφιστεύσειν: Usener; σοφιστεύειν: FP   32 γίγνεσθαι: suppl. Heeren   32 δὲ: suppl. Heeren   33 τὴν: suppl. Usener   33 καὶ οἳ μὴ: Usener; καὶ εἰ μὴ: FP; καὶ μὴ: Heeren

There are three preferential types of life, the kingly, the political, and thirdly the intellectual. Likewise there are three preferential types of making money:[195] the one derived from kingship, through which either one will be king oneself or be rich with money from a monarch; the second derived from political life, for he will take part in politics according to preferential reasoning;[196] and indeed he will marry and father children, as these are consistent with his <nature> as a rational creature who is communal and fond of fellowship.[197] So he will make money both from public office and from those of his friends who are in positions of authority. But as to whether he will be a sophist and will be rich in money through sophistry, the members of this sect disagreed with respect to what is meant. For they agreed that they will make money from educational activities and from time to time accept payments from those who are fond of learning. But there was some disagreement among them concerning what is meant, some saying that to be a sophist is the same thing as to share the beliefs of philosophy for payment, while others suspect that there is something worthless in sophistry, like trading in words, and they say that one need not make money from education from whoever happens along, as this way of making money falls short of the dignity of philosophy.[198]

They sometimes say that the way out from life can be appropriate for the worthwhile in numerous ways,[199] while for the worthless and for those who are not going to become wise only persistence in life is appropriate.[200] For virtue does not constrain

κατέχειν ἐν τῷ ζῆν οὔτε τὴν κακίαν ἐκβάλλειν·
τοῖς δὲ καθήκουσι καὶ τοῖς παρὰ τὸ καθῆκον
⟨παρα⟩μετρεῖσθαι τήν τε ζωὴν καὶ τὸν θάνατον.
Λέγουσι δὲ καὶ τὸν σοφὸν ἀνύβριστον
εἶναι· οὔθ' ὑβρίζεσθαι γὰρ οὔθ' ὑβρίζειν διὰ τὸ 5
τὴν ὕβριν ἀδικίαν εἶναι καταισχύνουσαν καὶ
βλάβην· μήτε δὲ ἀδικεῖσθαι μήτε βλάπτεσθαι
τὸν σπουδαῖον (ἀδικητικῶς μέντοι γέ τινας
αὐτῷ προσφέρεσθαι καὶ ὑβριστικῶς καὶ κατὰ
τοῦτο ἀδικοπραγεῖν). Πρὸς τούτῳ μηδὲ ⟨τὴ⟩ν 10
τυχοῦσαν ἀδικίαν εἶναι τὴν ὕβριν, ἀλλὰ
καταισχύνουσαν καὶ ὑβριστικὴν οὖσαν.
Ἀπερίπτωτον δ' ὑπάρχειν τὸν νοῦν ἔχοντα
τούτοις καὶ μηδαμῶς καταισχύνεσθαι· ἐν
ἑαυτῷ γὰρ ἔχειν τὸ Ι ἀγαθὸν καὶ τὴν θείαν 15
ἀρετήν, δι' ὃ καὶ πάσης ἀπηλλάχθαι κακίας
καὶ βλάβης.

SVF
3.578

W
2.111

Καὶ βασιλεύσειν τέ ποτε τὸν νοῦν ⟨ἔχοντα⟩
καὶ βασιλεῖ συμβιώσεσθαι καὶ εὐφυίαν
ἐμφαίνοντι καὶ φιλομάθειαν. Ἔφαμεν δ' ὅτι καὶ 20
πολιτεύεσθαι κατὰ τὸν προηγούμενον λόγον
οἷόν ἐστι, μὴ πολιτεύεσθαι δὲ ἐάν τι ⟨κωλύῃ⟩
καὶ μάλιστ' ⟨ἂν⟩ μηδὲν ὠφελεῖν μέλλῃ τὴν
πατρίδα, κινδύνους δὲ παρακολουθεῖν
ὑπολαμβάνῃ μεγάλους καὶ χαλεποὺς ἐκ τῆς 25
πολιτείας.

3.690

Λέγεσθαι δὲ μὴ ψεύδεσθαι τὸν σοφόν, ἀλλ'
ἐν πᾶσιν ἀληθεύειν· οὐ γὰρ ἐν τῷ λέγειν τι
ψεῦδος τὸ ψεύδεσθαι ὑπάρχειν, ἀλλ' ἐν τῷ
διαψευστικῶς τὸ ψεῦδος λέγειν καὶ ἐπὶ ἀπάτῃ 30
τῶν πλησίον. Τῷ μέντοι ψεύδει ποτὲ
συγχρήσεσθαι νομίζουσιν αὐτὸν κατὰ
πολλοὺς τρόπους ἄνευ συγκαταθέσεως· καὶ
γὰρ κατὰ στρατηγίαν ⟨κατὰ⟩ τῶν
ἀντιπάλων καὶ κατὰ τὴν τοῦ συμφέροντος 35

3.554

3 ⟨παρα⟩μετρεῖσθαι: Wachsmuth, comparing Plut. Stoic. rep. 20   10 ἀδικοπραγεῖν: von Arnim; δικαιοπραγεῖν: FP   10 πρὸς τούτῳ μηδὲ ⟨τὴ⟩ν τυχοῦσαν ἀδικίαν: Wachsmuth; πρός τε τὸ μηδὲν τυχοῦσαν ἀδικίαν: FP   18 ἔχοντα: suppl. Heeren   22 οἷόν ἐστι, μὴ: Heeren; οἷόν μή τι μή: FP   22 κωλύῃ: suppl. Heine   23 μάλιστ' ἂν: Usener; μάλιστα: FP   30 διαψευστικῶς: von Arnim; διαψευστῶς: FP   32 συγχρήσεσθαι: Zeller; συγχρήσασθαι: FP   34 κατὰ: suppl. Heeren

the worthwhile to live nor does vice force them out, but life and death is measured by what is appropriate and what is inappropriate.[201]

They also say that the wise man is free from outrage.[202] For he is neither treated outrageously nor does he act outrageously toward another, because outrage is injustice which makes one ashamed and a harm. But the worthwhile man neither suffers injustice nor is harmed (although some may deal with him unjustly and outrageously and in this respect act unjustly). In addition, a chance injustice is not an outrage, but only one which makes one ashamed and is outrageous. But the person with good sense does not get involved in these things and is in no way made ashamed, for he has the good and the divine virtue in himself, and as a consequence he is removed from all vice and harm.[203]

The man with good sense will sometimes be king and associate with a king who shows natural ability and the love of learning. For we said it is possible to take part in government in accord with preferential reasoning, but also not to take part if something <prevented him> and especially if he was not going to benefit his country, but assumed that great and difficult dangers would follow directly from political life.[204]

It is said that the wise man does not lie, but tells the truth in all cases. For lying does not occur in telling a falsehood, but in telling the falsehood in a false way and for the deception one's neighbours. However they believe that he will sometimes avail himself of the falsehood in numerous ways without assent: in accord with generalship against the opponents, and in accord with his foresight

πρόορασιν καὶ κατ' ἄλλας οἰκονομίας τοῦ βίου πολλάς. Ψεῦδος δ' ὑπολαμβάνειν οὐδέποτέ φασι τὸν σοφόν, οὐδὲ τὸ παράπαν ἀκαταλήπτῳ τινὶ συγκατατίθεσθαι, διὰ τὸ μηδὲ δοξάζειν αὐτόν, μηδ' ἀγνοεῖν μηδέν. Τὴν 5 γὰρ ἄγνοιαν μεταπτωτικὴν εἶναι συγκατάθεσιν καὶ ἀσθενῆ. | Μηδὲν δ' ὑπολαμβάνειν ἀσθενῶς, ἀλλὰ μᾶλλον ἀσφαλῶς καὶ βεβαίως, διὸ καὶ μηδὲ δοξάζειν τὸν σοφόν. Διττὰς γὰρ εἶναι δόξας, τὴν μὲν 10 ἀκαταλήπτῳ συγκατάθεσιν, τὴν δὲ ὑπόληψιν ἀσθενῆ· ταύτας ⟨δ'⟩ ἀλλοτρίους εἶναι τῆς τοῦ σοφοῦ διαθέσεως· δι' ὃ καὶ τὸ προπίπτειν πρὸ καταλήψεως ⟨καὶ⟩ συγκατατίθεσθαι κατὰ τὸν προπετῆ φαῦλον εἶναι καὶ μὴ πίπτειν εἰς τὸν 15 εὐφυῆ καὶ τέλειον ἄνδρα καὶ σπουδαῖον. Οὐδὲ λανθάνειν δὲ αὐτόν τι, τὴν γὰρ λῆσιν εἶναι ψεύδους ὑπόληψιν ἀποφαντικὴν πράγματος. Τούτοις δ' ἀκολούθως οὐκ ἀπιστεῖν, τὴν γὰρ ἀπιστίαν εἶναι ψεύδους ὑπόληψιν· τὴν δὲ πίστιν 20 ἀστεῖον ὑπάρχειν, εἶναι γὰρ κατάληψιν ἰσχυράν, βεβαιοῦσαν τὸ ὑπολαμβανόμενον· Ὁμοίως δὲ καὶ τὴν ἐπιστήμην ἀμετάπτωτον ὑπὸ λόγου· διὰ ταῦτά φασι μήτε ἐπίστασθαί τι τὸν φαῦλον μήτε πιστεύειν. Ἐχομένως δὲ 25 τούτων οὔτε πλεονεκτεῖσθαι τὸν σοφὸν οὔτε βουκολεῖσθαι οὔτε διαιτᾶσθαι οὔτε παραριθμεῖν οὔτε ὑφ' ἑτέρου παραριθμεῖσθαι· ταῦτα γὰρ πάντα τὴν ἀπάτην περιέχειν καὶ τοῖς κατὰ τὸν τόπον ψεύδεσι πρόσθεσιν. 30 Οὐδένα δὲ τῶν ἀστείων οὔθ' ὁδοῦ διαμαρτάνειν οὔτ' οἰκίας οὔτε σκοποῦ· ἀλλ' οὐδὲ παρορᾶν [ἀλλ'] οὐδὲ παρακούειν νομίζουσι τὸν σοφόν, | οὐδὲ τὸ σύνολον παραπαίειν κατά τι τῶν αἰσθητηρίων, καὶ 35

SVF
3.548
LS
41G

1.68
W
2.112
1.54

2.113

---

6 μεταπτωτικὴν: Usener; μεταπτωτήν: FP   11 ἀκαταλήπτῳ: Wachsmuth; ἀκαταλήπτων: FP; ἀκατάληπτον: most editors   12 δ': suppl. Heeren   14 καὶ: suppl. Salmasius   15 φαῦλον: Wachsmuth; μᾶλλον: FP   18 ἀποφαντικὴν: Heeren; ἀποφαντικοῦ: FP   21 κατάληψιν: Wachsmuth; ὑπόληψιν: FP   26 τούτων οὔτε: Mullach; τούτῳ μήτε: FP   26 πλεονεκτεῖσθαι: Usener; πλεονάζεσθαι: FP   33 ἀλλ': del. Mullach

of what is useful, and in accord with many other types of management of life.[205] They say that the wise man never assumes what is false nor does he assent at all to what cannot be apprehended, since he neither forms an opinion nor is ignorant in any matter. For ignorance is changeable and feeble assent.[206] But he assumes nothing in feeble fashion, but instead securely and firmly. Hence, the wise man also does not form an opinion either. There are two types of opinion: assent to what cannot be apprehended and weak assumption. These are alien to the disposition of the wise man. Hence, acting rashly and giving assent before apprehension is the mark of a rash, worthless man, and does not befall the naturally suitable and complete man,[207] the worthwhile person. For nothing escapes his notice, since obliviousness is a declarative assumption of a falsehood. Consistent with this, he does not mistrust, since mistrust is an assumption of a falsehood. But trust is civilised, since it is a strong apprehension, confirming what is assumed. Likewise knowledge is an apprehension irreversible by reason.[208] Because of this they say that the worthless man neither knows anything nor trusts in anything. In line with this, the wise man is not defrauded, cheated,[209] criticised, nor does he swindle nor is he swindled by another. For deception encompasses all these things as well as assent to what are falsehoods in the context. None of the civilised make a mistake about the way, or their home, or about the target — nor do they believe that the wise man fails to see or mishears, nor, overall, that he strikes a false note with respect to any of the organs of sensation,

γὰρ τούτων ἕκαστον ἔχεσθαι νομίζουσι τῶν[δε] ψευδῶν συγκαταθέσεων. Οὐδ' ὑπονοεῖν δέ φασι τὸν σοφόν, καὶ γὰρ τὴν ὑπόνοιαν ἀκαταλήπτῳ εἶναι τῷ γένει συγκατάθεσιν· οὐδὲ μετανοεῖν δ' 5 ὑπολαμβάνουσι τὸν νοῦν ἔχοντα, καὶ γὰρ τὴν μετάνοιαν ἔχεσθαι ψευδοῦς συγκαταθέσεως, ⟨ὡς⟩ ἂν προδιαπεπτωκότος. Οὐδὲ μεταβάλλεσθαι δὲ κατ' οὐδένα τρόπον, οὐδὲ μετατίθεσθαι, οὐδὲ σφάλλεσθαι· ταῦτα γὰρ 10 εἶναι πάντα τῶν τοῖς δόγμασι μεταπιπτόντων, ὅπερ ἀλλότριον εἶναι τοῦ νοῦν ἔχοντος· οὐδὲ δοκεῖν αὐτῷ τι φασὶ παραπλησίως τοῖς εἰρημένοις.   SVF 1.54

11n Γίνεσθαι δὲ καὶ διαλεληθότα τινὰ σοφὸν 15 νομίζουσι κατὰ τοὺς πρώτους χρόνους οὔτε ὀρεγόμενόν τινος οὔθ' ὅλως γινόμενον ἔν τινι τῶν ἐν τῷ βούλεσθαι εἰδικῶν ὄντων, διὰ τὸ μὴ κρίνοντι αὐτῷ παρεῖναι ὧν χρή. Οὐ μόνον δ' ἐπὶ τῆς φρονήσεως ἀλλὰ καὶ ἐπὶ τῶν ἄλλων 20 τεχνῶν τὰς τοιαύτας ἔσεσθαι διαλήψεις.   3.540

11o ['Εκ] πάντων τε τῶν ἁμαρτημάτων ἴσων ὄντων καὶ τῶν κατορθωμάτων, καὶ τοὺς ἄφρονας ἐπίσης πάντας ἄφρονας εἶναι, τὴν αὐτὴν καὶ ἴσην ἔχοντας διάθεσιν. Ἴσων δὲ 25 ὄντων τῶν ἁμαρτημάτων, εἶναί τινας ἐν αὐτοῖς διαφοράς, καθ' ὅσον τὰ μὲν αὐτῶν ἀπὸ σκληρᾶς καὶ δυσιάτου διαθέσεως γίνεται, τὰ δ' οὔ.   3.529 LS 59O

11p Καὶ τῶν σπουδαίων δὲ ἄλλους ἄλλων 30 προτρεπτικωτέρους | γίγνεσθαι καὶ πειστικωτέρους, ἔτι δὲ καὶ ἀγχινουστέρους κατὰ τὰ μέσα τὰ ἐμπεριλαμβανόμενα τῶν ἐπιτάσεων συμβαινουσῶν.   W 2.114

---

2 τῶν ψευδῶν: Meineke   4 ἀκαταλήπτῳ: Wachsmuth; ἀκατάληπτον: FP   8 ὡς: suppl. Heeren   17 οὔθ' ὅλως γινόμενον: von Arnim; οὔτε νομίζειν βουλόμενον: FP   18 εἰδικῶν: Meineke; ἰδικῶν: FP   18 ὄντων: Wyttenbach; ὄντα: FP   19 κρίνοντι: Usener; κρίνειν τι: F, κρίνειν: P   22 ἐκ: del. Usener   32 πειστικωτέρους: Usener; πιστικωτέρους: FP

and they believe that each of these (mistakes) belong to false assents.[210] They say that the wise man does not surmise, since surmise is "assent to what cannot be comprehended" in species. Nor do they assume that a man with good sense changes his mind, for changing one's mind belongs to false assent, on the grounds of erring through haste. Nor does he change his mind in any way, nor alter his opinion, nor is he confused. For all these things are marks of those who waver in their beliefs, which is alien to the person with good sense. They also say that nothing "seems to be" to him, in line with what has been stated.

11n They also believe that a person is wise without having been aware of it at first, since he is neither desiring anything nor has he completely arrived at any of the specific forms of wishing, because he does not judge that what is needed is present for him.[211] There will be similar types of apprehension not only with respect to intelligence, but also regarding the other expertises.[212]

11o As all wrong acts are equal and all right acts equal too,[213] so the stupid are all equally stupid, having the same, equal disposition.[214] But while wrong acts are equal, there are certain differences among them, to the extent that some of them occur from a harsh and difficult to cure disposition, while others do not.[215]

11p Of the worthwhile, some are more able to encourage and more persuasive than others; furthermore, some are shrewder about intermediates which involve changes in intensities.[216]

11q Εὐτεκνεῖν δὲ μόνον τὸν ἀστεῖον, οὔ τι μὴν πάντα· δεῖν γὰρ τὸν εὐτεκνοῦντα ἀστεῖα τέκνα ἔχοντα χρήσασθαι αὐτοῖς ὡς τοιούτοις. Εὐγηρεῖν τε μόνον καὶ εὐθανατεῖν τὸν σπουδαῖον· εὐγηρεῖν γὰρ εἶναι τὸ μετὰ ποιοῦ γήρως διεξάγειν κατ' ἀρετήν, εὐθανατεῖν δὲ τὸ μετὰ ποιοῦ θανάτου κατ' ἀρετὴν τελευτᾶν. SVF 3.601

11r Καὶ τά τε ὑγιεινὰ καὶ νοσερὰ πρὸς ἄνθρωπον λέγεσθαι καὶ ὡς τρόφιμα, καὶ τὰ λυτικὰ καὶ στατικὰ καὶ τὰ τούτοις παραπλήσια. Ὑγιεινὰ μὲν γὰρ εἶναι τὰ εὐφυῶς ἔχοντα πρὸς τὸ περιποιεῖν ὑγίειαν ἢ συνέχειν· νοσερὰ δὲ τὰ ἐναντίως ἔχοντα τούτοις. Παραπλήσιον δ' εἶναι καὶ τὸν ἐπὶ τῶν ἄλλων λόγον. 3.602

11s Καὶ μαντικὸν δὲ μόνον εἶναι τὸν σπουδαῖον, ὡς ἂν ἐπιστήμην ἔχοντα διαγνωστικὴν σημείων τῶν ἐκ θεῶν ἢ δαιμόνων πρὸς ἀνθρώπινον βίον τεινόντων. Δι' ὃ καὶ τὰ εἴδη τῆς μαντικῆς εἶναι περὶ αὐτόν, τό τε ὀνειροκριτικὸν καὶ τὸ οἰωνοσκοπικὸν καὶ θυτικὸν καὶ εἴ τινα ἄλλα τούτοις ἐστὶ παραπλήσια. 3.605

Αὐστηρόν τε λέγεσθαι τὸν σπουδαῖον καθ' ὅσον οὔτε προσφέρει τινὶ οὔτε προσίεται τὸν πρὸς χάριν λόγον. Κυνιεῖν τε τὸν σοφὸν λέγουσιν, ἶσον ⟨ὂν⟩ τῷ ἐπιμένειν τῷ κυνισμῷ, οὐ μὴν σοφὸν ὄντα ἐνάρξεσθαι τοῦ κυνισμοῦ. 3.638

Τὸν δὲ ἔρωτά φασιν ἐπιβολὴν εἶναι φιλοποιίας διὰ κάλλος ἐμφαινόμενον νέων ὡραίων· δι' ὃ καὶ ἐρωτικὸν εἶναι τὸν σοφὸν καὶ ἐρασθήσεσθαι τῶν ἀξιεράστων, εὐγενῶν ὄντων καὶ εὐφυῶν. W 2.115 3.650

Λέγουσι δὲ μήτε παρὰ τὴν ὄρεξιν μήτε παρὰ τὴν ὁρμὴν μήτε παρὰ τὴν ἐπιβολὴν γίνεσθαί τι περὶ τὸν σπουδαῖον, διὰ τὸ μεθ' 3.564 LS 65W

---

2 ἀστεῖα τέκνα ἔχοντα: transposed to before δεῖν by Usener 27 ὂν: suppl. Valckenaer 28 ἐνάρξεσθαι: Wachsmuth; ἐνάρξασθαι: FP 29 ἔρωτά: Canter; ἔρωντα: FP 34 μήτε ... μήτε ... μήτε: Wachsmuth; μήδε ... μήδε ... μήδε: FP 35 ἐπιβολὴν: Meurer; ἐπιβουλὴν: FP

11q Only the civilised man is fortunate in his children — certainly not everyone — for the man who is fortunate in his children, having civilised children, needs to experience them as such.[217] Only the worthwhile man has a fortunate old age and a fortunate death, for a fortunate old age is living out one's life in accord with virtue whatever the type of old age, and to have a fortunate death is to end one's life in accord with virtue whatever the type of death.[218]

11r Things which are healthy and things which make a person ill are spoken of in relation to man, as are things of the nurturing type, and the laxatives and astringents,[219] and the like. For things which are healthy are those which are naturally suitable for producing or preserving health, while things which make a person ill are the opposite to these. There is a similar reasoning about other matters.[220]

11s Only the worthwhile man is able to prophesy, having a knowledge that is able to distinguish the signs from the gods or spirits which touch on human life. As a result, the species of prophetic art are associated with him: the skill of dream interpretation, the skill of observing the flight of birds, the skill of making sacrifices, and any things which may be similar to these.

They say that the worthwhile man is stern to the extent that he neither addresses to anyone nor admits to himself speech for the purpose of ingratiation.[221] They say that the wise man will live like a Cynic, which is equivalent to sticking with the Cynic lifestyle; but certainly he will not start out on the Cynic lifestyle when he is a wise man.[222]

They say that erotic love is an inclination to forming an attachment resulting from the beauty displayed by young men in their prime.[223] As a result the wise man is erotic and falls in love with those worthy of erotic love — the well-bred and naturally suitable.

They also say that nothing contrary to desire, contrary to impulse, nor contrary to his inclination occurs in the case of the

ὑπεξαιρέσεως πάντα ποιεῖν τὰ τοιαῦτα καὶ μηδὲν αὐτῷ τῶν ἐναντιουμένων ἀπρόληπτον προσπίπτειν.

Εἶναι δὲ καὶ πρᾶον, τῆς πραότητος οὔσης ἕξεως καθ' ἣν πράως ἔχουσι πρὸς τὸ ποιεῖν 5 τὰ ἐπιβάλλοντα ἐν πᾶσι καὶ μὴ ἐκφέρεσθαι εἰς ὀργὴν ἐν μηδενί. Καὶ ἡσύχιον δὲ καὶ κόσμιον εἶναι, τῆς κοσμιότητος οὔσης ἐπιστήμης κινήσεων πρεπουσῶν, ἡσυχιότητος δὲ εὐταξίας περὶ τὰς κατὰ φύσιν κινήσεις καὶ 10 μονὰς ψυχῆς καὶ σώματος, τῶν ἐναντίων τούτοις ἐπὶ πάντων φαύλων γιγνομένων.

SVF 3.632

Ἀδιάβολον δ' εἶναι πάντα τὸν καλὸν κἀγαθόν, ἀπαράδεκτον ὄντα διαβολῆς, ὅθεν καὶ ἀδιάβολον εἶναι κατά τε τοῦτον τὸν 15 τρόπον καὶ τῷ μὴ διαβάλλειν ἕτερον. Εἶναι δὲ τὴν διαβολὴν διάστασιν φαινομένων φίλων ψευδεῖ λόγῳ· τοῦτο δὲ μὴ γίνεσθαι περὶ τοὺς ἀγαθοὺς ἄνδρας, μόνους δὲ τοὺς φαύλους καὶ διαβάλλεσθαι καὶ διαβάλλειν, δι' ὃ καὶ τοὺς μὲν 20 κατ' ἀλήθειαν φίλους μήτε διαβάλλειν μήτε διαβάλλεσθαι, τοὺς δὲ δοκοῦντας καὶ φαινομένους.

3.581

Οὐδ' ἀναβάλλεσθαι δέ ποτε τὸν σπουδαῖον οὐδέν, εἶναι γὰρ τὴν ἀναβολὴν 25 ὑπέρθεσιν ἐνεργείας δι' ὄκνον, ὑπερτίθεσθαι δέ τινα μόνον ἀνεγκλήτου τῆς ὑπερθέσεως οὔσης. Ἐπὶ γὰρ τοῦ ἀναβάλλεσθαι τὸν Ἡσίοδον ταῦτ' εἰρηκέναι·

W 2.116 3.648

Μήδ' ἀναβάλλεσθαι ἔς τ' αὔριον ἔς τ' 30 ἔννηφι·

καί,

Αἰεὶ δ' ἀμβολιεργὸς ἀνὴρ ἄτῃσι παλαίει· τῆς [δ'] ἀναβολῆς ἔκπτωσίν τινα τῶν προσηκόντων ἔργων ἐμποιούσης. 35

---

11 μονὰς: Canter; μόνας: FP   12 ἐπὶ: Meineke; περὶ: FP   12 πάντων: F; πάντα: P
30 ἔς τ' ἔνηφι: P; ἔς τε ἔννηφι: F; ἔς τ' ἔννηφιν: various manuscripts of Hesiod
33 ἄτῃσι: FP, manuscripts and quotations of Hesiod; ἀάτῃσι: Nauck   34 δ': del. Meineke

worthwhile man, because he does all such things with reservation and nothing adverse befalls him unforeseen.[224]

He is also gentle, gentleness being a condition through which they are gentle about doing what is befitting in every case and not being carried away into anger in any matter. He is also tranquil and proper, propriety being a knowledge of suitable motions,[225] while tranquillity is orderliness in relation to the motions in accord with nature and persistences of the soul and body, while the opposite to this occurs in the case of all the worthless.

Everyone who is fine and good[226] is free from slander, being impervious to slander; as a result, he is free from slander both in this way and by not slandering another. For slander is a disagreement between people, who are apparently friends, through false reasoning.[227] But this does not occur in the case of good men, but only the worthless slander and are slandered by one another. Accordingly, those who are truly friends neither slander nor are slandered by one another, but only those who seem to be and appear to be so.

The worthwhile man never delays, as delay is a postponement of activity through hesitancy, and he postpones anything only when the postponement is irreproachable. For Hesiod has stated this about delaying:

Do not delay for the morrow or the day after,
and

The dilatory man is always wrestling with ruin,[228]
since delay produces an abandonment of the fitting deeds.

12   Ταῦτα μὲν ἐπὶ τοσοῦτον. Περὶ γὰρ πάντων τῶν παραδόξων δογμάτων ἐν πολλοῖς μὲν καὶ ἄλλοις ὁ Χρύσιππος διελέχθη· καὶ γὰρ ἐν τῷ Περὶ δογμάτων καὶ ἐν τῇ Ὑπογραφῇ τοῦ λόγου καὶ ἐν ἄλλοις πολλοῖς 5 τῶν κατὰ μέρος συγγραμμάτων. Ἐγὼ δ' ὁπόσα προὐθέμην ἐπελθεῖν ἐν κεφαλαίοις τῶν ἠθικῶν δογμάτων ⟨τῶν⟩ κατὰ τὴν τῶν Στωικῶν φιλοσόφων αἵρεσιν διεληλυθὼς ἱκανῶς ἤδη τοῦτον τὸν ὑπομνηματισμὸν 10 αὐτόθι καταπαύσω.

8 τῶν: suppl. Diel

12 So much for these matters: Chrysippus has discussed all their paradoxical beliefs in many different places, both in the book "On Beliefs" and in the "Treatise on Reason" and in many other works in particular sections. But now that I have given an adequate account of whatever of the ethical beliefs in accord with the Stoic school of philosophers I intended to go through in survey fashion, I will here bring this summary to an end.

NOTES

1   **Zeno and the other Stoics**: Zeno of Cition (Cyprus), born ca. 333/2, founded the Stoic school of philosophy when he began teaching in the Painted Colonnade (Stoa) at Athens ca. 301/300, and died, aged 72, in 262/1 (Diogenes Laertius 7.28). Cited: 6a, 6e, 7g, 11g. Other Stoic sources quoted are: Chrysippus of Soli, ca. 280-206 (6a, 6e, 11g, 12), Cleanthes of Assos, died 232 BC (5b8, 6a, 6e, 11i), Diogenes of Seleucia, died ca. 152 BC (5b6, 6a, 7f), Antipater of Tarsus, died ca. 130 BC (6a, 7f), Archedemus of Tarsus, 2nd century BC (6a), and Panaetius of Rhodes, ca. 185-110 BC (5b5).

2   **Ethical part**: the Stoics traditionally divided philosophy into logic, physics, and ethics. Diogenes Laertius (7.84) gives the division of Stoic ethics deriving from Chrysippus as (1) impulses; (2) the good and the bad; (3) emotions; (4) virtue; (5) the goal; (6) primary value and acts; (7) the appropriately impelling and repelling. Arius, instead of beginning with the impulses to virtue (as in Diogenes and most particularly in Cicero, *De Finibus* 3), commences with the material objects which are necessary for the good life (goods and evils, virtues and vices — ch. 5), then moves on to the goal and happiness (ch. 6), and to things which are indifferent (ch. 7) or appropriate (ch. 8), and only then to the impulses (ch. 9) and passions (ch. 10), concluding with a discussion of the activities of the proper Stoic (ch. 11).

3   **Participate in substance (ousia)**: according to Stoic thought, only material objects can properly exist. Virtues and vices can exist as physical impulses: in this way they *participate* in substance. So Seneca, *Ep.* 117.2: "What is good is a substance (*corpus*), because what is good acts, and what acts must be a substance. What is good does good (*prodest*); furthermore, it must do something in order to do good; and if it does something, it is a substance." For the nature of *ousia* and its relationship to *hylê* (matter), see Chalcidius, *in Tim.* 290 and LS 27.

4   The world is thus divided into what is good in itself (cf. Cic. *Fin.* 3.33), that which is similarly universally bad, and things which fit neither category, the indifferents (literally, "the things which cannot be differentiated"). For such divisions as a feature of the Stoic system of definition, see LS 32.

5   Participates in virtue: if something contributes to virtue, it must be good in itself. For instance, an act which is done justly participates in justice and thus is a good.

6   The first item of each pair (pleasure and pain, health and sickness) was transposed by Wachsmuth; as indifferents, however, there is no need to list a "preferable" choice first — indeed, pleasure is virtually a "dispreferred" (Sext.

adv. Math. 11.73). This inclusion of *hêdonê* as an indifferent is a polemical act of the later Stoics, rejecting the Epicurean idea of pleasure as the goal or even as a good in itself, on the ground that there are pleasures which are disgraceful in themselves: Cic. *Fin.* 1.39, 3.57; Diog. Laert. 7.103.

7   From this list, it is clear that the important indifferents are not things about which we are absolutely indifferent (for instance, the number of grains of sand in the universe), but rather things which, unlike the good and bad, cannot simply be regarded as beneficial or harmful (Diog. Laert. 7.102). For instance, wealth may benefit, but it is also possible to use wealth badly.

8   The virtues are here defined as constant states of mind, whether they engage in deciding what should be done (such as intelligence) or act to produce an outcome (such as strength of mind). Note that, in accord with Stoic materialism, the soul is a substance, identified with the pneuma (5b7).

9   **Wish**: in Stoic thought this type of wish (*boulêsis*) is the positive form of rational desire (sometimes translated as "well-wishing" or "sensible desire").

10   These are individual responses to situations or intentions seeking a particular outcome, unlike the virtues which are permanent skills or traits (5c).

11   This is typical of the Stoic emphasis on empirical investigation: practical virtues/excellences require their possessor to excel at doing something — this will define them as best practice which has been put into action, best practice having been assessed by logical inference (cf. *SVF* 3.214).

12   I have translated *rhômê* as "strength of mind", comparing the description of the virtues of the soul in 5b4; so *adynamia* below is mental incapacity.

13   These virtues thus differ from the normal virtues which are, by the craft-analogy, given a particular area of expertise.

14   Wachsmuth transposed 5b1-5b13 (the discussion of virtues and vices) to this point instead of its position in the manuscript after 5g, arguing that this section of the text had fallen out of the codex and been re-inserted at the wrong point. While this is probably the best solution, it is clear that this whole passage is an expansion of 5b and interrupts the logical thread of the topic of what is good in itself (continued in 5c), which leads on to the discussion of what is a good based on the final end (5h).

15   **A naturally political creature**: this definition of the proper nature of man is derived from Aristotle (e.g. *Pol.* 1253a), who saw the formation of social groups, developing from families to communities, culminating in the *polis*, as a natural progression in man's search for the good life. Wachsmuth adds "rational" from ch. 6: the rationality of the human mind distinguishes humans from other forms of life, whose "virtues" would be appropriate to the nature of each (e.g. producing fruit for a plant). This correction is not, however, essential in this context.

16   That is, a soul which is without contradictory impulses must possess all the virtues in its appropriate reactions to any particular instance. The topic is developed in the section on impulses (9), treating the virtues as constant, steady dispositions which require a type of knowledge in each case to produce consistent results (cf. Sen. *Ep.* 31.8).

17   For the appropriate, see 8 below, defining it as "what is consistent in life, which, when carried out, has a reasonable defence."

18   For impulses, see 9 below and 11f on impulses in action.

19   The metaphors here appear to derive from book-keeping (LSJ, sv. ἀνταιρέω, συγκεφαλαιόω). Throughout this section the Stoic definitions tend to follow the etymological derivation of the term in question: for instance, circumspection (*eulogistia*) is interpreted as "good accounting" (*eu* + *logos*) and, above, soundness of judgment (*euboulia*) is defined as good planning (*eu* + *boulê*). Cf. "industriousness" below.

20   This would include correct deportment and appropriately masculine gesture for males (females also being expected to conduct themselves as appropriate to their sex), which were regarded as matters of a general societal interest in the ancient world.

21   Sextus Empiricus (*adv. math.* 9.153) gives an expansion of this derived from the Stoics: "the man who forgoes an old woman on the point of death is not showing self-discipline, but rather he who has the chance of pleasure with a Lais, Phryne, or other such courtesan, but refrains all the same." So, while few would desire a dying crone, it requires considerable reflection to decide that sex with a beautiful, available woman is not always correct, because it might not be in accord with the aim of true happiness. For correct reasoning vs. invalid argument, see LS 36-37.

22   There need not be a contradiction with 5b if "great-heartedness" is taken as being not a knowledge of any particular thing, but a general attitude that makes one act beyond one's innate abilities. As this must be a learned skill (it is not innate), it must therefore be a knowledge. The difficulty arises from making great-heartedness subordinate to the general virtue that deals with responses, courage, which suggests that, as part of the set of virtues encompassed by courage, great-heartedness does have a particular end in view.

   tois spoudaiois ... kai phaulois could be translated "in worthwhile and worthless people" instead of referring to things, but this would introduce the problem of a virtue occurring in the worthless. For "worthwhile" concerns, see 7f.

23   I have translated *philoponia* as "industriousness" which seems best to represent its normal use. However, the etymological derivation as "fondness of toil" is clearly still felt in the definition offered here. Cf. the strict definition of *philodoxia* in 10c.

24   Here instead of the traditional definition of the goal as happiness (*eudaimonia*), a fixed state, the goal is defined by the Stoics in active terms as living consistently with nature (expanded in 6a below).For both ideas, see the end of 5b5 and note 32 below.

25   The virtues have rules (each has its own sphere of action) and together they cover all the demands of life (since they provide for the life consistent with nature). For these rules (*theorêmata*) or "constituent theorems" as the principles of conduct of the virtues, see LS 1.384.

26   This extension of the virtues beyond the traditional definitions to other practices was regularly mocked by the Stoics' opponents as creating a swarm of virtues (e.g. Plut. *de virt. mor.* 2 441a = *SVF* 3.255). It leads to the inclusion of unusual excellences in the list of virtues, such as dialectics and physics (Cic. *Fin.* 3.72-3).

27   This is Hellenistic physiology, based on a theory of health as a correct balance of these elements as distributed by the pneuma through the body, while imbalance results in illness. As the Stoic soul was a physical component of the person, it too needed to be in proper balance for mental health (cf. Cic. *Tusc. Disp.* 4.30).

28   There will need to be correct mental exertion first to reach a decision, then to act or to avoid action (see ch. 9 for the Stoic psychology of action and the conclusion of 11m for erroneous acts).

29   In 5b3: the goal of living consistently with nature.

30   This is expanded by Diogenes Laertius 7.125: if something involves virtue, it has rules of action and is productive of what has to be done; what has to be done also has to be chosen, to be endured, assigned properly, and abided by. So anything associated with virtue will involve all the cardinal virtues: intelligence, bravery, justice, and self-restraint. It follows that all the virtues are linked.

31   Fr. 109 (van Straaten).

32   For a discussion of the implications of this definition of the goal as happiness ("eudaimonism") and its equation by the Stoics with living in agreement with nature, see LS 1.398-9. The analogy is facilitated by the use of the verb *keimai* ("set up"/"depend on") to apply to the target and happiness.

33   Diogenes of Babylon fr. 48, in *SVF* 3 p.219.

34   That is, some things should be chosen as "final goods", which are necessary attributes of the happy man and are the direct target of the virtues, as indicated above (5b4) — for instance, possessing intelligence; others are worth choosing as having a reason for this choice — for instance, a single intelligent act which is a step on the path to possessing intelligence. The topic is expanded in 5g.

35 See 5b5 for the argument for the unity of the virtues.

36 Although the idea of virtues having bodies seems odd (and was regarded as such in antiquity — Sen. *Ep.* 113), this simply reinforces the material view of thought processes offered by the Stoics. Pneuma/psyche was believed to exist in circulation in the arteries of the human body (cf. J. Annas, *Hellenistic Philosophy of Mind* [Berkeley/Los Angeles 1992] ch. 1,2).

The element of warmth is stressed to contrast human soul with the cold pneuma which exists in stones (LS 53, esp. 53 B [Hierocles]); cf. LS 47 and 1.287-8, 340-1 on the importance of heat (=fire) permeating the universe and the body and creating "tension"(cf. 5b4) within the muscles.

37 *SVF* 1.566.

38 A series of iambic dimeters may be used to complete a scene in comedy. They are then concluded by a catalectic dimeter (a line with a syllable suppressed in the final metron). So Aristophanes, *Clouds*1449-1452, has a succession of lines to be spoken in one breath, which if interrupted would be meaningless, but make a telling conclusion when the final line is recited. So people can either fail to complete their nature and continue to be buffoons ("the worthless") or follow their initial impulses to virtue and become serious members of society ("the worthwhile").

39 If an act is complete (*teleios*), it is done for its own sake and not as a step on the way to the goal of happiness; but the goal of happiness is the target of the virtues (5b5), which act in concert with one another. Hence, to be capable of a complete act indicates the possession of all the virtues.

40 The first two would not usually have been considered to be virtues, but they result from the Stoic acceptance of expertises which produce happiness as virtues (see note 26); the last two would have been regarded as bizarre and so require the following careful explanation.

41 This view contrasts with the Epicurean view of love as a longing for sexual pleasures (Lucret. 4.1058ff.). In Stoic thought, all human relations are based on the idea of familiarity (*oikeiosis*) — this begins with the child which experiences an affinity with itself; the fully developed adult will harbour affections for others of the species, rather than be alienated from his/her fellows. See also 11s below and Diog. Laert. 7.129.

42 For "the things in accord with virtue" (or "just acts"), see 8 below where these examples are given: "being intelligent", "acting justly".

43 Cf. Plut. *comm. not.* 28 (*SVF* 3.719), quoting Chrysippus: "love is a pursuit of a youth who is inexperienced but naturally endowed for virtue".

44   Contrast the definition of erroneous love in 10c: a desire for an attachment based on apparent beauty.

45   The maxim that the wise man does everything well was readily derided by the Stoics' opponents. Since the wise man will possess the virtues, which are the types of knowledge which deal with normal human relations and actions, he will do well what he needs to do. If he does not play the flute well, there is no reason to think that the wise man will need that skill for his happiness.

46   Sedley (LS 2.166), defending the manuscript reading, argues for "the general skills and the skills of a standard education". However, *enkuklios* is etymologised as identical with *katholou* (cf. Quint. 1.10.1; *PG* 36.914 [scholion on Gregory of Nazianzus]: ἐγκύκλιον παίδευσίν φασι καὶ τὴν καθόλου εἶναι, since this is the *cycle* through which the learner must pass).

47   For conditions, see 5f. A condition allows degrees of difference in skill, unlike the types of knowledge, which as "dispositions", are identical in all those who possess them: LS 1.263.

48   Thus a pursuit, such as those listed here, remains a specialised skill until it is developed into a more general type of knowledge; so it is only a start to gaining what is in accord with virtue. But, as a worthwhile condition, it can only be possessed by the worthy and this produces a similar paradox to 5b10. So a Stoic would be a bibliophile, since he knows the use of books, while others would be bibliomaniacs.

49   For the sub-types of the prophetic art, see 11s.

50   Probably foundations of temples and the erection of statues to the gods (LSJ, sv ἵδρυσις).

51   Since only the wise man will be in harmony with nature and so in harmony with the cosmos, only he can be considered to have entered the divine nature.

52   Above 5b2.

53   As justice is defined as apportioning what is due to each, the worship of the gods will involve due honour to the gods, which the impious will not be able to carry out appropriately in their ignorance.

54   **A civilised man:** *asteios*, a term derived from *astu* ("city"), indicating an urban and urbane attitude in comparison with the rustic attitude of the country folk. In Stoic usage, it preserves some of this meaning of urbanity, but also becomes a general term of approval, close to *kalos* ("fine"). I have translated throughout as "civilised". For a general discussion, see Schofield, *Stoic Ideal of the City* (Cambridge 1991) 136-40.

NOTES

55   The good is defined as what contributes to happiness — it may thus be viewed as the origin of a benefit (e.g. the virtue which results in a kindness) or as the benefit itself (e.g. doing someone a kindness). More indirectly, it is the agent of benefit (for instance, a friend who does the kindness). Finally, to avoid the problems of making a distinction between origin and agency, it can be simply defined as anything which benefits: cf. Sext. *adv. Math.* 11.22 (LS 60G).

56   The argument is linked to the Stoic concept of *oikeiosis* ("affinity"): aside from a person's own contributions to personal welfare, there is a natural bond with friends and acquaintances. When the circle of relationships is extended to all who can benefit, all those who have virtues must be included (cf. Hierocles in Stobaeus 4.671-3 = LS 57 G).

57   A disposition is a fixed mental feature — so a virtue, as an invariable state (e.g. a type of knowledge), is a disposition; a condition allows for variation in form and intensity in a mental state. For discussion of the topic, see Simplicius, *In Ar. Cat.* 237-8 (LS 47 S) and LS 1.376, indicating that disposition should be seen as a special (since it is unvarying) type of condition. Any individual *act*, while it may be derived from a mental feature, clearly cannot be described as a mental feature (as a condition or disposition).

58   For propensities, illnesses, and frailties, see 10e below.

59   "Intelligent walking" is a final good, since doing something intelligently is a good in itself. Cf. "stupid questioning" as an evil below — as stupid, such interrogation cannot produce a worthwhile conclusion.

60   For a discussion of the purpose of the distinction between "final" and "productive" goods, see LS 1.376. Joy, being a resultant benefit which does not produce another good, is described as final.

61   For instance, justice will contribute to producing happiness (as such it is productive); but one could not imagine a state of happiness without justice (even if it were not being used); hence justice is also a final good.

62   At this point the manuscripts offer the heading: "On What is Worth Choosing and What is to be Avoided". As there are no other section headings for Arius' topics (see note 2 above for the division of subject matter), it seems best to regard this as a marginal note and delete it from the text.

63   A reasonable choice is defined in 5i, using the language of public scrutiny (as if, for example, at a *dokimasia*): if something is judged to be satisfactory, valuable, and worthy of approval, then an adequate defence has been presented for that choice.

64 Cf. 7d for indifferents in motion or in a state.

65 This does not contradict 5f, which describes the virtues as "dispositions", in contrast to the pursuits which are "conditions", if the dispositions are taken as a sub-set of the conditions (LS 1.376).

66 Goods are here divided into those which are cooperative (one must be honoured by someone else, friendship requires a friend), and the self-contained, such as acting justly (since whether a recipient appreciates the value of a just act is irrelevant).

67 See 11m for Stoic epistemology. *Katalepsis* is explained according to Zeno in Cic. *Acad.* 2.145 by the metaphor of one hand holding a fist — thus grasping of knowledge is contrasted with a weak grip on impressions. In general, see LS 41 (where *katalepsis* is translated as "cognition").

68 The worthwhile person's knowledge is *rational*, since, as is stated, it is the inability of reason to change apprehension which creates true knowledge (LS 1.257).

69 On impressions, see LS 39; on reason, see LS 36. On knowledge (contrasted with opinion), LS 41.

70 Cf. 5b9 above.

71 While the normal use of these congratulatory terms suggests that anyone who has children or lives a long life is blessed, the Stoics use a strong etymology ("good-children-ness", "good old age", "good life") to limit these terms to the worthwhile experience of children, old age, or life, in accord with nature — hence their description as mixed goods. Cf. 11q, where the paradoxical nature of these Stoic definitions is stressed.

72 This is the distinction between goods and the preferred: what is chosen for itself alone and without regard for some further consequence must be a final good; what is selected after a rational consideration is simply a preference over other possible choices. This is developed in ch. 7.

73 *SVF* 1.179.

74 This is once again an etymological explanation: since those who live in conflict are unhappy, happiness is living *homologoumenôs* ("in agreement"), which is broken down into its elements of *homos* + *logos* ("same reason"-ly).

75 This probably does not indicate a change in Stoic thought after Zeno, but a clarification of the definition by introducing the term "nature", which will refer both to one's personal nature and to the universal nature of the world (Cicero, *Fin.* 4.14 has the goal, according to Zeno, as "living, making use of our knowledge of those things which occur naturally") — LS 1.400.

The discussion of the sufficiency of the predicate (*katêgorêma*) is indicative of the Stoic interest in linguistic problems (LS 33) — generally a minimum sentence will consist of a noun plus a predicate. The predicate "in agreement" (with what?) was therefore expanded by Zeno's successors to give a more complete definition.

76   SVF 1.552.

77   SVF 3.12. Chrysippus here clearly links the perception of what is natural with acquired knowledge — we do not have an innate awareness of what is natural, but achieve this as part of our intellectual development.

78   SVF 3.44 Diog.; cf. 7e-f below.

79   SVF 3.20 Arch.; cf. 8 below for the appropriate.

80   SVF 3.57 Ant.; for the "preferentially in accord with nature" as "right acts", see 8 and 8a.

81   Cf. 11f. The significant goal of this harmonious life (or "living in accord with nature") is obtaining agreement — it is this predicate ("in agreement", sc. with nature) which is being stressed in this second definition.

82   I have supplemented the lacuna in the text, following Stobaeus 2.7.3c which makes clear the distinction between the object aimed at (the target of happiness) which can be sought by various means and the final outcome (the goal of being happy).

83   It is impossible to achieve the goal without the virtues (the constituent parts) and virtuous activities (virtue as means).

84   Reading ἐπ' (Usener's emendation) to indicate participation (LSJ sv ἐπί III 1) against FP's ἀπ' ("derived from").

85   For the problems of identifying the goal with the concept of human *eudaimonia* ("happiness"), see LS 1.398-9.

86   This metaphor suggests a calm flow of life, rather than the ebbs and violent surges of most people's lives. This peacefulness can then be linked to the principle of "agreement" (non-contradiction) set out by Zeno in 6a.

87   This is typical Stoic linguistic analysis: while the target can be defined as an abstract noun, the achievement of the goal will be an actual occurrence, which will be expressed by a verbal expression ("being happy").

88   For the goods as either virtues or things which participate in virtue, see 5a above (examples in 5b).

89   A good is something which can benefit (5d) and is worth choosing (5h), but each person chooses what will benefit himself in each instance — so one chooses intelligence as a step towards "being intelligent"; likewise, one would choose to join a partnership, not "partnership" itself. See 11f below for further explanation. This also allows for the moral development of the individual — we cannot choose "being intelligent" as such, but only acts which are in accord with the virtue of intelligence. This prepares for the following discussion of preferables.

90   That is, everything bad is worth avoiding, while every harmful act must be avoided in order not to gain the associated vice.

91   Given that the good is what contributes to or is part of the happy life (and evil, the opposite), indifferents are things, or better, the acquisition of things (such as "the acquisition of wealth"), which do not contribute to happiness or continue that happiness.

92   As not stimulative of impulse or repulsion in accord with or contrary to nature: cf. 7c.

93   While achieving excellence in ourselves is in accord with nature, it is also part of our natural constitution that we are liable to externally originating flaws (deceptive images or physical wounds) — as beyond our control, such things cannot be regarded as either natural or unnatural.

94   The "first things in accord with nature" are those listed above: health, strength, etc.; "first things contrary to nature" are sickness and feebleness, etc. Hence, breaking one's arm is an indifferent without being in accord with nature (as it is not desirable). See LS 1.357-8 on selection of things in accord with nature and avoidance of those contrary to nature.

95   Even a paraplegic can live with dignity and so can, paradoxically, live a happy life, but paraplegia is not the natural state of the human body nor something one would seek.

96   Cic. *de Fin.* 3.56 gives illustrative examples: as preferred in themselves, preferable forms of deportment and facial expression; preferred for its results, wealth. He also gives health as an example which is both preferred for itself and for its results. Cf. Diog. Laert. 7.107.

97   *Euaisthesia*: the ability to use the senses well, such as a keen sense of smell, eyesight, hearing, touch, and taste.

98   *Kharopotês*: apparently an eye-colour (perhaps blue-grey), but also indicative of the eye's overall appearance (glassy-eyed or with distended pupil).

99   So, for instance, a quick mind would be preferred over keenness of sense perception.

100   These are the indifferents listed in 7a: health, strength, etc. in accord with nature; sickness, feebleness, etc. contrary to nature.

101   A generative principle is a basic (pro)creative force in the world: at the highest level this is identified with Zeus (who is also equivalent to the divine order in the universe) who seeds the world for its growth (LS 46 A, 1.277). Anything which arises from such basic principles cannot help but be in accord with nature. So healthiness in man is part of the natural development of things and in accord with nature. For motion and state, with reference to goods, see 5k.

102   That is, the mental acceptance of a signal from the senses (e.g. being able to hear someone speak) is an appropriate normal response and natural. This is also an example of a first thing in accord with nature *in motion* as a passing condition in contrast to the continuing state of soundness of body and mind.

103   So a sound hand participates in the overall state of soundness, while functioning senses (e.g. smell) participate in the general motion of sensation — in effect, those things "secondarily in accord with nature" are concrete examples of what is generally necessary for man to fulfil his nature.

104   This is a similar argument to 51 on the goods: some things naturally stimulate the desire for themselves alone, while others are valuable instrumentally (e.g. wealth, or reputation to assist in one's dealings with one's fellow men).

105   Von Arnim emends to *anenektikôs* ("by comparison, with reference to something else" — cf. *anapherein*, "to refer"); this seems better than Wachsmuth's text *anetikôs* ("in relaxed fashion") which would also need the emendation to *protreptikôs* ("in rousing fashion") above. Following von Arnim, the distinction is between indifferents which are to be sought for themselves (and so cause an direct impulse) and indifferents to be sought as instruments to obtain other desirable indifferents (causing an indirect impulse).

106   With typical Stoic precision, value (which is essential for choosing indifferents) is defined:
    (1) as intrinsic worth (as contributing to happiness);
    (2) the worth assigned by the person who has a choice of obtaining something ("market forces");
    (3) comparative value through preference over another object (wealth is preferred to poverty, but wealth may not have preferential value over health).

There is also a fourth use of value as "befitting" in the case of apportioning to each according to its value/due, which is the field of the virtue of justice (5b2).

107   Cf. 7a on the primary things in accord with nature and 7d on the generative principles and natural needs.

108   The objects evaluated do not have a value which allows them to be exchanged for one another (e.g. health for wealth), but they are nevertheless given some value ("health is a prized possession"; "public reputation is of little importance") which allows us to know whether they are important or not. Cf. the objects listed in 7b.

109   *Axiôma*: lit. "a valued thing" and so an "honour" or "dignity" — once again, an etymological derivation is used to boost the argument.

110   Zeno, by imposing a strong definition of what is good and bad as absolutes, created a large class of indifferents, many of which would in common judgement be considered good or bad. These were now to be classified as preferred or dispreferred indifferents.

111   So the good has the regal function of reigning above the council of preferred indifferents, which, however, are in attendance and closely related to the good.

112   That is, unlike the virtues which are both part of happiness and productive of it (5g).

113   The "appropriate" follows on from the topic of the preferred: the latter are things in accord with nature which are desirable, while the appropriate deals with actions in accord with nature. Like the preferred indifferents, the appropriate are not absolutes. See LS 59 and 1.364-8.

114   The appropriate is defined in terms of what is proper to the nature of the creature. The concept is thus not exclusive to rational creatures — dumb animals can act in an appropriate manner (for instance, in sustaining themselves and rearing their young) by instinct. In the case of humans, there is a choice of lifestyles according to age and circumstances.

115   See LS 1.365 for right acts: they are not only acts which are in accord with nature, but ones which accord with virtue. As virtues are complete in themselves, so right acts are complete too.

116   While marriage, for instance, is natural and consistent with human nature, it is only an intermediate step towards happiness. Both the worthwhile and the worthless may marry — but only the former will have the intelligence to make appropriate use of this act, in contrast to the latter who lack the virtues and thus the knowledge to make proper use of marriage.

117   Cf. the discussion in 6f: what benefits must be chosen, while other things are only worth choosing. An act such as honouring one's parents is in accord with the virtue of piety and complete (it is not done for some other reason), but, while a right act, would not be done if, for instance, such an act led to physical harm for one's parents.

118   For the "intermediate appropriate", see LS 1.366-7. The case is similar to that of the indifferents in accord with nature of 7. For instance, being healthy will usually be a desirable choice, but the foolish can also be healthy and misuse this blessing to the detriment of others (cf. Cic. *Fin.* 3.17). So preserving one's health is an intermediate appropriate unless it is made complete by the addition of virtue (e.g. by the proviso "intelligently"). But being healthy is normally desirable and as such is an appropriate which will not be rejected "except in special circumstances" (*aperistatôs*: cf. Diog. Laert. 7.109) because of its general usefulness.

119   While it is ambiguous whether *autothen* ("on the spot" or "immediate") refers to either the *phantasia* or the *kathêkon*, the overall meaning is generally clear. For instance, after a sensation which stirs interest (e.g. the smell of a donut), there needs to be a mental response ("impression") in the thinker ("I like donuts") which acts as the basic impulse for action ("Eat donut"). Note the emphasis on "the appropriate" (what is in accord with nature). Since the definition is concerned with man (and not animals, see below) and he is a rational creature (cf. 6 above), an impulse must be a rational impulse.

120   Clearly creatures other than humans have impulses (e.g. a cat towards catching mice), but because they lack a rational component, their impulses are of a different type from those of humans.

121   The pattern is as follows:

Rejective Impulse	Impulse Towards Something
(two types: [a] rational; [b] irrational)	(two types: [a] rational; [b] irrational) + Impelling Disposition

(each of [a] and [b] is sub-divided into two forms:
[a] response to a present situation;
[b] impulse with regard to the future.
See LS 53Q and 1.321-2 for the Aristotelian background for this psychology.

122   The first four here can be taken as types of impulse with regard to the future:
prothesis (proposal) — general planning;
epibolê (inclination) — a plan to do something which will lead to a second impulse (e.g. to make friends in order to gain sexual favours later);
paraskeuê (preparation) — a preparatory act, although the consequential act may not occur;
encheirêsis (undertaking) — perhaps an act which is part of an uninterrupted sequence of acts.

123   These are forms of desire *(orexis)* for good in the present:
hairesis (choice) — a correct choice by analogy;
prohairesis (policy)— a preliminary choice;
boulêsis (wish) — a correct desire;
thelêsis (willingness) — a freely chosen correct desire (as against correct desires which may be impelled, for instance, by necessity).

124   The argument seems to be that if I choose to eat a donut, there is not only an active impulse towards eating it, but also an evaluation that eating this donut is in itself a good thing (a predicate is already included in the mental assent: "Nice donut!" = this donut is good to eat). For the Stoic use of the term *axiôma*,"proposition", see LS 34.

125   For an explication of the Stoic views on "passion" *(pathos)*, see LS 65, 1.419-421.

126   For the significance of "agitation" *(ptoia)* or "fluttering" (like a bird), see LS 1.421-2: the impulse of the soul is depicted as changing so rapidly that it does not appear to be obeying the choice of reason. But this should not be seen as a dualistic view of the *hêgemonikon* (the reasoning part of the soul), with one part fighting another. Rather, the reasoning centre is not providing a constant plan of action (cf. *SVF* 3.564 = LS 65 W), but flip-flopping in its assents.

127   LS 65C and 41; "feeble" opinion is opposed to knowledgeable (an apprehension which is secure and irreversible by reason: 5l). For "fresh" stimulation, see 10b below and LS 1.421.

128   The use of "irrational" does not mean that the process has not been evaluated, but rather that the act does not conform to normal rational choices (as the motion in the soul is excessive). The effect of this is to reinforce the moral responsibility of individuals for their acts, rather than excuse them as outside their control.

129   Inwood (*Ethics and Human Action* 142) suggests that this description is heavily influenced by Poseidonius or Platonizing philosophy to suggest a dualistic nature of the soul, wherein the rational part is unable to control the passionate section. While the horse simile and Euripidean quotation show a dualistic treatment of the theme, it is not, I think, necessary to assume that Arius is diverging from Stoic thought — a mistaken impression leads to an excessive response (a passion), which can be rationally evaluated as bad in its outcome as it is being undertaken, but can hardly be corrected at this time.

130   The appeal to the authority of the classics of Greek literature is a typical feature of Hellenistic argument. Chrysippus, from whom this description is probably derived, for instance, quotes Menander (fr. 567 Koerte[2] = Plut. *de virt. moral.* 450c = *SVF* 3.390) to illustrate the discrepancy between reason and action.

NOTES 119

131 Euripides 840.2 N².

132 The example is knowingly chosen as a jibe at the Stoics' rivals, the Epicureans, whose physics were based on the existence of atoms.

133 This description emphasizes the *immediate* nature of the stimulus — an older stimulus may be replaced by a more recent ("fresh") one, in line with the agitation of the soul of 10, if there is no rational control. This concept of freshness allows for the change in the strength of the passions, as the opinion which led to a passionate response is reevaluated (LS 65 O, 1.421).

134 This "fresh opinion" is a process of evaluation of the result of some act (which has originally had a different evaluation as desirable, since no one actively seeks an unfavourable outcome) — in this example, as something to be rejected, resulting in a subsequent emotional reaction of pain, although the primary emotion was either to want something (now found undesirable) or to reject something (now found to have been desirable).

135 For the appetites, see LS 65 E and 1.419-20.

136 Cf. this view of (sexual) desire as an appetite with the sexual response of the worthwhile in 5b9 and 11s.

137 By listing *philodoxia* along with the other *philo-* compounds, what would normally be treated positively as the "love of fame", a desire for *good* opinion, is demoted to a mere appetite for opinion.

138 This is defined as bad, since the civilised do not rejoice at others' sufferings, while the worthless can take no true satisfaction in anything at all (Plut. *Stoic. Repugn.* 25 = SVF 3.672).

139 *Goêteia* is defined as *trompe-l'oeil* — as a type of visual trickery. This would be offensive as a manipulation of impressions (since the Stoics placed considerable emphasis on the senses, such as sight and hearing: cf. 11m) and as intentionally deceptive (again, not the mark of the wise man: 11m).

140 Superstition is here etymologically derived from *deos* ("fear") + *daimones* ("spirits").

141 For this whole section, compare Cic. *Tusc. Disp.* 4.17, which offers a similar list of types of mental suffering. Note that it is not suggested that the Stoic will not respond emotionally to his surroundings (for instance, at the premature death of a child), but that this response will be controlled and will not cause an upset in one's mental balance (cf. *SVF* 3.416).

142 This approximately conforms to traditional views of envy as jealousy (a bad thing) or as a goad to achievement by rivalry (a positive). But, for the Stoics, the latter can only be an appetite to gain what is viewed as desirable or to imitate a person who is felt to be better: neither is anything other than opinion.

143   Cf. 11d on tolerance as a fault.

144   That is, the first group have an external reference (pity at others' pain, fear of reproach from others, joy at harm to others, shame at others' opinion of us), while the second are internal (pain in our minds, terror from our own expectations).

145   Meineke's emendation *hôs* ("as") seems preferable here, explaining that this group of proclivities is based on a *pathos*: so depression (*epi+lupia*) is a tendency to distress (*lupê*), and irascibility (being *orgilos*) a tendency to anger (*orgê*). These passions contrast with proclivities to certain acts (not passions) listed in the next sentence: for instance, the tendency to theft is not linked to a named *pathos*, but to a deed (*ergon*). Von Arnim's "or" produces a difficulty in explaining how the unnatural deeds listed in this sentence differ from those listed next.

146   The emphasis is on the continuous state produced by a proclivity: an adulterer is someone who is always ready to commit adultery, rather than a person who engages in single adulterous acts; so too a person of nervous disposition differs from someone who is anxious on occasion (cf. Cic. *Tusc. Disp.* 4.27). This can further develop into a pronounced preference for such activities (e.g. a "libertine"), as described in the next sentence.

147   That is, an acceptance of an undesirable impulse has become fixed in the mind (just as the material in a rock is arranged in a particular disposition) and is no longer the result of a reasoned, but mistaken choice — the result is an unhealthy state beyond the ability of the sufferer to resist, such as satyriasis, alcoholism, or kleptomania.

148   That is, mental illnesses. The parallels between mental and physical states are constantly stressed by the Stoics. Aversions too can develop into fixed states (Cic. *Tusc. Disp.* 4.23).

149   For an elucidation of the metaphor here, see A.A. Long, "The Harmony of Stoic Virtue", *Oxford Studies in Ancient Philosophy*, Suppl, Vol. 1991, 97-116. A right act is an appropriate act, which is complete, and so it must contain all the *numbers* — that is, it has the sum of all the parts or, in musical terminology, it has gone through all the scales in proper tune (which results in an *harmonious* life). See also LSJ, ἀριθμός I.4.

150   8 above.

151   *Hamartêma* thus embraces both acts of commission and omission. Cf. 8b.

152   Since what is just is not arbitrary or dependent on changeable circumstances, the worthwhile use a secure standard of justice in their dealings with others in their society. They will seek to apportion what is due to others and so take part in the administration and education of their states.

This will be particularly true of governments which are progressing to being "complete" — that is "complete" by having all the desirable features of government, the ones which are in accord with nature. The foolish, not unexpectedly, will follow a perverted variant of this — courting the mob (instead of seeking to control its ways) and disseminating mistaken advice (as, for instance, does Diogenes of Oenoanda by publishing Epicurus' teachings). Cf. the anti-Cynic tone of the following discussion and Epict. 3.22.

153   Cf. Schofield, *Stoic Idea of the City* (Cambridge 1991) 119-127 on Stoic attitudes to politics and marriage, and especially 126 on the pejorative tone of καταβαίνειν. See further: W. Deming, *Paul on Marriage and Celibacy*(Cambridge 1995) and K. Gaiser, *Für und wider die Ehe* (Munich 1974). The provision that one's country be moderate is added to allow for its possible improvement into a just state — otherwise, suffering on its behalf would be useless.

154   This defines three types of friendship:
   (1) a community of purpose;
   (2) a friendly relationship with one's neighbours, as expressed in friendly acts (this is a manifestation of friendship and an external good);
   (3) an internalised friendship, which is part of one's intellectual capacities through which friendly acts are produced, one of the mental/rational goods.

155   Cf. 11b above.

156   If a worthless person were able to benefit or be benefitted in accord with virtue, she would be participating in the virtue — which would automatically mean that she was not worthless.

157   The skill of household management is investigated as a significant feature of Greek society (since social life above the individual was organised around the *oikos*) and as an intermediate stage of interaction with one's fellows below to the organisation of the city. See, for instance, Xenophon's *Oeconomicus* and Aristotle, *Politics* 1 for discussion of household management and its relationship to money-making.

158   Cf. 8b and 11a for the definition of complete right acts. The examples listed here are indifferents, unlike right acts (springing from the virtues) and wrong acts (resulting from the vices).

159   Right acts are acts occasioned by the virtues or in accord with the virtues (e.g. walking around intelligently is a good derived from the virtue of intelligence; cf. 5g).

160   Cf. 6f, on the difference between things worth choosing (goods) and those which must be chosen (benefits).

161   Cf. 9b: there are assents "to" some things, but impulses "toward" other things.

162   See LS 31J and 1.202: one cannot actually choose "being intelligent", since the verbal form is an incorporeal (unlike "intelligence") and is simply a predicate applied to something ("he is intelligent"). So although a choice is for a good, we are actually choosing the source of benefit ("intelligence").

163   That is, as the virtue of self-restraint acts to acquire a benefit based on knowledge of what is worth choosing, modesty (5b2) will also act in the same way in deciding what must be avoided, the virtue of bravery in cases of what must be endured, and so on.

164   This Stoic view that virtue alone produces happiness (and vice alone unhappiness) is regularly attacked as counter-intuitive in cases where, for instance, there is a serious deficiency of the externals which would normally be considered good and numerous apparent bodily evils are present (Gellius, *Noct. Attic.* 18.1.4).

165   Note the typical appropriation of traditional attributes such as strength, eminence (originally, "tallness"), and power, by redefining them as ethical values. Contrast, for instance, the male military *aretê* of an Achilles with the rational excellence denoted by *aretê* in Stoic thought.

166   For *prohairesis* (policy) as "a choice before a choice", see 9a.

167   Note the emphasis on completeness — happiness is defined as a state which is self-sufficient (since, if it lacked anything, there would be a further, more complete state to aim at).

168   Virtue is here defined in terms of what each excellence *produces* to create complete happiness: that is, as productive, rather than final virtues (cf. 5b3).

169   Once again, appeal is made to (frequently, dubious) etymology in these proofs: virtue is good (*agathon*) because it leads (*agein*) to the good life; worthwhile (*spoudaion*) because it deserves the greatest regard (*spoudê*); beautiful (*kalon*), because it calls (*kalein*) those deserving it; advantageous (*sympheron*), because it brings (*pherein*) what together contribute (*syntenein*) to the good; useful (*khrêsimon*), as being beneficial in use (*khreia*); enough (*apokhrôn*), because it provides for our usage (*khrêsis*) and our needs (*khreia*).

170   As goodness cannot be damaged, the wise (who have all the virtues) cannot be harmed. Whatever must be attendant to the good can only befall the wise also — if such things occurred to a worthless person they could not benefit him (as in his ignorance, he is incapable of being helped). See 11g above for the necessary goods.

171   This distinction between "innate" slaves and purchased workers was a noted feature of Stoic ideology (e.g. Sen. *Ben.* 3.22, quoting Chrysippus; Athen. *Deipn.* 6.267b).

172   Cf. Diog. Laert. 7.121: "freedom is the possibility of self-directed action (*autopragia*), while slavery is the absence of this. There is also another type of slavery, to be under someone else's control, and a third type, being the property of and under the control of another, to which is contrasted control (*despoteia*),

also a worthless thing in itself." Only the wise will be able to do what is needed to achieve true wealth and power, while the worthless will choose incorrect goals and incorrect methods and suffer for this (cf. *SVF* 3.356).

173   11b above.

174   11d above. For the Stoic insistence on law as the basis of civic life, see LS 1.435.

175   Hence the law will be in accord with nature and not merely arbitrary (cf. Diog. Laert. 7.128).

176   Thus, even if the wise man is not exercising his ability to govern, he maintains the character of a governor.

177   Cf. 11g on life experiences, and 5b10 above for the limitations of "everything".

178   The law is the expression of nature's will in the universe and a true state is one in which there is the rule of law. Hence the worthless man who fails to understand what is naturally required will live in a group of humans, but one which is not governed by true law. Rather than a true city, governed justly, this will be closer to the grouping of a robber band (cf. Cic. *Rep.* 3.33). And, given that civic rights in the Greek world were based on citizenship, to be deprived of one's city either by becoming a fugitive or being punished by exile was a very heavy punishment indeed.

179   11d above.

180   The city is described as an *oikêtêrion kataskeuasma* — an arrangement for domestic living; as such it is parallel to the traditional Greek *oikos*, where there is grouping first around the family, but including the other members of the household as well (for instance, slaves), who would be under the disciplinary control of the master of the household.

181   The city is civilised (*asteios*) not as a city (*astu*) per se, which is merely a dwelling place, but as a place for lawful interaction among men. This argument is repeated in Eusebius, *Praep. Ev.* 15. 15.3-5 = LS 67L, who quotes Arius Didymus as his source. For Cleanthes' syllogism and the difficulties involved, see Schofield, *The Stoic Idea of the City* 130-135.

182   This section lists all the vices to which the worthless are prone. As almost all humans are to be considered worthless in comparison with the rare worthwhile individual, it might be objected that this paints a bleak picture of mankind (so Alexander Aphrod. *de Fato* 28 = *SVF* 3.658). The Stoic answer is that, rather than placing the stress on the vices, they are indicating that the worthless cannot be exempt from any of these errors and mistakes (Sen. *Ben.* 4.27).

183   That is, the stupid man's ruling intellect cannot stand the strain of reasoning because it is warped, unlike the firm, reliable mind of the wise man. For this physical description of the mind, cf. 5b4 on mental strength and the beauty of the body — the stupid man from his vices and passions has lost the appropriate tension and the proportionality of the parts of the soul.

184   *Philoponia* ("industriousness") is here given its full etymological force as "fond of toil" (*philos* + *ponos*). Cf. 5b2.

185   Clarification of this passage can be obtained from 5b5 where the virtue of justice is defined as acting to provide what is in accord with the merit of each (cf. 5b2) and 7f where "contribution" is explained as providing a natural need (here defined as something which is known to be worthwhile). Just as they cannot claim to be industrious, the unworthy cannot profit from the virtues associated with justice as they have no appreciation of their value.

186   Apart from impiety in action, there is an impious state of mind which the worthless man must have (just as the worthwhile man has a pious disposition, that is, the virtue of piety); like the virtues, the vices act in unison (cf. 5b5). Hence, every act of the worthless is impious (and stupid, unjust, etc.).

187   For instance, it is wrong to say that a person who is a mile out of town is in town, just as it is wrong to say the same of a person a hundred miles out of town. In neither case is the person in town, so the two statements are equally erroneous as the results of the vice of stupidity. But the nature of the error (the position of the person, which is something indifferent) differs between the two examples. Cf. Diog. Laert. 7.120.

188   Heeren's supplement simplifies the argument, but it may be preferable to amend εἶναι to ἐνεστάναι ("is present"), comparing Stobaeus 1.8.42 and Plut. *comm. not.* 1081c-1082a (=LS 51 B, C). The alternative is to omit Heeren's supplement and take the statement as a comment on the nature of time, which does not really exist, but only subsists.

189   That is, the act of lying is the same, but the object lied about and the deception of the listener differ in each case.

190   On right acts as acts in accord with virtue and completely appropriate acts, in contrast with intermediate acts, see 8 above.

191   *TrGF* 2.516. Note the paradoxical nature of these claims that *natural* ability and good *breeding* can be acquired.

192   In the ancient world, an unwillingness to tell the truth was regarded as a typical feature of slaves (who, after all, were concerned not to displease their owners). For the Stoic view of who is truly free and who slavish, see 11i.

193   Cf. Diog. Laert. 7.124, adding that *polyphilia* ("having numerous friends") is one of the goods.It could, however, be viewed negatively: C.E. Glad, *Paul and Philodemus* (Leiden 1995) 165-75.

194   Cf. 5f where drunkenness is listed among the illnesses and frailties. According to some of the Stoics, it was, however, possible for a Stoic sage to be intoxicated, since this is the result of an external and unnatural influence (alcohol) making it difficult to exercise normal rational judgement. Depression and dementia could have the same effect (Diog. Laert. 7.118).

195   According to Diogenes Laertius (7.188), there was considerable debate about how the wise man should derive his livelihood. Chrysippus also added the proviso that, although one should seek in life what is needed for self-preservation, it would be quite wrong to do this by depriving another of the same (Cic. *Off.* 3.42).

196   Cf. 11b above.

197   Cf. 6 above.

198   These misgivings have a long history, being frequently expressed in the works of Plato. As not everyone is capable of profiting from philosophical teaching (for instance, due to the power of their impulses towards wrong acts), it cannot be correct to offer such teaching to all. Chrysippus suggested that the wise man should merely offer to do as much he can in the necessary amount of time (Plut. *Stoic. repugn.* 20 = *SVF* 3.701). A similar argument was also made against the first two preferential ways of earning a livelihood: deriving an income from a king must not involve submitting to him, and deriving it from friends must not make friendship a marketable commodity for gain (Diog. Laert. 7.188).

199   The wise man can end his own life to benefit his country or friends or even to avoid horrible pain, incapacity, or incurable disease (Diog. Laert. 7.130). The topic was of considerable interest to the Stoics as the causes for living or dying are not goods or evils, but intermediates, judged according to whether they were in accord with or opposed to nature (Plut. *Stoic. repugn.* 18 = *SVF* 3.759). Cf. A.J.L. van Hooff, *From Autothanasia to Suicide* (London 1990) 188-191.

200   Because only in living is there a possibility of wisdom, which is totally impossible in death; cf. Plut. *Stoic. repugn.* 14 = *SVF* 3.761.

201   So even those who are fortunate in possessing happiness would leave this by ending their lives in order to avoid something unbecoming.

202   "Free from *hybris*", that is, free from the effects of a type of assault which seeks to degrade the victim or abusive violence. Contrast assault for the purpose of robbery with a racist attack — only the latter is *hybris*.

203   The paradoxical statement that the wise man cannot be insulted is founded on the need for mental distress to have been caused by the action, which is impossible in his case. So too the desire to cause injustice is thwarted

by the inability of the unjust to deprive the wise man of his due worth. Cf. Stob. *Flor.* 7.21: "Chrysippus says that the wise man feels pain, but cannot be tortured, as he does not permit it in his soul."

204   11b above.

205   The manner is more significant than the truth value of a statement which may be known to be incorrect. As the wise man himself does not assent to the truth value of the statement, he is not deceiving himself and can use an untruth: for instance, to encourage a patient to follow a course of treatment.

206   As the wise man only offers his assent to the truth and not to what is false, vacillating assent shows a confused judgement. For instance, the wise man may honour the gods due to knowledge of what is appropriate conduct (itself based on the apprehension of this, which has been scrutinised by reason), but the fool, when he honours the gods, will lack the capacity of knowing whether this conduct is really correct. Cf. LS 41.

207   By his natural suitability, such a man is in accord with nature, and he is complete, as possessing all the virtues.

208   Cf. 51 above.

209   *Boukoleisthai*: lit. "to be grazed on"; the civilised and worthwhile will not metaphorically "be grazed" on by others, as if by cattle fattening themselves!

210   A mirage is a real perception, but only the wise man can correctly note that it does not represent something other than a mirage. A stupid man, however, will offer false assent to this perception and be of the opinion that the mirage is real.

211   The text is uncertain here and has been emended by von Arnim, among others, to give more clarity. The general meaning is, however, clear: the movement from ignorance to wisdom is so sudden that the man on the point of wisdom may not recognise it himself, although he would note that he was no longer seeking anything else. But he would not be able rationally to deduce that he had obtained what he desired. Cf. Philo *de agric.* vol.2 p.127 Wendl (=*SVF* 3.541): in the case of the newly-arrived wise man it is impossible to recognise two things at once — his arrival at the end and the mental grasping (*katalepsis*) of this arrival. It would appear from Philo that the Stoics would define this as "an elevated form of ignorance, close to real knowledge". Cf. also the Sorites argument: LS 37 E,F.

212   That is, there will be an intermediate step with regard to any type of knowledge (just as there was with intelligence to produce a wise man) where the possessor has gained the skill but cannot be sure in his own mind that he has arrived at his final goal.

213   Cf. 111 above.

214   That is, the disposition, "stupidity", since this is the vice which produces wrong acts.

215   For instance, some errors may occur from the mistaken belief in an atomic basis of physics, which is much easier to cure than the belief that pleasure is a worthwhile goal: 10a above. For wrong acts as forms of sickness in dispostion (and so, curable), see , e.g., 11e.

216   Although it might appear that there would be no need for persuasiveness among the wise, as they are not going to accept what is mere opinion or be moved from accepted judgements, there is need for use of persuasion on those who have false beliefs (cf. 11o). Some will also be better than others in, for instance, divining the outcome of some act: these are the intermediate things mentioned in 8a and 11l. For example, some of the worthwhile would be better than others in predicting the course of a disease (an indifferent in itself) and the methods of treatment (intermediates, since they are not absolutely fixed). Hence the proviso that the matter must involve an indifferent (if it is a good or an evil, there will be no doubt about the outcome) and one which is variable (as reflected in different intensities).

217   This alters the traditional view of being blessed with children from merely indicating surviving offspring to placing the emphasis on the children's own moral development (cf. Arist. *Eth.* 1.8). Only the worthwhile can be blessed with children, as only they have the right attitude toward them. Cf. 5m.

218   These two are paradoxical definitions, placing the emphasis on the life in accord with virtue rather than the traditional ease of living in old age and lack of suffering at death. On ways out of life, see 11m above.

219   These are technical terms for substances that can loosen the bowels or arrest diarrhoea (LSJ, sv. στατικός, λυτικός).

220   That is, they are judged by their natural ability to produce states in accord with nature (the preferential indifferents of 7a).

221   Cf. Diog. Laert. 7.117, who compares the use of "severe" (*austeros*) to describe the worthwhile with "severe" or "bitter" wine whose proper use is for pharmacology rather than for drinking. Thus the pleasure of the listener or for himself is of no consequence to the worthwhile. This lack of regard for common politenesses links the Stoics with the Cynics, whose disregard for traditional practices was notorious.

222   There is a clear link between the Stoic emphasis on nature and the ethical thought of the Cynics (which involved a rejection of anything which was not clearly "natural" and an acceptance of all things which appeared to be natural

functions — including the public exercise of bodily functions). Although they differed in their view of the more extreme Cynic practices (cf. Cic. *Fin.* 3.68), the Stoics recognised merit in the austere lifestyle and even considered whether Cynicism might not be a short-cut to virtue (Apollodorus Ephillus in Diog. Laert. 6.104, 7.121). Cf. Epictetus' depiction of the ideal Cynic (*Diss.* 3.22); for diversity within Cynicism, see A.J. Malherbe, "Self-Definition among the Cynics", in *Paul and the Popular Philosophers* (Minneapolis 1989) 11-24; id., *The Cynic Epistles* (Missoula 1977).

223   Cf. Diog. Laert. 7.129: "Youth is the flowering of virtue" according to Chrysippus in his *Peri Erôtos*; cf. 5b9.

224   As the wise man will not undertake a course of action without reckoning its consequences, he will not experience disappointment. For instance, a wise man might stand for office and fail to be elected — but he will not be discouraged, since rejection is something indifferent.

225   Cf. 5b2.

226   *Kalos kagathos*: "a real gentleman" in common usage.

227   Slander or recrimination can only occur within the group, which is why it is defined as occurring between familiars or friends. As these people are using "lying words", which are derived from "false reckoning", they are neither wise nor true friends (who will use "true reasoning", *orthos logos*).

228   Hesiod, *Works and Days* 410, 413 Rzach.

BIBLIOGRAPHY

Long and Sedley, *Hellenistic Philosophers*, offers an essential bibliography of work on Stoic ethics organised by subject matter up to the mid-1980s. This is extended further by Engberg-Pedersen, *Stoic Theory of Oikeiosis*. Other works listed here include a selection of general studies on the Stoics, more recent works which throw light on problems of Stoic ethics, and some essential studies of Arius.

Annas, J. *The Morality of Happiness* (Oxford 1993).
Annas, J. *Hellenistic Philosophy of Mind* (Berkeley, Los Angeles 1992).
Bett, R. *Sextus Empiricus, Against the Ethicists* (Oxford 1997).
Cooper, J.M. 'Eudaimonism, the Appeal to Nature, and "Moral Duty" in Stoicism', in Engstrom, Whiting, *Aristotle, Kant, and the Stoics*.
Engberg-Pedersen, T. *The Stoic Theory of Oikeiosis* (Aarhus 1990).
Engstrom, S., Whiting, J. eds. *Aristotle, Kant, and the Stoics* (Cambridge 1996).
Fortenbaugh, W.W. ed. *On Stoic and Peripatetic Ethics: The Work of Arius Didymus* (New Brunswick, N.J. 1983) = *Rutgers University Studies in Classical Humanities* vol. 1.
Göransson, T. *Albinus, Alcinous, Arius Didymus* (Göteborg 1995).
Hahm, D.E. 'The Ethical Doxography of Arius Didymus', *Aufstieg und Niedergang der römischen Welt* II.36.4, 2935-3055, (bibliography) 3234-3243.
Hülser, K. *Die Fragmente zur Dialektik der Stoiker*, 4 vols. (Stuttgart 1987-8).
Inwood, B. *Ethics and Human Action in Early Stoicism* (Oxford 1985).
Inwood, B., rev. of Göransson, *Albinus, Alcinous, Arius Didymus*, in *Bryn Mawr Classical Review* 7(1996) 25-30.
Long, A.A. ed. *Problems in Stoicism* (London 1971).
Long, A.A. *Hellenistic Philosophy* (London 1974).
Long, A.A. 'Arius Didymus and the exposition of Stoic ethics' in Fortenbaugh, *On Stoic and Peripatetic Ethics* 41-65; repr. Long, *Stoic Studies* 107-133.
Long, A.A., Sedley, D.N. eds. *The Hellenistic Philosophers*, 2 vols. (Cambridge 1987).
Long, A.A. *Stoic Studies* (Cambridge 1996).

Nussbaum, M. *Therapy of Desire* (Princeton, N.J. 1994).
Reesor, M.E. *The Nature of Man in Early Stoic Philosophy* (London 1989).
Reesor, M.E. *The Politics Theory of the Old and Middle Stoa* (New York 1951).
Rist, J.M. *The Stoics* (Berkeley/Los Angeles 1978).
Runia, D.T., Mansfeld, J. *Aetiana:the Method and Intellectual Context of a Doxographer*(Leiden 1997).
Sandbach, F.H. *The Stoics* (London 1975).
Schofield, M. *The Stoic Idea of the City* (Cambridge 1991).
Tieleman, T. *Galen and Chrysippus on the Soul* (Leiden 1996).

Greek-English Glossary

This list excludes the commonest Greek words in the text (forms of the verb "to be", "to have" [ἔχειν — often equivalent of "to be"], particles, conjunctions, articles, prepositions, pronouns). It is intended to be a guide to the usage in the English translation, not a general vocabulary — usually only one or two English renderings are offered. Semantic groupings are generally listed together, for instance the adjectival, nominal, and verbal forms associated with οἰκονομία; the resulting grouping may be contrary to strict alphabetic order. Verbs are listed by the infinitive which most closely follows the usage in Arius — so ἀφορίζεσθαι is listed by its middle form. Adjectives used as neuter substantives are listed as such.

Arius' vocabulary displays the standard features of Koine Greek: there are a considerable number of alpha-privative formations, adjectival forms derived from the verbal form (e.g. -τικός creations), and new nominal forms (e.g. ἀδίκευσις, ἀδικοπράγημα). There are also a number of technical Stoic terms (e.g. κατάληψις, ἀφορμή). Some words have shifted their meaning from Classical Greek — where significant, these are noted in the glossary with references to H.G. Liddell, R. Scott, H.S. Jones, *A Greek-English Lexicon, 9th Edition and Supplement* (Oxford 1996).

ἀβέβαιος	unstable 11m	ἁγιστεία	ritual 5b12
ἀβλαβής	free from harm 11n	ἄγνοια	failure to understand 5b(x3), 5b1(x5), 5b12, 5b13(x3), 11m
ἀγαθός	good 5a, 5b6, 5b12, 5i, 6e, 11d (x3), 11g(x2), 11h, 11s(x2)		
(τὸ) ἀγαθόν	a good 5d(x2), 5i, 5o, 6b, 6e, 6f(x2), 7, 10, 10b(x2), 11c, 11h, 11i(x3), 11m(x2)	ἀγνοεῖν	to fail to understand 11g, 11m
		ἄγριος	wild 11k
(τὰ) ἀγαθά	good things 5a, 5b, 5b1(x2), 5c, 5d, 5e, 5f, 5g(x4), 5h, 5k(x2), 5l, 5m, 6d, 6f, 7(x2), 7g(x2), 10c, 11b(x2), 11c(x3), 11d, 11f(x5), 11g(x3), 11i(x2)	ἀγροικία	rusticity 11k
		ἄγροικος	rustic 11k
		ἀγρός	rural
		(κατ' ἀγρόν	= in the fields 11d)
		ἀγχίνοια	shrewdness 5b2(x2)
ἀγανεκτεῖν	to be annoyed 11i	ἀγχίνους	shrewd 11m, 11p
ἀγαπᾶν	to be affectionate 11m	ἄγειν	to lead 5b11, 10a, 11n

ἀγωνία — anguish 10b, 10c

ἀδιάβολος — free from slander 11s(x2)

ἀδιαπτώτως — unerringly 5b5(x2)

(τὸ) ἀδιάφορον — indifferent 5a, 5b9, 7(x3), 7a(x3), 7g
(τὰ) ἀδιάφορα — indifferents 5a, 7(x2), 7b(x3), 7c, 7d, 7f, 8a

ἀδικία — injustice 5a, 5b(x2), 5b1, 11m(x2)
ἀδικεῖν — to act unjustly 10c, 11d, 11e, 11m
ἀδίκευσις — acting with injustice 5f
ἀδικητικῶς — unjustly 11m
ἀδικοπράγημα — unjust act 11e
ἀδικοπραγεῖν — to do unjust deeds 11m

ἀδοξία — lack of reputation 5a, 10c

ἀδρός — powerful 11g(x2)

ἀδύνατος — impossible 11m
ἀδυναμία — incapacity 5b(x2)
(cf. δύναμις)

ἀήττητος — invincible 5b2, 11g

ἆθλον — prize 11i

αἰδημοσύνη — modesty 5b2(x2)

αἱμύλος — soothing 11m

αἱρεῖσθαι — to choose 5b5, 6f(x3), 7f, 10, 11f(x3), 11h
αἵρεσις — choice [11m: "school"] 5h, 5i, 5l, 6a, 6b, 7, 9a(x4), 11f, 11m(x2), 12

αἱρετός — worth choosing 5b1(x2), 5b6(x3), 5h(x2), 5i(x2), 5o(x3), 6f(x3), 7(x2), 10e(x2), 11f(x3), 11g, 11h
αἱρετέος — ought to be chosen 6f(x3), 11f(x3)
(cf. προαίρεσις)

αἰσχύνη — shame 10b, 10c, 10d
αἰσχρός — shameful 5d, 5e

αἰσθάνεσθαι — to have awareness 5b7
αἴσθησις — (sense-)perception 5c(x2), 7d
αἰσθέσεις — senses 7d
αἰσθητήριον — organ of sensation 7a, 11m

αἰτία — cause 5b6, 11l
αἴτιον — causative/cause 5d, 10b(x4), 11i

ἀκάθαρος — impure 5b12

ἀκαταγώνιστος — unconquerable 11g

ἀκατάληπτος — what cannot be apprehended 11m(x3)
(cf. κατάληψις)

ἀκατάστατος — unstable 5b13

ἀκολασία — lack of self-restraint 5a, 5b(x2), 5b1
ἀκολασταίνειν — to show lack of self-restraint 11e

ἀκολουθεῖν — to be consistent with 5b7, 11m
ἀκόλουθος — consistent with 5b10, 6, 8(x3)
ἀκολουθῶς — consistently 5b3(x2), 5b9, 5b11, 8, 11m
ἀκολουθητικός — able to follow 11d, 11i

GLOSSARY

ἀκούειν	to listen 11k, to be understood 5b1	ἀμέτοχος	without participation 11i (cf. μετέχειν)
ἀκροχολία	outburst of rage 10e	ἄμετρος	immoderate 11k
(κατ') ἀλήθειαν	true, truly 11i(x4), 11s	ἄμικτος	unmixed 5m
ἀληθεύειν	to tell the truth 11m	ἀμοιβή	exchange value 7f(x2)
ἀληθινός	true 11n		
ἄληπτος	worth shunning 7e(x3)	ἀμφιβήτησις	disagreement 11m
ἀλλοιωθείσας	changed 5k	ἀναβάλλεσθαι	to delay 11s(x3)
		ἀναβολή	delay 11s(x2)
ἀλλοτριούμενος	alienated from 11k (cf. οἰκειούμενος)	ἀνάγεσθαι	to be led 10a
ἄλογος	irrational 8, 9, 10(x2), 10a(x2)	ἀνάγωγος	unmanageable 11i
		ἀναγκαῖος	necessary, principal (dogma) 5, 6d(x7), 7, 7g, 11h
ἀλυπία	not feeling distress 5l	ἀναγκάζειν	to force 11g(x2)
		ἀνάγκη	attachment 11m
ἀλυσιτελής	unprofitable 5d	ἄναγνος	unclean 5b12
ἁμαρτάνειν	to do wrong 11d(x4), 11g, 11i, 11l, 11m	ἀναλαμβάνω	(to take up), to repeat 5
ἁμάρτημα	wrong act 8a, 11a, 11e(x4), 11k(x5), 11l(x5), 11o(x2)	ἀνάληψις	acquisition 5b12
ἁμαρτία	wrong 11l	ἀνάλογον/κατὰ τὴν ἀναλογίαν/ κατὰ τὸ ἀνάλογον analogously, by analogy 5b, 5c, 6f, 11f; 5d, 7g; 5b10, 5b11, 5g, 7d, 7f	
(τὸ) ἁμαρτητικόν	the wrongful 11m		
ἀμβολιεργός	dilatory 11s (cf. ἀναβολή)	(ἐξ) ἀναλογισμοῦ	by comparison 9a
ἀμελετήτως	spontaneously 11k	ἀνάλωσις	expenditure 11d
ἀμέμπτως	without incurring blame 5b2	(τὰ) ἀναλώματα	expenses 11d
ἀμεριαῖος	momentary 11g	ἀναξίως	undeservedly 10c (cf. ἄξιος)
ἀμετάπτωτος	irreversible 5k, 5l(x2), 11m	ἀναστρέφεσθαι	to conduct oneself 5b5, 5b9, 11d

ἀναφέρειν to refer 5k, 6b
ἀναφορά reference 10, 11i
ἀναφορικῶς with reference to 6b

ἀνδραποδώδης slavish 11k
ἀνδρεία bravery 5a, 5b(x2), 5b1, 5b2(x4), 5b5

ἀνέγκλητος irreproachable 11s

ἀνελέσθαι to pick up 7

ἀνεμποδίστως without impediment 11k

ἀνενδεής free from want 11h
(cf. ἐνδεία)

ἀνεορτάστος barred from festive rites 5b12

ἀνενεκτικῶς by reference to something else 7e
(cf. ἀναφέρω)

ἀνήμερος savage 11k

ἀνία annoyance 10b, 10c

ἀνοίκειος unfitting 5d
(cf. οἰκεῖος)

ἀνομήματα lawless acts 11e

ἀνόσιος unholy 5b12
(cf. ὅσιος)

ἀντaναιρέτικος marking off (LSJ: "striking a balance") 5b2

ἀνταπόδοσις return 11k

ἀντέχεσθαι to lay hold of 7e

ἀντικείμενος opposite 11e

ἀντίπαλος opposition 11m

ἀντιτίθεσθαι to be opposed to 7b, 7f, 9

ἀνύβριστος free from insult 11m
(cf. ὕβρις)

ἀνυπέρβατος not overstepping the proper bounds 5b2

ἀνυπέρβλητος unsurpassable 11h

ἀνυπεύθυνος answerable to none 11m

ἀνυπομενετός not worth sustaining 11f

ἀνυπομενετέος must not be sustained 11f

ἀνυπόπτως unhesitatingly 5i, 11h, 11k(x2)

ἀνωτάτω above all 5b5, 11m

ἀξία value, due 5b1(x2), 5o, 7, 7b(x4), 7f(x7), 7g(x5), 11d, 11h, 11k
(κατ') ἀξίαν in accord with one's value/merits 5b5, 7f, 11d, 11k(x2)
ἀξιόλογος worthwhile 11k
ἄξιος worthy 5b9, 11h(x2), 11i
ἀξίωμα proposition 9b(x2); dignity 7f, 11m
ἀξιωματικός meritorious 11g
ἀξίωσις evaluation 11i

ἀξιαπόλαυστος worth (sexually) enjoying 5b9

ἀξιέραστος worthy of erotic love 5b9(x2), 11s

ἀξιοφίλητος worthy of friendship 5b9

GLOSSARY

ἀπαγορευτικός forbidding 11d, 11i

ἀπαλλάττειν to get away, to remove 10b, 11h, 11m

ἀπαξία lack of value 7, 7b(x2), 7f(x2), 7g(x3) (cf. ἀξία)

ἀπαραβάτως unerringly 6a

ἀπαράδεκτος impervious 11s

ἀπαρεστός displeasing 11k(x2)

ἀπατᾶν to deceive 10a
ἀπατή deception 10c, 11m(x2)

ἀπεῖναι to be absent 10c(x2)

ἀπειθής disobedient 10, 10a(x2), 10b(x4)

ἀπειρία lack of experience 11k
ἄπειρος having no experience 11i

ἀπεκλογή rejection 6a, 7
ἀπεκλεκτικός for rejection 7
ἀπεκλεγόμενος rejecting 6a

ἀπελέγχεσθαι to be convicted 11k

ἀπερίεργος simple 11m

ἀπερίπτωτος unconcerned (not falling into) 11m

ἀπεριστάτως except in special circumstances 8a

ἀπέχων having in full 11a

ἀπιστεῖν to mistrust 11m
ἀπιστία mistrust 11m

ἄπιστος mistrusting 11m

ἄπλαστος unaffected (i.e. natural) 11m

ἁπλοῦς straightforward 11m

ἀπογεννᾶν to create 5g(x2)

ἀποδεκτός worth accepting 11f(x2)
ἀποδεκτέος ought to be accepted 11f(x2)
ἀποδεκτικῶς acceptably 11i
ἀποδέχεσθαι to accept, agree with 11i, 11m
ἀποδοχή acceptance 7b

ἀποδημεῖν to live abroad 11e

ἀποδίδοναι to interpret 5d, 6a(x3), 8

ἀποικονομεῖσθαι to get rid of 11k

ἀποκρίνεσθαι to answer 11e
ἀπόκρισις answer 5c

ἀπολαμβάνειν to gain back 11d

ἀπόλαυσις (enjoyment), pleasure 11k

ἀπολείπειν to accept 11m
ἀπολείπεσθαι to lack 5b8, 11g

ἀπολογία defence 8

ἀπονέμειν to apportion 5b5, 11d
ἀπονέμεσις apportionment 5b2, 5b3
ἀπονεμητικός apportioning 5b1(x2), 7f

ἀπονία lack of pain 7e

ἀποπροηγμένος dispreferred 7b(x6), 7g(x3)

ἀποστρέφεσθαι to turn their backs on 10a

ἀποτελούμενος completed 5b2
ἀποτελοῦσθαι to be completed 11l

ἀποτιθέναι (ἀποτεθειμένος) to set aside 10c

ἀποτυγχάνειν to fail to get 10

ἀποφαίνειν to declare 11c
ἀποφαντικός declarative 11m

ἀποχρᾶν to be enough 11n

ἀπρεπής unsuitable 5b2, 5d

ἀπρόληπτος unforeseen 11s

ἀπροσδόκητος unexpectedly 10c

ἀρέσκειν to be the view (opinion) 11g, 11k(x2)
ἀρεστός satisfying 5i(x2), 11h

ἀρετή virtue (excellence) 5a(x2), 5b(x5), 5b1(x3), 5b2(x2), 5b3(x2), 5b4, 5b5(x5), 5b7(x3), 5b8(x4), 5b9(x3), 5b10, 5b11, 5c, 5e(x2), 5f(x2), 5g, 5i, 5k(x5), 5l(x2), 6, 6d, 6e(x4), 6f, 7, 7b, 8, 11d(x2), 11e, 11f, 11g(x4), 11h, 11i(x4), 11k(x9), 11m(x7), 11q(x2)

ἀριθμοί the sum total of features 11a
(cf. LSJ ἀριθμός I.4)

ἀρρώστημα frailty 5f, 6d, 10e
(cf. νόσημα)

ἄρτιος sound; (of numbers) even 7, 7c, 7d
ἀρτιότης soundness 5b4, 7a, 7d

ἀρχή office 11m; first element (=atom) 10a; (starting point) foundation (cf. LSJ 1a) 11k
ἀρχεῖν to govern 11i(x4)
ἄρχεσθαι to begin 5
ἀρχηγός fundamental 10
ἀρχικός governing 11i

ἀσέβεια impiety 5b12, 11k(x3)
ἀσέβημα impious act 11k(x4)
ἀσεβής impious 5b12
(cf. εὐσέβεια)

ἄση vexation 10b, 10c

ἀσθένεια feebleness 5b(x2), 7a, 10e
ἀσθενής feeble 10, 11m(x2)
ἀσθενῶς in a feeble fashion 11m

ἄσκησις practice 5b4

ἀσμενισμός self-gratification 10b, 10c

ἀσπάζεσθαι to embrace 11m

ἀστεῖος civilised (*hence often* = "fine") 5b12, 11d(x3), 11i(x4), 11m(x2), 11q(x2)

ἀσύμφορος disadvantageous 5d

ἀσυμφωνία disharmony 11k

ἀσυνήθης unaccustomed 10c

ἀσφαλής secure 5l
ἀσφαλῶς securely 11m

GLOSSARY

ἀσώματα	incorporeals 11f	ἀφραίνειν	to act stupidly 11e
ἀτακτήματα	unruly acts 11e	ἀφρόνευσις	acting with stupidity 5f
ἀτάκτως	in unruly fashion 10b	ἀφροσύνη	stupidity 5a, 5b(x2), 5b1, 11k
ἀτάραχος	calm 5k	ἄφρων	stupid 5b12, 5c(x6), 5g(x2), 11i(x2), 11k(x7), 11o(x2)
ἀτελής	incomplete 5b8, 11g(x2)	ἀφωνία	speechlessness 10c
ἀτεχνία	lack of expertise 5b(x3)	ἀχάριστος	ungrateful 11k
ἄτη	ruin 11s	ἄχθεσθαι	to be worried 11i
		ἄχθος	worry 10b, 10c
ἄτιμος	dishonoured 11i(x2)	ἄχος	sorrow 10b, 10c
ἄτομος	indivisible 10a	ἀχώριστος	inseparable 5b5, 5b7
αὐθάδης	headstrong 11i	ἄωρος	premature 10c
αὐλή	court 7g	βαρυνεῖν	to become burdensome 10c
αὔλησις	flute-playing 5b10	βασιλεία	kingship 11i, 11m(x2)
αὐλητής	flute-player 5b10		
αὐξάνειν	to extol 11g	βασιλεύς	king 7g, 11m(x2)
		βασιλικός	kingly 11g, 11m(x2)
αὔριον	(to)morrow 11s	βασιλεύειν	to be king 11m(x2)
αὐστηρός	stern 11s	(τὸ) βέβαιον	solidness 5l
		βεβαίως	firmly 11m
αὐτάρκης	self-sufficient 11h	βεβαιοῦν	to confirm 11m
		βεβαιότης	firmness 11m
αὐτοτελής	complete in itself 5o	βίαιος	violent 11k
ἀφελής	guileless 11m	βιαστικός	(forcing), overpowering 10a
ἀφίστασθαι	to abandon 10a(x2)	βιάζειν	to force 10a, 11g(x2)
ἀφορίζεσθαι	to define 9	βίος	life 5b1, 5b4, 5b10, 5b12, 5k, 5l(x2), 6b, 6e(x3), 7, 7b, 8, 11b, 11g(x4), 11h(x2), 11i, 11k(x2), 11m(x4), 11s
ἀφορμή	repulsion 7, 7a, 7c(x4), 9(x2), 11i; initial impulse 5b3, 5b8		
		βιοῦν	to live 11k(x2)

βλαβερός	harmful 5d	γραμμή	line 5b5(x3)
βλαβή	harm 11m(x2)		
βλάμμα	harmful thing 11i	(τὰ) γράμματα	writings 11b
βλαπτικός	harmful 11k	δαίμων	spirit 5b12, 10c, 11s
βλάπτειν	to harm 5d(x3), 11i(x4), 11m	δάκτυλος	finger 7
βλέπειν	to consider 5b5	δειλία	cowardice 5a, 5b(x2), 5b1
βουκολεῖν	to cheat (LSJ II) 11m	δεῖμα	terror 10b, 10c, 10d
βούλεσθαι	to want/wish 5b7, 6a, 11f(x2), 11n	δεινός	terrible 5b1(x4), 5b2, 10c
βούλησις	wish 5b, 9a(x4), 11f, 11k	δεισιδαιμονία	superstition 10b, 10c
βουλητός	worth being wanted 11f(x3)	δεκτικός	receptive 5l, 7a(x2)
βουλητέος	must be wanted 11f(x3)	δεῖν	to need 5b5(x4), 5b9(x2), 5b12(x3), 10a, 11d, 11k(x2), 11m, 11q
γάμος	marriage 11b		
γαμεῖν	to marry 8, 11m	δεόντως	rightly 9, 11d
γένος	family 11g, 11m	δέος	fear 10b, 10c
τῷ γένει, κατὰ τὸ γένος in genus, in overall classification, generally 9, 10 (cf. εἶδος)		δεσπόζειν	to lord it over 11g(x2)
		δεσποτικός	tyrannical 11k
ἐκ γένους	(from one's family), inherited 11m	δεύτερος	second 5d, 7g, 11c, 11m
γενναιός	noble 11g	κατὰ τὸν δεύτερον λόγον secondarily 5b5(x4)	
γέρας	privilege 11i(x2)	δῆλος	clear 5b10, 6e
γῆρας	old age 5m, 11q	δηλοῦν	(to make clear), explain 11l
γνώμη	judgement 10a(x2)	δημοκοπεῖν	to court the mob 11b
γνῶσις	recognition 10a	διαβάλλειν	to slander 11s(x5)
γνώριμος	acquaintance 5e	διαβολή	slander 11s(x2)
γνωριμότης 5l	acquaintance(ship)	διαγνωστικός 11s	able to distinguish
γοητεία	charlatanry 10b, 10c	διαδέχομαι	to take over 6a
γονεύς	parent 7b		

GLOSSARY

διάθεσις (fixed condition), disposition 5b1, 5f(x11), 11i(x3), 11k, 11m, 11o(x2)

διαίρεσις division 5b6, 5n

διαιτᾶσθαι to be criticised 11m

διακεῖσθαι to be inclined 11i, 11k

διαλανθάνειν to escape notice 11n

διαλεκτικός skilled in dialectic 5b12
διαλεκτικῶς dialectically (= by logical reasoning) 5b9

διαλέγεσθαι to discuss 8, 12
διαλογισμός calculation (= mental reckoning) 10c

διάληψις intermediate state, distinction 11n

διαλλάττειν to vary 11l

διαμαρτάνειν to make a mistake 11m

διανοία mind 5b7(x3), 7b, 9(x3)

διάπτωσις failure 10c

διάστασις disagreement 11s
διιστάναι to disagree 11m
διεστηκώς made of different parts 11c

διαστροφή distortion 11k

διατείνειν to extend 5d, 8, 11h

διάταξις organisation 11d

διαφέρειν to differ 5b5, 5o(x2), 6c, 6f, 7a, 11f(x2), 11g(x2)

διάφορος different 5b5
διαφορά difference 11l, 11o

διαφωνοῦν to be in disharmony 11b, 11k

διαψευδεῖσθαι to subject to falsehood 11g, 11l (x3)
διαψευστικῶς in a false way 11m
διάψευσις falsehood 11l

διδάσκειν to teach 10a

διδόναι (to give), permit 7f, 11i (e.g. διδόντων τῶν πραγμάτων)

διεξάγειν to live out 11q
διεξαγωγή lifestyle 11k

διέξοδος way out 5b2

διέρχεσθαι to give an account 7, 12

διηνεκῶς continually 6a(x2)

δικαιοπραγεῖν to act justly 8, 11e
δικαιοπραγία acting justly 5l
δικαιοπράγημα a justly performed act 11e
δίκαιος just 5b12, 11b
δικαιῶς rightly 11i
δικαιοσύνη justice 5a, 5b(x2), 5b1, 5b2(x4), 5b5, 5b12, 7f, 11e
δικαίωμα just act 11e
δική judgement (=a form of justice) 11i

διό, διότι, διόπερ hence 5b5, 5b7, 5b8, 5b9, 5b12, 5b13, 7a, 10, 11d, 11f, 11k, 11l, 11m

διοιδοῦν to boil over 10c

διομολογεῖσθαι to agree 11m

διττός	of two types 11m	ἐγκρατῶς	with self-control 11i
διττῶς, διχῶς, διχῇ	in two ways 5b6, 5b9, 7, 9	ἐγκύκλιος	everyday 5b11
διχόνοια	discord 11k	ἐγχείρησις	undertaking 9a(x2)
διωθεῖν	to reject 8a	ἔθός	custom 11k
δόγμα	belief 5, 5b4, 5b10, 11k, 11m(x3), 12(x3)	εἴδησις	awareness 10a
δογματίζειν	to hold a belief 5b9	εἶδος	species, manifestations 5b12, 5e, 9(x3), 9a, 9b, 10b, 11i, 11s (cf. γένος)
δοκεῖν	to seem 10c(x2), 11m, 11s	εἰδικός	specific 11n
δοκιμάζειν	to price 7f	εἰκών	image 11l
δοκιμαστός	(valued), prized/priced 5i(x2), 7f(x3), 11h	εἶπον	they said 11d
δοκιμαστής	(valuer), appraiser 7f(x2)	(τὰ) εἰρήμενα	those things stated 5b1, 7b(x2), 7f, 11m (cf. τὸ ῥηθέν = the thing said 5b4, 5k, 6a)
δοκιμαστικῶς	in a prized manner 11i		
δόξα	opinion; (good opinion), reputation 5a, 7e, 10(x2), 10b(x2), 10c, 10e, 11m(x2)	εἰρωνεύεσθαι	to dissemble 11m(x3)
		εἰσδύνειν	to burrow into 10c
δοξάζειν	to form an opinion 10b(x4), 11m(x2)	ἐκβάλλειν	to force out 11m
δόσις	contribution 7f(x2), 11k(x4)	ἐκβεβαιοῦσθαι	to strengthen 11k
		ἐκκεῖσθαι	to be set forth 6c, 6e
δοῦλος	slave 11i	ἔκκλισις	avoidance 10b
δουλεία	slavery 11i		
δύναμις	capacity 5b4, 5l	ἐκλέγεσθαι	to select 5o, 6a, 7g, 8a
(ὡς) δυνατόν	as much as possible 11m	ἐκλεκτικός	selective 5k, 7, 7f
δυνάμενος	able 11b	ἐκλογή	selection 6a, 7, 7g
δύνασθαι	to be able 6e, 7b, 11d, 11g, 11k, 11l	ἑκούσιος	voluntary 9a
δυσίατος	difficult to cure 11o	ἔκπληξις	consternation 10b, 10c
δύσχρηστος	useless 5d		
ἐγκράτεια	self-control 5b2(x2)	ἔκπτωσις	abandonment 11s

GLOSSARY

ἐκρήγνυμι	to break out 10c	ἐναντίως	(oppositely), the opposite 8, 11i, 11r
ἐκτός	external 5e(x8), 7a, 7b(x6), 11c	ἐναντιωτικός	in opposition 11k
		ἐναποκεῖσθαι	to be stored up 10c
ἐκφέρειν (ἐξήνεγκον)	to express 6a(x2)	ἐνάρχεσθαι	to start out on 10c, 11s
ἐκφέρεσθαι	to be carried away 10a, 11s		
		ἐνδεής	lacking 10c
ἐκφύγειν	to escape from 10	ἐνδεία	want (lack) 11h
ἔλεος	pity 10b, 10c, 10d	ἐνέργεια	activity 5e(x2), 5f(x2), 6d(x2), 10c, 11i, 11k, 11s
ἐλεύθερος	free 11i, 11m	ἐνεργεῖν	to act 8, 11i
ἐλευθερία	freedom 11i	ἐνέργημα	activation 8, 11e, 11k
ἐλλείπειν	to lack 11g, 11l	ἔνθερμος	warm 5b7
ἐμμενετός	worth persisting in 6f, 11f	ἔννηφι	the day after 11s
ἐμμενετέος	must be persisted in 6f, 11f	ἐνοικοῦν	to inhabit 11i
ἐμμενητικός	able to persist 5b2	ἔνοχος	subject to 11k, 11m
ἔμπειρος	experienced in 5b12 (practical)	ἐνσκιροῦσθαι	to become ingrained 10e
ἐμπειρία	experience 5b12, 6a, 11d, 11g, 11i		
		ἐντυγχάνειν	to happen upon 11b(x2)
ἐμπεριλαμβάνεσθαι	to be involved 11p		
		ἐξάγεσθαι	to carry out 5b9
ἐμποδός	in the way 7	ἐξαγωγή	way out 11m
ἐμποιεῖν	to produce 10c, 11s	ἐξαπατᾶν	to deceive thoroughly 10a, 11g(x2)
ἐμφαίνειν	to display 10c, 10d, 11b, 11m, 11s		
ἔμφασις	display 5b9	ἐξαρκεῖν	to suffice 11h
ἐναντίος	opposite, opposed 5b13, 5d, 6c, 7b, 10e, 11g, 11i, 11k(x3), 11m, 11s	ἐξεργαστικός	able to accomplish 5b2, 11k
τοὐναντίον, ἐκ ἐναντίων	conversely 11g(x2), 11i(x2)	ἐξηγητικός	able to interpret 11d, 11i
ἐναντιοῦσθαι	(to be opposed), adverse 11s	ἑξῆς	next 5a, 9b

ἕξις	condition (which is variable) 5b11, 5e(x2), 5f(x8), 5k(x3), 5l, 7b, 7f, 9. 10e, 11d(x2), 11k, 11m(x3), 11s	ἐπιεικής	tolerant 11d(x3)
		ἐπιθυμεῖν	to have an appetite for 10(x2), 10c(x2)
ἐξομολογεῖσθαι	to confess 10a	ἐπιθυμία	appetite 5b9, 10(x2), 10b(x2), 10c(x4), 10e
ἐξώφορος	published 11k	ἐπιλαμβάνειν	to gain 11k
ἑορτάζειν	to carry out festive rites 5b12(x2)	ἐπιλυπία	taking offence 5f, 10e
ἑορτή	festival 5b12	ἐπιμέλεια	care 11d
ἐπαινεῖν	to praise 11h	ἐπιμελής	careful 11m
ἐπαινετός	praise-worthy 5e, 5i(x2), 11h	ἐπιμένειν	to stick with 11s
		ἐπίμονος	steadfast 7b
ἐπαίρεσθαι	to be elated 10b		
ἔπαρσις	elation 10, 10b	ἐπιπλεῖον	in the main 7b
ἔπανδρος	manly 5k	ἐπιπλοκή	tie 11m
ἐπαφρόδιτος	charming 11m	ἐπιπόλαιος	superficial 11k
ἐπεί, ἐπειδή	since 5b7, 5b9, 9b, 10, 11i, 11k, 11m	ἐπισημασία	celebration 5b12
		ἐπίσης	equally 11l(x2), 11o
ἐπέρχεσθαι	to go through, to give an account 7, 12	ἐπιστάσθαι	to know 11m
		ἐπιστήμη	knowledge 5b(x3), 5b1(x5), 5b2(x19), 5b5, 5b9(x3), 5b11, 5b12(x2), 5l(x3), 5m, 11b, 11k, 11m(x2), 11s(x2)
ἕπεσθαι	to follow 11b		
ἐπιβάλλειν	to befall 7f(x2), 11g(x2), 11i, 11k, 11s	ἐπιστήμων	knowledgeable 5l(x2), 11m
ἐπιβολή	inclination 5b9, 9, 9a, 10c, 11s(x2)	ἐπιστημονικός	(knowledgeable), intellectual 11m
ἐπιβλαβής	harmful 11b		
ἐπιγίγνεσθαι	to be in addition 5b4, 10	ἐπιστασία	superintendence 11i
		ἐπισυρμός	mockery 11m
ἐπιδέξιος	clever 11m	ἐπίτασις	intensity 11p
ἐπιδοτική (τέχνη)	(the skill of) giving (= charity) 5l	ἐπιτελεῖν	to complete 5b10, 6a

GLOSSARY

ἐπιτέλεσις	completion 9a	ἑτοίμως	readily 11k
ἐπιτευκτικός	able to hit 5b2	εὖ	well 5b10(x4), 6e, 10b, 11d, 11h, 11i
ἐπιτυγχάνειν	to achieve 10c(x2)		
(ὁ ἐπιτυγχάνων = whoever happens along 11m)		εὐαισθησία	good perception 7b, 7e
ἐπιτήδευμα	pursuit 5b11(x2), 5f, 5k, 6d	εὐανάληπτος	easily able to gain 11m
ἐπιτηρεῖν	to keep watch 10c		
ἐπιφέρεσθαι	to approach 10b(x2); to be led (LSJ III.2) 11m	εὐάρμοστος	accommodating 11m
ἐπιχαιρεκακία	joy at another's misfortunes 10b, 10c, 10d	εὐβουλία	soundness of judgement 5b2(x2)
ἐπίχαρις	gracious 11m	εὐγένεια	good breeding 11m(x2)
ἐρᾶν	to love 5b9(x2)	εὐγενής	well-bred 11m, 11s
ἔρασθαι	to fall in love 5b9, 11s	εὐγηρεῖν	to have a fortunate old age 11q(x2)
ἔρως	erotic love 5b9(x3), 5l, 10b, 10c(x2), 11s	εὐγηρία	good fortune in old age 5m(x2)
ἐρωτικός	erotic 5b9(x2), 5l, 11s		
ἐρωτικῶς	erotically 5b9		
ἐρωτομανής	mad with erotic love 5b9	εὐδαιμονεῖν	to be happy 5b5, 6c, 6e(x2), 8a, 11g
ἐργάζειν	to produce 11d	εὐδαιμόνημα	happy act 11e
ἔργον	deed 10d(x2), 11d, 11k(x3), 11s	εὐδαιμονία	happiness 5g, 6, 6c, 6d, 6e(x5), 7, 7g, 11g(x4)
		εὐδαιμόνως	happily 7a
ἔρχεσθαι	to come to; result in (LSJ IIB4) 5h, 5i	εὐδαίμων	happy 6e, 7, 11g(x2)
ἐρωτᾶν	to pose a question 11e	εὐδόκιμος	highly prized 11i (cf. δοκιμαστός)
ἐρώτησις	questioning 5g	εὐεμπτωσία	proclivity 10e(x2)
ἔσχατον	last 6b	εὐεπιτήδευμα	properly pursued act 11e (cf. ἐπιτήδευμα)
ἑταιρία	comradeship 5l		
ἕτοιμος	ready 11k(x3)	εὐεργετεῖν	to be benevolent 11e
		εὐεργετικός	benevolent 11i

εὐζωία 5m(x2)	good fortune in life	εὑρετικός 5b2(x2)	able to discover
εὐθανατεῖν death 11q(x2)	to have a fortunate	εὕροια	smooth flow 6e, 8a
εὐκαίρημα	opportune act 11e	εὐσέβεια 5b2(x2), 5b12(x3), 11k	piety
εὔκαιρος	opportune 11m	εὐσεβής	pious 11g
εὐκαταφορία	propensity 5f, 10e	εὐστάθεια	balancing 5b3
εὐκοινωνησία 5b2(x2)	good fellowship	εὐσταθής	balanced 5b5
εὐκρασία	proportion 5b4(x2)	εὐστοχία 5b2(x2)	soundness of aim
		εὔστοχος	keen in aim 11m
εὐλαβητός	worth avoiding 11f		
εὐλαβητέος 11f	ought to be avoided	εὐσυναλλαξία	fair dealing 5b2(x2)
εὐλαβητικός	able to avoid 5b2	εὐσχημόνημα	dignified act 11e
		εὐσχημόνως	with dignity 7a
εὔλογος (= rationally defensible) 5h, 5i, 8, 9a	reasonable	εὐτάκτημα	orderly act 11e
εὐλόγως 11h	reasonably 5i, 11h,	εὔτακτος	orderly 5k
		εὐτάκτως	in orderly fashion 11i
εὐλογιστεῖν (act reasonably) 6a	to be circumspect	εὐταξία 5l, 11s	orderliness 5b2(x2),
εὐλογιστία 5b2(x2)	circumspection	εὐτεκνία (having) children 5m(x2)	good fortune of
εὐλογίστως	circumspectly 5o	εὐτεκνεῖν one's children 11q(x2)	to be fortunate in
εὐμετάπτωτος	easily changing 11i		
εὐμηχανία	ingenuity 5b2(x2)	εὐτελής	cheap 7b
εὔνοια	good will 5l, 11m	εὐτύχημα	prosperous act 11e
εὔνους	well-disposed 11h	εὐτυχής	prosperous 11g
εὐνόμημα	lawful act 11e	εὐφραίνεσθαι	to be cheerful 11e
εὐποιητικός 5b2, 11i	disposed to do good	εὐφροσύνη 5g, 5k, 6d	cheerfulness 5b, 5c,
εὐπορεῖν	to be rich 11m(x2)	εὐφυής 5b9, 11m(x3), 11r, 11s	naturally suitable
εὐπορία	affluence 11d	εὐφυία 7b(x3), 11m(x2)	natural suitableness
εὕρεσις	discovery 5b3		

GLOSSARY

εὐχή	prayer 5b12	ἡσυχία	rest 5k
		ἡσύχιος	tranquil 11s
εὔχρηστος	useful 5d	ἡσυχιότης	tranquillity 11s
εὐψυχία 5b2(x2)	stout-heartedness	ἥττη	defeat 10c
		θάνατος	death 5a, 7f, 10c,
ἐφίεσθαι	to aim at 6c	11b, 11m, 11q	
ἐφικνεῖσθαι	to accomplish 11g	θαρραλεότης	intrepidness 5b2(x2)
		θάρρος	confidence 5b, 5g
ἐφιστάναι	to fix one's mind on		
(ἐπιστήσας = having considered 11l)		θεῖος	divine 5b12(x2), 11g, 11m
		θεός	god 5b2, 5b12(x6),
ἔχθρα	enmity 11k	10c, 11k(x9), 11s	
ἐχθρός 11k(x4)	enemy 5e, 5g, 11b,	θεοφιλής	dear to the gods 11g
		θέλησις	willingness 9a(x2)
ζῆλος	envy 10b, 10c(x2)		
ζηλοτυπία	jealousy 10b, 10c	θεραπεία	service 5b2, 5b12(x3)
ζῆν 5b7, 6a(x8), 6e(x6), 7a, 7b, 11h, 11l, 11m(x2)	to live 5b3(x2), 5b5,	θερμός	warm 5b4
		θέσις	decree
		(θέσει = by convention 11b)	
ζωή	life 5a, 6, 7f, 8, 11m		
ζῷον 5b1, 5b7(x2), 6, 8(x2), 8a, 9, 11a, 11m	(living) creature	θεωρεῖν 6f(x2), 9	to view 5b5(x3),
		θεώρημα	rule of behaviour
ἡγεῖσθαι 11d, 11k	to think 5b7, 6c, 7,	(cf. "theorem") 5b4, 5b5, 5b12	
		θεωρητικός	rule-based 5b12, 11d
ἡγεμονικός 10	controlling 5b7(x2),	θήρα	hunt 5b9
		θηρευτικός	able to hunt 11m
ἡδέως	gladly 11k	θηριώδης	savage 11k
ἡδονή 10(x3), 10b(x2), 10c(x4)	pleasure 5a, 7b,	θνητός	mortal 6
		θόρυβος	commotion 10b, 10c
ἠθικός	ethical 5(x2), 12	θρυλοῦν 10a	to say commonly
ἠλίθιος	silly 11i		
ἡμιάμβειος	iambic half-line 5b8	θυμός	temper 10b, 10c

θυσία	sacrifice 5b12	καθιστάναι	to bring (into a state) 11m, (καθεστώς) stand 5b4
θυτικός	sacrificial 11s		
ἰατρός	doctor 11m	καθόλου	overall 5b2, 5b9, 5b11, 5e(x3), 5o, 11e, 11g(x2)
ἰδιαζόντως	in a special way 10a		
ἴδιος	personal 5b3, 5b5, 11d, 11m	καθυπολαμβάνειν	to surmise 5i
ἰδιότης	specific type 10d		
ἰδίως	in a special sense 9(x2)	καιρός	occasion, opportunity 5c(x2), 10c, 11k
ἵδρυσις	foundation (esp. of temples) 5b12	κακοδαιμονεῖν	to be unhappy 6a, 6c, 11f
		κακοδαιμονία	unhappiness 5g(x2), 6d
ἱερεύς	priest 5b12(x2)	κακοδαιμονικός	creating unhappiness 11i
ἱκανός	adequate 5b4(x2), 11h	κακοδαίμων	unhappy 11g
ἱκανῶς	adequately 7, 11i, 12	κακοπαθεῖν	to suffer harm 10c
ἵμερος	yearning 10b, 10c	κακοποιεῖν	to do harm 11g(x2)
		κακοποιητικός	ready to do harm 11b
ἱπποκένταυρος	centaur 11l		
ἵππος	horse 10a		
ἰσοδυναμεῖν	to be equivalent 6e	κακός	bad 5a, 5d, 5i, 6e, 7, 10, 10b(x2), 11i(x2)
ἴσος	equal 6e, 10a, 11d, 11l(x3), 11o(x3), 11s	(τὰ) κακά	(bad things), evils 5a, 5b, 5b1(x2), 5c, 5d, 5e, 5f, 5g(x4), 6d(x2), 7(x2), 10c, 11g(x5), 11i(x3)
ἰσότης	equality 5b2		
ἰσχύς	strength 5b(x2), 5b4(x3), 7a, 7d, 11g	κακία	vice 5a(x2), 5b(x4), 5b1, 5b8, 5b9, 5b10, 5b12, 5b13, 5c, 5e(x2), 5f(x2), 5g, 6d, 6f, 7, 11d, 11f, 11g, 11k(x9), 11l, 11m(x2)
ἰσχυρός	strong 11g(x2), 11m		
καθαρμός	purification 5b12	κακῶς	badly 5b10, 11g, 11i
καθήκειν	to be appropriate 5b12, 5l, 10b(x2), 11m	καλεῖν	to call 5b7, 5b11, 5k, 10e, 11h
(τὸ) καθῆκον	appropriate 5b2(x2), 5b3, 5b9, 6a, 7b, 8(x5), 8a(x4), 9, 11a(x3), 11m	κάλλος	beauty 5b4(x3), 5b9, 7e, 10c, 11g, 11s
καθηκόντως	appropriately 11m	καλός	fine 5d, 6e(x2), 11g, 11h, 11k, 11s
καθικνοῦσθαι	to take up home 10c	καλῶς	well 5b9, 6e

GLOSSARY

καπηλεύειν	to trade in 11m

καρτερία	perseverance 5b2(2)

καρφός	twig 7

καταδεής	(lacking), falling
short 11m

καραισχύνειν	to make ashamed
11m(x3)

καταλαμβάνεσθαι to be
apprehended, to be aware 11i

καταλείπειν	to admit (LSJ 2b)
5b11

κατάληψις	apprehension 5l, 7d,
11m(x2)

κατανέμειν	to assign 11i

καταπαύω	to bring to an end 12

κατασκεύασμα arrangement 11i
κατασκευή	training 11m(x3)

κατάστασις	state 7a

καταστρεπτικῶς self-referentially
7e(x2)

κατάσχεσις	attitude 11c

κατατάττειν	to classify 5b6

καταφαίνειν	to reveal 11k

καταφεύγειν	to take refuge 11i

κατεπείγειν	to urge on (together
with something) 10c

κατέχειν	to hold (together)
11m(x2)

κατηγορεῖν	to classify 8a
κατηγόρημα	predicate (= a
statement completing a noun) 6a,
6b, 9b, 11f(x3)

κατοικεῖν	to dwell together 11i

κατονομάζειν	to give a name
(accordingly/correspondingly) 6f,
9, 11f

κατορθοῦν	to do right 11g
κατόρθωμα	right act 8(x3),
8a(x2), 11a, 11e(x4), 11l, 11o

κεῖσθαι	to be set up, depend
on 5b5(x2), 5l

κεφάλαιος	main (e.g. idea,
function) 5, 5b5(x3), 12
κεφαλή	head 7

κιθαρῳδία	lyre-playing 5b10
κιθαρῳδός	lyre-player 5b10

κίνδυνος	danger 11m

κινεῖν	to set moving 5i, 9,
11d
κινητικός	stimulative 5o, 7,
7c(x2), 7e(x2), 9b, 10
(τὸ) κινητικόν	stimulation 10b(x2)
κίνησις	motion 5b2, 5k(x2),
7d(x2), 10, 10d, 11s(x2)

κλέπτειν	to steal 11e
κλέπτης	thief 10e
κλοπή	theft 5g
(κλοπαί = acts of theft 10e)

κοινός	common (to) 5b5,
11b(x2), 11c, 11d, 11i, 11m
κοινότερος	more generally 5b1,
5d(x2)
κοινωνία	association 5b2, 5l
κοινωνικός	communal 11m

κοινῶς	in general, in the usual sense 10a, 11k; cooperatively (11k)	λῆσις	obliviousness 11m
κόλασις	punishment 11d(x3)	λέγειν	to say, speak, call 5b2, 5b4, 5b5, 5b7, 5b10(x2), 5b11, 5b12, 5b13, 5o, 6b(x4), 6e(x2), 6f, 7, 7a(x2), 7c, 7d, 7f, 7g, 9(x4), 9a, 9b, 10, 10a(x2), 10b, 11b, 11c, 11d, 11e, 11f(x2), 11g(x2), 11h, 11i(x3), 11l, 11m(x6), 11s(x2)
κόσμιος	modest 11s		
κοσμιότης	modesty 5b2(x2), 11s		
κοσμιῶς	modestly 11i	λέγεσθαι	to be spoken of 5b6, 5b7, 5b9(x2), 5b11, 5d, 5h, 6b(x2), 7(x3), 7a, 7f(x4), 7g(x2), 8, 9, 10c, 10e, 11c(x3), 11d, 11i(x3), 11k, 11m(x2), 11r, 11s
κότος	rancour 10b, 10c		
κρατεῖν	to govern 10a		
κρείττων	greater 10c, 11h	(τὸ) λεκτέον	(what must be spoken), sense 7
κρίνειν	to decide 5b2, 5b4, 11n	λογικός	rational 5l, 6, 8, 8a, 9(x4), 11a, 11m
κρίσις	judgement 7f, 10a, 11l(x2)	λόγος	conversation, reasoning, reason, meaning, word 5b2, 5b4, 5b8, 5b10, 5l(x2), 6a, 6f, 7a, 7g(x2), 8, 10, 10a(x4), 10b(x4), 10c, 11d, 11e(x2), 11f, 11i(x2), 11k(x3), 11m(x5), 11r, 11s(x2), 12 (κατὰ τὸν δεύτερον λόγον = secondarily 5b5(x3))
κριτικός	capable of (literary) criticism 5b12		
κτῆσθαι	to possess 11m		
κτῆσις	possession 7b, 11d		
κυνίζω	to be a Cynic 11s		
κυνισμός	Cynicism 11s(x2)	λογόφιλος	fond of talking 11k
κυριός	in control 7b	λευκός	white 5b5
		λευκότης	(whiteness), pale skin 7b
κωλύειν	to prevent 5b2, 11g(x2), 11m		
		λήρησις	raving 11m
λαλία	chatter 11k	λοιπός	other 5, 5b1 (καὶ τὰ λοιπά = and so on 5b5)
λαμβάνειν	to acquire, get 8a, 11i, 11l, 11m (εἴληπται = it is taken, understood 10a)	λυπεῖσθαι	to feel pain 10a, 11e
		λύπη	pain 5b, 5c, 5g, 10(x3), 10b(x2), 10c(x10), 11i
ληπτός	worth acquiring 5o(x4), 7e(x4)	λυσιτελής	profitable 5d, 11h
		λυτικός	laxative 11r
λανθάνειν	to be unaware 11g, 11m	μαίνεσθαι	to be mad 5b13

GLOSSARY 149

μανία	madness 5b13(x3)	μεταδιδάσκειν	to teach (new things) 10a
μακάριος	blessed 11g		
μακαρισμός	blessing 10c	μεταδιδόναι	to share 11m
		μετάδοσις	(sharing), return (of a favour) 11k
μανθάνειν	to know 10a		
μαντικός	prophetic, able to prophecy 5b12(x2), 5f, 11s(x2)	μεταδοτική (τεχνή)	expertise in sharing (= generosity) 5k
μάντις	prophet 5b12	μεταλαμβάνειν	to gain a share 11g
μαχομένως	in conflict 6a	μεταμέλεια	regret 11i(x3)
μεγαλοψυχία	great-heartedness 5b(x2) (cf. μικροψυχία)	μετάνοια	changing one's mind 11m
		μετανοιεῖν	to change one's mind 11m
μέθη	drink 11m		
μεθύσκεσθαι	to get drunk 11m	μεταπίπτειν	to waver 11m
		μεταπτωτικός	changeable 11m
μειγνύναι (μεμιγμένος = composite 5m)	to mix	μετατίθεσθαι	to alter one's opinions 11m
μέλαινα	black 5b5		
μελανότης	(blackness), dark skin 7b	μεταφέρειν	to transfer 11k
μελέτη	practice 11m	μετέχειν	to participate 5a(x3), 7d, 11g, 11i(x2)
μέλλειν (μελλουσα = future 10c)	will be 9, 11m(x2)	μετοχή	participation 7d(x2)
		μέτοχος	participating in 6e
μελός	limb 5b4	μέτριος	moderate (not excessive) 11b
μέρος (τὰ κατὰ μέρος = particulars 5l, 12)	part 5, 5b4, 5b7(x2), 5b11, 5g(x2)	μηδετέρως	in neither way 7c
		μῆνις	wrath 10b, 10c
μέσος (τὸ μέσον = intermediate [between good and bad], i.e. an indifferent 8a, 11d, 11l, 11p)	middle 8	μιαρός	defiled 5b12
		μικρός	little 7b
		μικροψυχία	small-mindedness 5b(x2)
μεταβάλλεσθαι	to change one's mind 11m	μίμησις	imitation 10c

μισανθρωπία 10e	hatred of mankind	νοσεῖν	to be sick 11k
		νοσερός	making ill 11r(x2)
		νόσημα	illness 5f, 10e(x3)
μισθός	payment 11m(x2)	νόσος	sickness 5a, 7a, 7f
μισογυνία	hatred of women 10e	νουνέχεια	sensibleness 5b2(x2)
		νουνεχόντως	sensibly 5b9
μισοινία	hatred of wine 10e	νοῦς	good sense 5b9, 5l, 11d, 11i, 11m(x5)
μνήμη	memory 7b		
		ξενία	hospitality 5l
μοιχεία	adultery 10e		
μοιχός	adulterer 10e	ξηρός	dry 5b4
μοναρχικός	of a monarch 11m	ὁδός	way, path 5b11, 5k, 11m
μονή 11s	persistence 5k, 11m,	ὀδυνή	mental pain 10b, 10c, 10d
μόνος	only 5b9, 5b11, 5b12(x2), 5f(x2), 5g(x4), 5k(x2), 7f, 11d(x2), 11e, 11i(x7), 11k(x2), 11m(x5), 11n, 11q(x2), 11s(x3)	οἴεσθαι	to think 5b10, 11m
		οἰκεῖος	having an affinity 5d, 5k, 7, 11b, 11m(x2)
		(οἰκείως ἔχειν	to have an affinity 11k)
μοχθηρός	base 5e		
ναυαρχία	admiralship 11i	οἰκειοῦν	to have an affinity 11k
(οἱ) νέοι	youths 5b9, 11s	οἰκία	home 11d, 11m
		οἰκονομία	(household) managment 11d, 11m
νεῦρον	sinew 5b4		
		οἰκονομικός	skilled in household management 11d(x2), 11g
νοεῖσθαι	to be thought of 7		
νομίζειν 11k, 11m(x3), 11n	to believe 11d(x2),	οἰκονόμος	manager of a household 11d
νομιστέος	must be thought 11g	οἰκονοῦν	to manage a household 11d
		οἶκος	household 11d(x2)
νομικός 11d(x2), 11i	learned in the law	οἰκητήριον 11i(x3)	dwelling (place)
νόμιμος 11i	law-abiding 11d(x3),		
		οἶνος	wine 11m
νομοθετεῖν	to make laws 11b	οἰνοφλυγία	drunkenness 5f
νομοθέτης	law-maker 11d		
νόμος 11i(x4), 11k(x2)	law 5b12, 11d(x5),	οἰωνοσκοπικός	skilled in observing birds 11s

GLOSSARY

ὄκνος 11s	hesitancy 10b, 10c,	ὀρέγεσθαι	to desire 11f(x2), 11h, 11n
ὄλβιος	fortunate 11g	ὀρεκτέος 11f(x3)	must be desired
ὅλος 5b10	whole 5b1, 5b4(x2),	ὀρεκτός	worth desiring 6b, 10b, 11f(x3)
ὁμήλικος group 5l	of the same age	ὄρεξις 11s	desire 9, 9a, 10b, 11f,
ὁμιλία 11m	association 5k, 10c,	ὀρθός	correct 5b2, 5b10, 10a, 11h, 11i
ὁμιλητικός	affable 11m	(ὀρθὸς λόγος = correct reason 5b2, 10a, 11a, 11d, 11e(x2))	
ὁμοδογματία 5l	agreement in beliefs	ὀρθῶς	correctly 5b2
		ὁρίζειν	to define 5b1, 6e, 8
		ὅρος	definition 6e, 7f
ὁμονοεῖν	to be in concord 11b	ὁρμᾶν	to impel 9
ὁμόνοια 11m(x2)	concord 11b, 11k,	ὁρμή	impulse 5b2, 5b3, 5b5(x2), 5b13, 5c(x2), 5o, 7, 7a, 7c(x4), 7e(x2), 9(x11), 9a(x4), 9b(x4), 10, 11f, 11s
ὁμολογία 6b	agreement in beliefs	ὁρμητικός	able to impel 9(x2)
ὁμολογοῦσθαι to agree, be in agreement 6, 6b		ὅρουσις	impulsion 9(x2)
ὁμολογουμένως in agreement (sc. with nature) 5b5, 6a(x3), 6e, 11d		ὅσιος ὁσιότης	holy 5b12 holiness 5b12
ὀνειροκριτικός 11s	dream interpreter	οὐδέτερος οὐδετέρως	neither 5b1(x8), 11e in neither way 7b
ὄνομα ὀνομάζειν ὀνομασία	(name), term 7f, 11n to name 5l, 11e nomenclature 7g	οὐσία	substance 5a, 5b7
		ὄψις (δι' ὄψεως = visual 10c)	appearance
ὄντως	really 10b(x2)		
ὀξύτης	quickness 7b	πάθος	passion 6d, 9b(x2), 10(x6), 10a(x7), 10d, 10e, 11i
ὁρᾶν	to see 10a, 11k	παιδεία παιδεύειν	education 11m(x2) to educate 11b
ὀργή 11s	anger 10b, 10c(x6),		
ὀργιλότης	irascibility 10e	παιδοποιεῖσθαι 11m	to father children

παλαίειν	to wrestle 11s
παλαίωσις	maturity (aging) 10c
παντελῶς	overall 7b
παραγγέλλειν	to prescribe 5b1, 11k
παράγγελμα	prescription 11k
παράδειγμα	example 7g
παράδοξος	paradoxical 12
παραδοχή	reception 11k
παραιτητικός	able to be begged off 11d
παρακεῖσθαι	to be associated 6b, 11b, 11f, 11i(x2)
παρακολουθεῖν	to follow closely 11m
παρακούειν	to mishear 11m
παραλαμβάνειν	(to take over), accept, employ 5b9, 7f(x2), 10
παραλείπειν	to omit 11a
παραμετρεῖσθαι	to be measured 8a, 11k
παράνομος	lawless 11k
παραπαίειν	to strike a false note 11m
(τὸ) παράπαν	at all 11m
παραπλήσιος	similar, like 5b(x2), 5b1, 5c, 5e, 5f(x4), 5k, 6d, 7a, 7b, 7e, 11e, 11i, 11r(x2), 11s

παραπλησίως	likewise, in a similar fashion 6d, 10a, 11m
παραριθμεῖν	to cheat 11m(x2)
παρασκευάζειν	to prepare 11k
παρασκευαστικός	preparative 5h
παρασκευή	preparation 9a(x2)
παρατηρεῖν	to carefully observe 5l
παρατηρητής	careful observer 11m
παραχρῆμα	on the spot 5b2, 10c
παρεῖναι	to be present 10b(x3), 11h(x2), 11n
παρεκβαίνειν	to transgress 5b12
παρέχεσθαι	to provide (enable) 7f; show (itself); (also aor. infin. παρασχεῖν) 5b2, 5b3(x2), 5b5, 5b13, 11d
παροιμία	proverb 11m
παρορᾶν	to fail to see 11m
παρορμᾶν	to be eager for 11k
πατάττειν	to strike 5b5
πατρίς	country 11b, 11m
πειθαρχικός	obedient to command 11i
πειστικός	persuasive 11p
(οἱ) πέλας	(those nearby), neighbours 11c(x2)
πένης	poor 11i
πενία	poverty 5a, 7f, 11i

GLOSSARY

πένθος	grief 10b, 10c	(οἱ) πλησίον	(those nearby), neighbours 5b2, 11b, 11m
πενταχῶς	in five ways 9	πλούσιος	rich 11i
περιγίγνεσθαι	to result from 5b4	πλουτεῖν	to be rich 11i
περιέχειν	to encompass 9b(x2), 11m(x3)	πλοῦτος	riches 5a, 7e, 7f, 10c, 11i
περιπατεῖν	to walk 11e(x2)	πνεῦμα	breath 5b7
περιπάτησις	walking around 5c, 5g	πόθος	craving 10b, 10c
περιπίπτειν	to encounter 5b2, 10, 11g(x2)	ποιεῖν	to do, act, make 5a, 5b2, 5b5(x2), 5b8, 5b9, 5b10(x9), 6a(x2), 7a, 7g, 10a(x2), 11d, 11g, 11i(x2), 11k(x8), 11m, 11s(x2)
περιποιεῖν	to acquire 11g, 11k, 11r	ποιητέος	what must be done 5b1(x4), 5b5(x2), 11d(x2), 11i(x2)
περιποίησις	acquisition 11d	ποιητικός	productive 5g(x6), 5h(x3), 7b, 7e(x2)
περιττός	odd(-numbered) 7, 7c		
		ποιητής	poet 5b12
πηγή	source 5d, 11l	ποιότης	quality 11l
πηρᾶν	to disable 7d	πολεμικός	contradictory 11m
πήρωσις	disability 7a(x2)	πολέμιος	at war 11b
πιθανός	trustworthy 11m	πόλις	city 11i(x8), 11k
πικρία	ire 10b, 10c	πολιτεία	(government), political life/system 11b(x2), 11i, 11m(x3)
πίπτειν	to befall 11b, 11k, 11m	πολιτεύεσθαι	to take part in politics 11b, 11m(x3)
πιστεύειν	to trust 11m		
πίστις	trust, belief 11m(x2)	πολιτικός	political 5b1, 6, 11g, 11m
πλεονάζειν	to be excessive 10	πόνος	suffering, toil 5a, 5b2, 7b, 11b, 11k(x2)
πλεοναχῶς	in various ways 5d		
πλεονεκτεῖν	to defraud (LSJ II.2) 11m	πρᾶγμα	thing, object 5b2, 5b9, 7f(x3), 7g, 10a, 11m
		πραγματεία	effort 11h
πλῆθος	mass 11m	πρακτέος	must be done 5b2

πρακτικός practical, able to do something 9, 9a, 9b, 11d(x2), 11i
πρᾶξις action 5b2, 5b8, 9a(x2), 11k
πράττειν to act, do 5b2(x2), 5b3, 5b4, 5b5(x4), 6e(x2), 8, 9(x2), 11a, 11e(x2), 11g, 11i, 11k

πρᾶος gentle 11s
πραότης gentleness 11s
πράως gently 11s

πρέπειν to be suitable 5b2

πρεσβεύειν to be an ambassador 8

προαίρεσις policy 9a(x2), 11g

προβαίνειν to advance 11k

προδιαπίπτειν to err through haste 11m

προείπειν to say above 11a (esp. τὰ προειρημένα 5b6, 5d)

προηγεῖσθαι to lead the way 10
προηγούμενος preferential 6a, 7g, 11m(x4)
προηγουμένως primarily 5b5(x3)
(τὸ) προηγμένον preferred 7b(x9), 7g(x5), 8
προῆχθαι (to be elevated), to be preferred 7f

πρόθεσις proposal 9a(x2)

προθύμως eagerly 11k

προκαταλαμβάνειν (προκατειλημμένος) to prejudice 11k

προκεῖσθαι to be proposed 5b2, 11g

προκοπή progress 7b, 11b

προπετής rash 11m
προπίπτειν to act rashly 11m

προόρασις foresight 11m

προσαγορεύειν to call, describe 7f, 8, 11h

προσδεῖσθαι to need in addition 5b12

προσδιαρθροῦν to add further 6a

προσῆκων fitting 10c, 11s

πρόσθεσις assent 11m

προσιέναι to approve 11s

προσκοπή aversion 10e

προσοχή attention 5k

προσπίπτειν to befall 11s

προστακτικός ordering 11d, 11i
προστάττειν to order 11d, 11i

προστάτης (chief), head 11d

προστιθέναι to add on 6a, 9; (mid.) to embark on 11g

πρόσφατος fresh 10, 10b(x4)

προσφέρειν (τινι λόγον) to address (LSJ AI3) 11s
προσφέρεσθαι to deal with 11m; bring in addition 7b, 8a

προτείνειν (to hold out), to point 7

προτιθέναι to propose 5b5, 12

GLOSSARY

προτρέπειν to encourage
11k(x7)
προτρεπτικός encouraging 5b9,
11m, 11p

πρῶτος first, primary
5b2(x3), 5d, 6a, 7a, 7d(x2), 7g, 10(x2),11
πρώτως in the first sense 5d

πτοία agitation 10(x2)
πτοιώδης agitated 5b13(x2)

ῥήτωρ orator 5b12

ῥιπτασμός thrashing around
10c

ῥώμη strength of mind
5b(x2)

σαρκάζειν to be sarcastic 11m

σαφής clear 6a, 11l

σεμνός majestic 11g

(τὸ) σημαινόμενον (what is meant), meaning 6b, 7f, 11c, 11i, 11m(x2)
σημεῖον sign 5b12, 11s
σημείωσις indication 9a

σκληρός harsh 11d

σκοπεῖν to examine 5b5, 11k

σκοπός target 5b2, 5b5(x3), 6b, 6c(x2), 6e, 11m

σοφιστεία sophistry 11m
σοφιστεύειν to be a sophist 11b, 11m(x3)
σοφός wise 5b8, 5b10(x2), 5b11, 5b12(x2), 11b, 11g(x2), 11i, 11l, 11m(x11), 11n, 11s(x2)

(κατὰ τοὺς) σμερματικοὺς λόγους
in accord with generative principles 7d(x2)

σπουδαῖος worthwhile 5b2, 5b8, 5b9(x3), 5b11, 5d, 5e(x2), 5k, 5l, 5m(x2), 6c, 7f, 11b(x4), 11d(x3), 11g(x6), 11h, 11i(x9), 11k(x6), 11m(x8), 11p, 11q, 11s(x4)
σπουδή (effort), regard 11h

στασιώδης quarrelsome 11i

στατικός astringent (LSJ I.1)
11r

στέρεσθαι to be deprived 11i

στοχάζεσθαι to aim 5b5, 6c

στρατηγία generalship 11i, 11m
στρατηγικός fit for command
11g

συγγενής kin 5l
συγγενικός of kin 5l

συγγνώμη forgiveness
(συγγνώμην ἔχειν = to forgive 11d(x3))

συγγράφειν to compose 11b(x2)
σύγγραμμα treatise 6e, 12

συγκαταβαίνειν to stoop 11b

συγκατάθεσις assent 7b, 9b(x4), 11m(x6)
συγκατατίθεσθαι to assent 11m(x2)

συγκαθιέναι (to stoop down), humbly enter into (LSJ II.2) 5b12

συγκεφαλαιωτικός able to surmise
5b2

συγχρῆσθαι to make use 11m

συμβαίνειν to occur 5b5, 5d(x4), 6a, 9, 10a, 10e, 11h, 11i(x2), 11l, 11p

συμβάλλεσθαι	to contribute 7g	συνιστάναι (συνεστηκέναι)	to be composed of 5b4
συμβλητικός	contributing 7		
συμβιοῦν	to associate with 11m	συνεῖναι	to live with 11k
συμμετρία	proportion 5b4(x2)	συνέχειν	to hold 11r
σύμμετρος	moderate 7b	(συνεχόμενος = in the grip 11i)	
		συνεχῶς	continually 11i
συμπληροῦν	to make complete 5g(x2)	συνήθεια	intimacy; (customary) usage 5l, 6b
συμπίνειν	to drink in company 5b9	(τὸ) σύνολον	totally 11m
συμπόσιον	drinking party 5b9(x2)	συντείνειν	to extend 5b12; contribute 11h(x2)
συμποτικός	convivial 5b9		
συμποτικῶς	convivially 5b9	συντελοῦν	to produce 11k
συμφέρειν	to be useful 5d, 10a, 11d, 11h, 11m(x2)	συνυπακούειν	to understand 5b10
συμφερόντως	expediently 5b2	συστέλλεσθαι	to contract (draw back) 10b
συμφυής	inborn 5b7	συστολή	contraction 10, 10b
συμφωνεῖν	to be in harmony 11b	σύστημα	composite 5l(x2), 11i(x2)
συμφωνία	harmony 5l		
σύμφωνος	in harmony 5b1, 5b3, 6a	σφάλλεσθαι	to be confused 11m
συναγωγή	collection 11d	σφόδρα	very much, especially 10e
συναλλάττειν	to deal with 5b2	σφοδρότης	violence 10a
		σφοδρός	violent 10b
συναμφότερος	both together 11i	σχέσις	state 5k(x4), 7d(x2)
σύνδεσις	attachment 11m	σῶμα	body 5b4(x4), 5b7(x2), 6c, 7a, 7b(x8), 7d, 7e, 11s
συνεγγίζειν	to come close 7g	σωματικός	bodily 7a
συνειθίζειν	to grow accustomed 5l	σώφρων	restrained 5k
		σωφρονεῖν	to show self-restraint 8a, 11e, 11f
συνεργεῖν	to work in partnership 7b, 7g	σωφρόνημα	restrained act 11e

GLOSSARY

σωφόνως with self-restraint 11g
σωφροσύνη self-restraint 5a, 5b(x2), 5b1, 5b2(x4), 5br, 5b13, 5f, 5l, 11e, 11f

τάξις post, order 5b2, 5b12, 7
τάττειν to order, classify, assemble 7g, 11d, 11k

τείνειν to touch on 11s

τεκμήριον proof 11k

τεκνογονία fathering children 11b
τέκνον child 5m, 7b, 11q

τέλειος complete 5b4, 5b8, 8(x2), 11a, 11b, 11g(x2), 11l, 11m
τελειοῦν to complete (τελειωθείς = completed 5b8, 8a)
τελικός final 5g(x6), 6b
τελικῶς completely 5b6
τέλος goal 5b3, 5b5(x3), 5k, 6a(x2), 6b(x5), 6c, 6e(x3), 7

τελευτᾶν to end (one's life) 11q

τετραχῶς in four ways 9

τεῦξις attainment 5b5
τυγχάνειν to accomplish 6c

τέχνη expertise 5b(x3), 5b4, 5b5, 5b10, 5b11(x2), 5k(x2), 7b, 11n
τεχνικός expert 5l
τεχνολογία prescription of rules 8a

τήρησις guarding 11d

τιμᾶν to honour 11k
τιμή honour 5b12, 5l, 7f, 11i(x2)

τίμιος held in honour 11i

τιμωρεῖσθαι to take revenge 10c
τιμωρία vengeance 10c

τόνος tension 5b4(x2), 5l

τόξοτης archer 5b5

τόπος place, topic 8, 11i, 11m

τραῦμα wound 7a

τρέπειν to turn 11k(x2)

τρίχες (θρίξ) hair 7, 7c

τρίτος third 6b, 7f(x2), 11i, 11m
τριττός three-fold 7f
τριχῶς in three ways 6b, 7f(x2), 11c, 11i

τρόπος way, fashion 5b5(x2), 5b10(x2), 5b11, 6a, 6e, 7, 11c, 11d, 11m(x4), 11s

τρόφιμος nurturing 11r

τυγχάνειν to hit, to obtain, to occur 5b3, 5b5(x4), 6a, 6e, 10, 11m

τυραννικός tyrannical 11k
τυραννίς tyranny 10a

ὑβρίζειν to act outrageously 11m(x2)
ὕβρις outrage 10e, 11m(x2)
ὑβριστής hooligan 10e
ὑβριστικός outrageous 11m
ὑβριστικῶς outrageously 11m

ὑγίεια health 5a, 5b4(x3), 7a, 7b, 7d, 7e, 7f, 11k, 11m, 11r

ὑγιεινός	healthy 7d, 11r(x2)	ὑπονοεῖν	to surmise 11m
ὑγρός	wet 5b4	ὑπόνοια	surmise 11m
ὑπάγειν	to subsume 10b	ὑποπτωτικός	submissive 11i
		ὑπόστασις	substance 5b7

ὑπάρχειν to exist, belong to, be possible, consist 5b6, 5b12, 5c(x6), 5i, 5l, 6, 6e, 11b, 11g(x2), 11i(x2), 11k(x3), 11m(x5)

ὑποτάττεσθαι to be subordinate 5b2(x4), 5b5

ὑπείκειν	to fail, give way 11k	ὑποτοπεῖν	to suspect 11m
ὑπεξαίρεσις	reservation 11s	ὑστερεῖν	to deprive 11i
ὑπεράγειν	to surpass 7b	ὑψηλός	eminent 11g(x2)
		ὕψος	eminence 11g
ὑπερέχειν	to have more 11l		
ὑπεροχή 11m	position of authority	φάναι	to say 5a, 5b1, 5b6, 5b7(x2), 5b8, 5b9, 5b12(x3), 5d, 5k, 5l, 6, 6c, 7a(x2), 7b, 7c, 7f(x7), 8, 10, 11b, 11c, 11d(x3), 11e, 11g, 11k, 11m(x9), 11s
ὑπέρθεσις 11s(x2)	postponement		
ὑπερτίθεσθαι	to postpone 11s		
ὑπογράφειν 5b12, 5b13, 5d	to describe 5b11,	φαίνειν (φαινόμενος 11s(2))	to appear apparently 10(x2),
ὑπογραφή 10a, 12	description, treatise	φανερός	obvious 5n
ὑπολαμβάνειν 11d, 11f, 11g, 11m(x5)	to assume 6a, 10e,	φαντασία	impression 5l, 7a, 7b, 9, 10c
ὑποληπτέον 10	it must be assumed	φαῦλος	worthless 5b2, 5b8, 5b9(x2), 5b10, 5b12(x4), 5b13, 5d, 5e, 6c, 11b(x2), 11d(3), 11g(x7), 11i(x7), 11k(x17), 11m(x8), 11s(x2)
ὑπόληψις 11m(x3)	assumption 10,		
ὑπομένειν 11b	to endure 5b5(x2),	φευκτός 5b1(x2), 5i, 7(x2), 10b	worth avoiding
ὑπομενετός 6f, 11f	worth maintaining		
ὑπομενετέος maintained 6f, 11f	what must be	φθονερία φθόνος 10d	enviousness 5f, 10e distress 10b, 10c,
ὑπομονή	endurance 5b2, 5b3		
ὑπομνηματίζειν	to note 11k	φιλάλληλος 11m	fond of one another
ὑπομνηματισμός	summary 5, 12		

GLOSSARY

φιλαργυρία   fondness for money
5f, 10e

φιληδονία   fondness for
pleasure 10b, 10c

φιλήκοος   fond of listening 11k

φιλία   friendship 5b9,
5l(x8), 11c(x3), 11k, 11m(x4)
φιλικός   friendly 11c
φιλικῶς   in a friendly way
11i, 11k

φιλιππία   fondness for
horseriding 5b11

φιλογεωμετρία   fondness for
geometry 5k

φιλογραμματία   fondness for
literature 5b11, 5k
φιλογράμματος   fond of literature
5b11

φιλογυνία   fondness for women
10e

φιλοδοξία   fondness for (good)
opinion 10b, 10c

φιλοινία   fondness for wine
10e

φιλοκυνηγία   fondness for dogs
5b11

φιλόλογος   fond of discussion,
scholarly 6b, 11k

φιλομάθεια   fondness for
learning 11m
φιλομαθεῖν   to be fond of
learning 11m

φιλομουσία   fondness for music
5b11, 5k

φιλόμουσος   fond of music 5b11

φιλοπλουτία   fondness for wealth
10b, 10c

φιλοποιία   fondness for
forming an attachment (= making
friends) 5b9, 10c, 11s

φιλοπονία   (fondness for toil),
industriousness 5b2(x2), 11k
φιλόπονος   fond of toil 11k

φιλοσοφεῖν   to philosophise
11k(x2)
φιλοσοφία   philosophy 5, 11k,
11m(x2)
φιλόσοφος   philosopher 11g,
11k, 12

φοβεῖσθαι   to fear 10(x2), 10a,
11e
φόβος   fear 5b, 5c, 5g,
10(x2), 10b(x2), 10c(x9)

φορά   motion 9(x4)

φρένες   brains 5l
φρονεῖν   to be intelligent 5b7,
6f, 8, 8a, 11e, 11f
φρόνησις   intelligence 5a,
5b(x2), 5b1, 5b2(x4), 5b5, 5b7, 5l, 6f,
11e, 11f, 11n
φρονιμεύμα   intelligent act 5f, 11e
φρονιμός   intelligent 5b10,
5c(x6), 5g(x2)
φρονίμως   intelligently 11e,
11g, 11i

φυγάς   exile 11i

φύλλον   leaf 7

φύσις   nature 5b1, 5b3(x3),
5b5, 5b8, 5b12, 5m(x2), 6(x2),
6a(x8), 6e(x2), 7a(x11), 7b(x3),

7c(x2), 7d(x4), 7e(x4), 7f(x4), 7g, 8, 8a(x2), 10, 10a(x4), 10e(x2), 11b, 11i, 11m(x5), 11s

φωνή	sound 10c
χαίρειν	to be joyful 11e
χαρά	joy 5b, 5c, 5g, 5k, 6d
χαροπότης	brightness of the eyes 7b
χάρις	favour, ingratiation 5b12, 11k, 11s (χάριν = for the sake of 5b5, 10a, 11b)
χείρ	hand 7d, 9a
χόλος	rage 10b, 10c
χρῆσθαι	to use, experience 6e, 7f, 11g(x2), 11i, 11q
χρησιμός	useful 7b, 11h
χρῆσις	use 5f, 5m(x2), 11h, 11i
χρηστότης	kindness 5b2(x2), 5l
χρηστικός	making use, using 6d
χρεία	need, use 7b, 7f, 11h, 11h
χρή	(one) should, ought (= obligatory) 5b12, 8a(x3), 11i(x2), 11n
χρήματα	money 11d(x2), 11m
χρηματίζεσθαι	to make money 11d, 11m(x3)
χρηματισμός	skilled in money-making 11m(x2)
χρηματιστέος	money ought to be made 11d
χρηματιστικός	money-making 11d(x3), 11g
χρονίζω	to continue over a long time 11m
χρόνος	time 5b12, 11n
χρῶμα	colour 5b5(x2)
χώρα	(place), rank 5d, 7g
ψεκτός	blameworthy 5e
ψεῦδος	falsehood 11g, 11l(x4), 11m(x6)
ψευδής	false 7a, 11l(x2), 11m(x3), 11s
ψεύδεσθαι	to lie 11m(x2)
ψευδώνομος	falsely named 11m
ψόγος	reproach 5b2, 5b9
ψυχή	soul 5b(x2), 5b1, 5b2, 5b4(x5), 5b7(x4), 5e(x8), 5f(x2), 7a, 7b(x7), 9, 10(x3), 10a, 10b(x2), 11c, 11i, 11s
ψυχρός	cold 5b4
ὠμός	cruel 11k
ὡραῖος	in their prime (=handsome) 11s
ὠφελεία	benefit 11c, 11d, 11h
ὠφελεῖν	to benefit, confer a benefit 5d(x3), 11b(x3), 11d(x5), 11h(x2), 11i(x3), 11m
ὠφέλημα	benefit 6f(x2), 8a, 11f(x2), 11i
ὠφέλιμος	beneficial 5d, 11h